Praise for *Back to the Womb*

From her own experience and the shared experiences of fifty-nine mothers in Hawai'i, Alexandra comes to understand that childbirth is at the fulcrum of our human connection with our home, Mother Earth. It resonates through time, binding us with our ancestors, our culture. All of us are born from the womb of a woman, and this book shines moonlight on the significance of that fact.

—Ibu Robin Lim, Bumi Sehat Foundation

As someone who has been immersed in the world of birth for decades, I highly recommend Back to the Womb for expectant moms, new moms and anyone interested in stories of birth and reclamation. Dr. Alexandra Kisitu's book is a testament to the power of understanding our origins and honoring pregnancy, birth and postpartum. This book is a transformative and enlightening read that will leave you with a deep sense of connection to the essence of birth and life itself.

—Debra Pascali Banaro, World-Renowned Inspirational Speaker, Filmmaker, Doula Trainer, Childbirth Educator and Author

Back to the Womb

Reclaiming Birth Sovereignty

**CALUMET
EDITIONS**
Minneapolis

First Edition January 2024
Back to the Womb: Reclaiming Birth Sovereignty
Copyright © 2024 by Alexandra Kisitu, PhD
All rights reserved

10 9 8 7 6 5 4 3 2 1

ISBN: 978-1-962834-04-9

Cover and book design by Gary Lindberg

Cover art by Catie Atkinson

Back to the Womb

Reclaiming Birth Sovereignty

ALEXANDRA KISITU, PhD

CALUMET EDITIONS

Minneapolis

Table of Contents

Introduction

We are all born. All of us emerge from a mother's womb and need constant care for the first few years of our lives if we're to survive. As humans, we must care for our infants more intensely and much longer than other mammals. We have an instinctive and biological need to do so. Pending any major disruptions, the mother's instinct is designed to protect her young, and this immaculate design spans back to time immemorial.

Moms and dads alike are designed to connect and bond with their children. We see similar sentiments across the animal kingdom. This is for our survival as a species and also to fulfill our deep need for love. In the words of Brené Brown, "we are hard-wired for connection." Of course, life is complicated, and so not all babies receive the love and connection they need. Mothers often have to leave their newborns in the care of strangers because they have to go back to work to afford life's expenses. Sometimes, fathers are absent because they cannot handle the responsibility of taking care of a family, or they feel inadequate because they were never taught how to care for children. There is a myriad of reasons for why such things happen. This is unfortunate and often the result of pressures from unhealthy familial and societal structures. Nevertheless, it is still part of our design to take care of our young, and we must do everything we can to protect this design.

The purpose of this book perhaps is to show people a loving alternative to how we birth our babies, to birth mothers and babies into spaces of connection, freedom, and love, to show women they can follow their instincts, to show men that they are also invited into this space of love, and to hopefully find our way to back to the womb so that we can reclaim our humanity.

It is 2023, and I know most of us can feel the collective despair many of our fellow human beings are experiencing and perhaps the despair we have felt internally. It's been a tumultuous couple of years. Things we never thought would happen came to fruition. The world shut down. We went through a collective trauma. We saw social unrest. We saw the worst of war. And people profited from our fears and pain. They profited (and continue to profit) from paradigms of division, the antithesis of love and connection. I don't know how to solve all the world's problems, and I bet you don't either. But I would offer us a starting point. It is the point where we all had to start—in our mother's womb. It is where we were shaped. And where she was shaped as well. Our mothers' experiences, thoughts, and emotions during her pregnancy shape us for the rest of our lives (and in many complex ways). We can go back even further, though, to our conception. Did you know that there is a 1 in 400,000,000,000,000 that you'd be born? And yet, here you are, literally beating the odds. I often imagine all the events, relationships and circumstances that had to happen just to be conceived. And, then, to be born! We all have experienced this. We all can come back to this place in the womb. And knowing that means we all are connected. We certainly don't spend our days celebrating the miracle that is birth, but I think that, given these odds and given where we are in the world today, we should.

How we come into this world and how we are born deeply impacts us. Some people are born at home, some in the car, some in a hospital, some outside. Some babies come out of their mother's vaginas, others through a cut in her lower abdomen. Sometimes, we are separated from our mothers right away. Sometimes, we come out and lay directly on her chest, skin-to-skin, and begin to suckle the nourishing colostrum she provides in the early days of our lives. Some of us are poked, or cut, or bathed right away. Some babies need resuscitation and surgery after birth to survive. Some babies lose their moms during childbirth or are adopted shortly after they are born. These early experiences shape us in profound ways and have lasting impacts on our brains, the depth of our bonds with others, our immune systems and our nervous systems.

Birth trauma can make us more susceptible to disease, infections, mental and emotional disturbances, relationship issues, colds/flus, nervous system dysregulation, etc., in the immediate aftermath and later in life. There is even a term for the trauma of being separated from one's birth parents shortly after birth, for instance, called the primal wound (see Nancy Verrier's book *The Primal Wound*). The mother and the child have a vital connection on a physical, psychological, physiological, and spiritual level, and when this is disrupted, the mother and the baby suffer tremendously. If you've given birth, you understand that your pregnancy and birth experiences deeply impact you as a mother as well. Studies have proven that a mother's emotional health affects the baby. Even breathwork, prayer, meditation and yoga have been proven to support mothers and babies and improve their health. We are shaped by birth much more than we give credit for, and birth experiences and outcomes impact not only us as individuals but our collective world.

Imagine a world where mothers are honored, fathers feel included and encouraged, and babies are born through gentle birth practices. Imagine each individual soul coming into this world in a peaceful manner. In fact, many midwives live by the mantra, "Peace on earth begins at birth." They say this as they know that birth shapes how we interact with one another, our nervous systems, our behaviors, etc. This is not exclusive to the baby. Birth shapes mothers and fathers and extends to how we relate to one another in society as well. Being born is the most important event in our lives and means we've beaten the odds. We are the product of a million different circumstances that led to our conception. Such a mundane yet phenomenal event, isn't it? Our society views birth as nothing more than a brief moment in a woman's life, and yet, it is *everything*. This book honors birth and all that it is, with a focus on all its expansions, spiritual openings, interconnections and physical sensations. As you read this book, you might be surprised to find out about the history of birth, and you might even find yourself challenging some core beliefs you hold dearly around birth and life. The womb holds room for all of this. I know this because I have been blessed to have birthed two children of my own, so far. And the ways in which I birthed were quite unconventional and spectacularly expansive.

Our birth stories (whether we are the one doing the birthing or the one supporting the laboring mother) are personal, intimate, spiritual, physical, hard, beautiful, and sometimes painful and traumatic. We all carry our own stories—in our memories, in our cells and in our bodies. This book shares a variety of stories, including those that led mothers to birth in the places and spaces of their choice. To be honest, I was never particularly interested in pregnancy, birth, babies or mothering before my own experiences. I wasn't sure I even wanted to be a mother. I could never imagine expanding and birthing and nursing. I couldn't envision my body changing so much, growing another human, and nourishing a baby with my body. But, as you will quickly learn, I became enamored with all things birth once I experienced it for myself. My own birth experiences made me curious about other women's experiences.

My birth story began years before I became pregnant with my daughter, Isabella. About five years before she was born, I fell pregnant early in my relationship with my husband. My body changed so much in those first couple of months. I was really sick in the beginning, thinking I had just caught an awful flu. It was February and major flu season in Minnesota at the time. I was so sick that I lost about ten pounds in those early weeks. I didn't imagine it was a pregnancy causing this—as I always learned that women gained weight during pregnancy. I remember feeling a level of fatigue I had never felt before. My face broke out in pimples, my boobs started swelling and I was so fascinated by it all, albeit overwhelmed.

These changes came quickly, and yet, in my head, I still couldn't fathom that my breasts would produce milk and my belly would stretch enough to make room for a whole baby. Around nine weeks along, I went to my first prenatal appointment. I was excited about it all, and despite having mixed feelings about the pregnancy, I was really starting to feel joy around it all. I asked my sister, Katie, to join me at the appointment. You know how doctors' appointments can be—lots of paperwork, lots of waiting, cold rooms, nervous energy. We waited such a long time in a generic waiting room—a staple of doctor's offices. The nurse finally called us back to the exam room, and we went through a slew of tiring questions and vitals. The doctor *finally* came in and immediately asked me when I wanted to schedule the abortion. I was shocked. There was no sense of love, support, excitement, education, etc. I chalked her coldness up to the fact that she probably sees many young women coming in to schedule abortions, but I felt offended that she made that assumption without asking me what my plans were. I was, after all, in a committed relationship, fully employed and done with my college degree (I was a double major and graduated with *summa cum laude* honors even). Surely, she wouldn't think of me as incapable of being a mother—not that anything can prepare you to be a mother anyhow. And, not that those qualifications excuse such bold questions—all women should be treated as capable and should be given an opportunity to discuss any choices they want to make with their doctors.

Upon her abortion question, I immediately felt that I needed to protect myself and my baby. Those mothering instincts kick in quickly. It was clear from that moment on that I was just a patient who was to undergo procedures. I wasn't to be honored as a person capable of bringing a soul through, a powerful being and creator, a woman who deserves care and informed consent. I learned that day that most mothers probably felt the same as I did. I left that appointment feeling very sad about it all.

The next time I went in—probably around ten weeks or so—I was able to get an early ultrasound. Ultrasounds in the early weeks are usually done trans-vaginally; that is, they put a wand up your vagina and do imaging. I wasn't asked if I wanted to have this done. It was just assumed I would be a good patient and undergo the procedure. The technician called another person into the room once the imaging was complete. They were whispering and letting me know they were having a hard time seeing whether the sac was developing. They said I would have to come back in next week to see if everything was developing okay. The baby was there on the ultrasound moving around with its little head and hands and feet. So, I left without too much worry.

Each week I went, I wasn't told much except to keep waiting until the next appointment. They'd know more then. Many more unnecessary trips to the clinic and unnecessary ultrasounds occurred in the following weeks (that ended up costing me thousands of dollars, unfortunately—another staple of healthcare in America). Each week, more whispers, more inconclusive results, more gowns, more invasive procedures. Around week thirteen or fourteen, I started bleeding and cramping. I'm sure they had predicted this would happen. But I was still surprised. I already had a little low-belly pouch. My boobs already started swelling to get ready to feed my baby. Everything would be okay, I thought. After all, I believe in miracles and prayers.

I went in for another checkup because the bleeding and cramping became more intense. An older male doctor came into the room. He was not warm, and he was unfamiliar. So many doctors and technicians. I never remembered their names, but I remember how it felt to be around them. This one felt more uninterested than the rest. Cold, even. It seemed that he didn't care about what was happening to me. He was simply there to do another procedure. He did not communicate with my husband, nor did he acknowledge what I was going through. He prepared his tray of tools in the sterile, cold room with the fluorescents beaming down on us. Getting ready to peer into the entrance of my womb, but without regard for its sacredness. He carried a sort of long swabbing stick with a cotton ball at the end of it. He told me to lay back, and he inserted the stick and swabbed my cervix. It hurt. And it felt violating. If he would have explained what he was doing and why, I may have felt better about it all. But he treated me like a routine. I felt so dehumanized. He pulled out a blood-soaked swab, looked at me, and then exited the room without saying anything. I got my clothes back on and was told by a nurse to go home and wait it out. Just rest. More orders. Apparently, I wasn't in control of anything.

My memory is foggy, but I believe a few hours after that, my cramping and bleeding picked up. I laid on the couch that evening, trying not to cry. I distracted myself by watching *The Notebook*. My roommate at the time came home from work and sat down to watch it, too. She did not know that my womb was cramping and getting ready to birth—or expend, I suppose, would be the better word. I wanted to be left alone. I wanted to yell at her to leave. I wanted silence. To go into a cave. I felt guilty to be sitting with these feelings. I later learned these feelings were so intensely instinctual. I went to my bedroom, and my husband (who was my fiancé at the time) came over to be with me as we weren't yet living together; that would come a couple months later.

In the middle of the night, I felt several intense contractions. It was hard to sleep as the pain of my womb cramping would wake me up every couple of minutes. I had never felt my uterus move like that. And, when the sun came up, I knew it was over. The cramping had stopped. I went to the bathroom, and the baby slid out of me. Just like that. How can a life end so soon, be so anticlimactic? It was so tiny and barely covered the palm of my hand. It must've stopped growing around nine or ten weeks by the size of it. But my body carried it until fourteen weeks. A mother has a hard time letting go, after all. But I later found out that parenting is full of moments of grief and letting go, letting them grow, honoring their life paths, and loving them despite our pain. The womb carries it all. I never watched *The Notebook* again.

I knew that soul had left me. And while my emotions would take years to process the loss, my physical body was already shifting and healing. My belly was already going down. My breasts knew that there would be no baby to feed. My husband took me to the doctor that morning, and they did yet another ultrasound. They were thrilled that I did not have to get a D&C, which is where doctors scrape any remaining tissue out of the uterus generally to prevent infections. They were elated. I did a good job on my miscarriage, apparently. It was April 24, 2009. I felt empty. They asked if they wanted me to send the tiny fetus in for testing to see what went wrong. I felt even more violated by that. The baby was gone. I did not need any other proof. But, I strangely, and I know this might sound cold, but I strangely did not want anything to do with the dead fetus. I had wrapped it up and brought it to the doctors that day. But when they asked to take it from me, I did not want them to do so. Instead, I ended up flushing it down the toilet. That felt cold, too. What else should I have done? That moment still haunts me. They sent me home with a congratulations that I didn't need more procedures. Without a word of sympathy or mental health support, or even any knowledge of how to take care of my body after the miscarriage, they just sent me home.

I learned that day that life sometimes isn't honored—even by the systems that are supposed to protect life. Systems sometimes take away our humanity. And, so I made it my mission to learn about birth and start making choices for my body that honored my humanity. Although we did not carry that baby to term, I found the blessings in the loss over time. Any mom can confirm that loss sticks with them forever. And my experience wasn't as terrible as many other losses that mothers endure. But it was my loss, and I was determined to make something out of it.

A few years later, my sister started learning about birth and exploring her options as well. She asked me to come on a tour of a birth center in Saint Paul, Minnesota, which was called Health Foundations. The freestanding birth center offered a place for women to get prenatal care, breastfeeding education and support, mother support classes, midwives, nutritional support, and two very beautiful birthing rooms with large tubs. It was such a beautiful place—clean, warm, inviting. Void of gowns, fluorescent lights, and sterile dispositions.

My sister also started learning more about birth and introduced me to the documentary *The Business of Being Born*. Almost everyone in the natural birth community has seen this documentary. It essentially explores the history of obstetrics, critiques the for-profit business model that oversees birth and can lead to harmful interventions and explores birth options and choices. Watching that documentary opened my eyes to why my own experience was so cold, expensive, routine and empty. I also was determined to hire a midwife should I become pregnant again. And pregnant is what I became!

In August 2013, we conceived our daughter, Isabella, who is the most beautiful, creative, sweet, empathetic and spiritual child I've ever met. She is an old soul and just the epitome of a Taurus. She's amazing! My pregnancy with Isabella was so easy. I felt so healthy and happy. I loved my growing belly, and I loved feeling so feminine. At eleven weeks, I had my first appointment with the HealthEast midwives in Saint Paul. The first appointment went well. I explained that I wanted a natural birth—that is, I wanted zero interventions and no medications during birth. They seemed on board. But I quickly learned that even if they were on board, I was still in a medical system designed to maximize profits and reduce litigation.

My next appointment, sometime around sixteen weeks, did not go well at all. You don't get to choose what midwife will be at your birth (it is whoever is on call that day), and you see rotations of midwives for your prenatal appointments. Unsurprisingly, this appointment was with a different midwife.

When my husband and I entered the room, she did not acknowledge us. She was texting her friend and taking notes on the computer. After waiting about five minutes for her to wrap up what she was doing, she started complaining about my birth plans. She said that I should plan to reconsider using an epidural because "childbirth is hell." She also told my husband and me to sleep now because the first three months of a child's life are absolutely horrible. I left feeling so discouraged. But we had a hospital tour to do, and preparations were underway, so I kept myself in the system. We visited the hospital a couple of weeks later. The moment the automatic doors opened, I felt like turning around and running away. My intuition was trying to protect me, but I just kept walking in. The lady giving us the tour was nice. But it did not feel right. I couldn't see myself birthing there.

The next week, we had the anatomy scan, and it was confirmed to me that my baby was, in fact, a girl. I had dreams about her and knew I was having a girl. The confirmation of my intuition gave me a boost of confidence. She was healthy and beautiful on the ultrasound. After that appointment, I was to schedule a glucose test in the weeks ahead. It is a routine test that mums are told to take to assess whether they may have gestational diabetes. Up to this point, I had not consumed much sugar in the months before the pregnancy and during the pregnancy. I was very sensitive to sugar as I had been balancing my gut health, and I was hesitant to take the glucose test. On top of that, the liquid test is essentially corn syrup (hello GMOs and pesticides) and was full of additives and synthetic food coloring (all of which are banned in Europe due to the health risks). I called the doctor's office and asked to speak to the midwife about whether I could forgo the glucose test. She called me back and was absolutely irate. She yelled at me for questioning the test and the ingredients and told me she would drop me as a patient if I did not do it. I hung up the phone. I needed time to think. If she reacted with such anger over a simple question of whether I could forgo a test, how would she treat me during childbirth should she be the one on call? How would any of them treat me if I said no to their regimen of interventions? I was twenty-four weeks pregnant. Where would I give birth?

Sometimes, people will introduce you to ideas, people and places that seem insignificant at the time, and later, they become the spaces, people and places that are the most influential in your life. When my sister introduced me to the freestanding birth center, Health Foundations, little did I know it became the birthplace of my daughter and where she would take her first breaths of life. After doing a lot of soul searching, becoming frustrated with the medical midwives at HealthEast, and feeling that the tests and birth suggestions did not fit my values, I decided to reach out to Health Foundations to see if I could transfer care there. The initial phone call with their receptionist was so cheerful, and she reassured me that I would be welcomed and taken care of there.

My first appointment with a midwife named Amanda was wonderful. Firstly, walking into the birth center just felt right. It is essentially a home with a cozy reception area, updated fixtures and furniture, and exam rooms that felt comfortable and cozy (i.e., no fluorescent lighting, no sterile exam feelings, etc.). The place felt welcoming, clean and comfortable. I was able to tour the birthing suites there too. There are two birthing suites complete with beautiful windows, a large bed, a comfortable couch, a large birth tub, and a bathroom with a shower. There were birth balls, birth stools and other equipment, but overall, any medical equipment was intentionally placed out of sight.

The appointment with my midwife was a breath of fresh air. She was even wearing regular clothes! She felt so comfortable, answered all my questions, allowed me to have power over my choices (and supported those choices), and informed me on how to prepare for birth and manage my pregnancy in a holistic way. The birth center also offered newborn classes, birth prep classes and breastfeeding classes. I felt really happy to be there. The midwives made it clear that they were there to support birth in a holistic way, to honor my choices and to help my husband and me through birth and transitioning into parenthood.

I was taking really good care of my body as well and was encouraged to do so. I regularly got massages and visited my acupuncturist weekly. I wasn't eating any unhealthy foods, and I was making sure to relax and do yoga and deep breathing. I was committed to birthing my baby in the way that felt best for me. Every woman's pregnancy and birth journey, as well as what they want, is uniquely individual. Every labor is uniquely individual. Every birth and every baby are uniquely individual.

While writing this book, I toiled with whether I should tell my own individual birth stories. I wondered whether it would matter to the premise of this book. But, truthfully, my births laid the foundation for this book since they thrusted me into the world of birth, honoring women's divine power, understanding how dads can support their partners, and seeing that birth is such a sacred, spiritual experience. I must tell my story so you know why and how it is so important that I write this book. As you probably picked up on, by the time I was almost done with the pregnancy of my daughter, I was already rejecting much of the American medicalized paradigm on birth and women's bodies. I have always been someone who goes against the grain and questions things—but to have that be embodied for me on a cellular level was even more impactful. I was determined to give birth the way I wanted and with whom I wanted. The birth center offered this opportunity.

Despite my assertions that I did not want an epidural or that I was going to birth without medication, coworkers, random ladies, other moms, and even strangers would tell me I couldn't do it or sarcastically say "good luck" or they would tell me horror stories of their pain or their emergency C-sections, and thank God they were in a hospital and not irresponsible at a birth center. I heard it all. But I did it. On May 18, I went into labor, and two days later, she was born. I will now share with you my birth story with my daughter, Isabella. I wrote this when she was three days old when I was so raw from birth. It's important I share this with you and the stories of many other birthing women.

Isabella's Birth Story

It's nine thirty-two in the morning, on a warm, sunny Friday in May. My baby is cuddled into my chest, and I can feel her breathe; I can feel the warmth and softness of her new skin. It is a miracle beyond words or thoughts or any other means of perception. It is beyond the measurement of the senses. I feel her on the outside, the way I once did on the inside—only now it is the ultimate reality that she is born. Her little not-quite three-day-old body is in my arms, and my experience birthing her is all around me, has shook me to my core, and remains with and in me forever. I have been transformed. Her existence was a reality before I was ever pregnant with her. Somehow, I know she is and always was. It's just that her spirit and body joined inside of me, came through and out of me, and is now in front of me.

Here is Isabella's birth story:

At eleven thirty-four in the evening on Sunday, May 18, my water broke. I was lying on my left side in bed when I felt a warm gush of water flow out of me, soaking my underwear. I quickly got up and went to the toilet, where a little more water gushed out, and then trickled for a few minutes. I laughed to myself because we had had a BBQ earlier that evening and had a bunch of friends over. I kept joking with my husband that after all the work of having friends over, cooking, grilling, etc., it would be funny if I went into labor that evening. When I yelled to him, "Henry, I think my water broke!" he was a bit skeptical until he got out of bed to see for himself. He was as surprised as I was that this was the real deal. I called the midwife overnight paging line to see what to do next.

When the midwife called back, she asked what the color of the water was, how far apart my contractions were, and then told us to rest until the contractions were five minutes apart for an hour. The water was clear—a great sign—and then, throughout the night, I lost my mucous plug. At one point, my contractions were five minutes apart for about forty-five minutes, but then they slowed to seven to eight minutes apart. They were very irregular but still powerful. I didn't get much rest that evening, but I managed to relax and breathe between contractions. That night, I was excited, full of anticipation, and just finally relieved that my baby would be here soon. As the night progressed, my contractions became more powerful, but I reminded myself that each one would bring me closer to my baby.

Morning arrived like a breath of fresh air. I thought to myself, today is the day! I called the midwives at the birth center at eight in the morning as instructed, and since my contractions were still irregular, they told me to stay at home for a few more hours until they picked up. They called back around ten in the morning to check on me. The contractions were about five to seven minutes apart and becoming stronger. I had to change positions and really focus on my breathing to get through them. I quietly noticed at this time that my contractions were felt mostly in my back—in my hip joints and sacrum. The midwives instructed me to come at noon to get my first round of antibiotics since I was positive for Strep B (this is a routine precaution for strep B carriers—about 25 percent of healthy women are carriers). Although later I learned that antibiotics for Strep B aren't always necessary, and the risk to my and my daughter's gut health was not fully explained.

As noon approached and contractions required my full attention, I was dreading going to the car. To be confined in the car during a contraction seemed to be the most uncomfortable situation for my body. Luckily, I only had two contractions on the way there. On our way to the birth center, I remember thinking I hope my baby comes soon. I am ready to hunker down and no longer travel in the car. When we arrived, my contractions slowed to about seven minutes apart. I felt disappointed. I thought they would have picked up by now. I thought to myself, it's been twelve hours so far, and my baby hasn't come yet. I received my first round of antibiotics, and since my labor wasn't picking up, they decided to send me home to rest.

Before we left, while we were waiting for my IV drip to finish, we heard a woman laboring in the birthing suite next to us. She moaned a few times, and then there was a long moment of silence. She moaned again. I felt happy for her to be so progressed in her birth, but I also felt scared for the time that my contractions would be so powerful to make me moan/yell out like that. I never saw this woman or her baby, but I felt close to her as she endured her birth. And then, after a long pause, we heard a baby cry. Tears began to fall from my eyes at the sound of the baby making its first cry. I looked at my husband, "Oh, they have their baby now! It is so sweet.... I want our baby to come out soon, Henry. When will our turn come?" I could see his eyes reflect the desperation in mine, but he reassured me that our baby would come to us. He knew I was becoming discouraged with the length of labor. The way he looked at me throughout the next phase of Isabella's birth is beyond words. His support and love and the connection we had throughout the rest of the labor helped me to birth our baby. I will say more on this later, but I never knew how much love I could feel for my husband until this day came upon us. He is my best blessing—along with my daughter.

Once my IV drip finished, the midwife decided to send us home because my contractions were still not picking up. I was to call when they became three minutes apart, lasting a minute long for an hour. I was discouraged to be sent home, to have to labor in the car, and to be moving to a new space again. We ended up going home for four more hours. I tried to rest, but although my contractions were five minutes apart, they began to challenge me. I wanted to cry and scream, but instead, I followed my mom's directions to relax and stay ahead of the surges. I just breathed, rested, and ate in between. When four in the afternoon arrived, we left for the birth center again for round two of my antibiotics.

This time, when we went outside to get into the car, it was raining and thunderstorming. The rain was cold on my body, and the thunder was so loud, but it was a nice distraction as we made our way back to the birth center. I remember walking up the ramp to the door of the birth center when a surge stopped me. I grabbed onto the railing and breathed slowly. I looked down at my feet, in flip flops, looking at all my toes and watching the raindrops fall on them. I thought about my baby's toes and how I longed to see them. The surge released me, and we entered the birth center.

My contractions were still five or more minutes apart. I felt like I was making progress, but I still wondered why it was now seventeen hours after my water broke, sixteen hours since contractions started, and I was still waiting for my baby. I felt ready for my baby, but the midwife didn't think I was progressing. I knew it was time to call my doulas. Amy and Nicole arrived at the birth center shortly after we called them, and they were a breath of fresh air. Since my contractions were still more than five minutes apart, we were sent home again. This time, since I didn't want to ride in the car, we all went to my sister's apartment. Her apartment was about three doors down from the birth center, so we could walk there instead of enduring the car yet again. My doulas were with me. My husband was with me. And my mom and sister were with me. I felt like I could keep going with their love and support. The new energy brought me confidence.

When we arrived at my sister's, we chatted, snacked, worked through contractions, did some yoga, laughed and cried. At one point, I was on the couch with my mom, and I asked her why my baby wasn't coming. I didn't want to keep enduring the pain. I was scared, and I didn't know why my body was taking so much time to birth my baby. My doulas reassured me that I was strong and that I could do it. They said everything about my birth is normal, and this is the birth I am meant to have. My husband held me through contractions and kissed me. He made me feel warm and safe when I wanted to give up. My mom cried with me. My sister lovingly prepared tea and food for us. She made us feel warm and safe in her space.

One of my doulas did reiki on me to help move energy and ease my pain. Her warm hands radiated healing energy in my chakras and down my spine. When eight in the evening rolled around, I needed to go back to the birth center for another round of antibiotics. This time, as we walked to the birth center, my heart felt more open, and I felt lighter. I know this was because of the reiki and the healing power of my doula, Nicole. I did have a powerful surge on my way there. I was stopped in my tracks. My doulas guided me to wrap my arms around a nearby tree for support. I held the tree, and it held me back. I could feel its roots securing me in my space as the surge built in power. The rain was still lightly falling from the sky. I felt I was holding all the elements of the world and the circle of life in my arms. My legs started to quiver, and then I was released from the contraction.

A note I wanted to make is that I chose to give birth at Health Foundations Birth Center in Saint Paul, Minnesota. I wanted to have a natural birth without medications and medical interventions. I wanted control over my body and my decisions. I wanted to be treated like an educated, healthy woman—not a patient in need. I wanted to be supported by women who would respect that my body was designed to carry and birth a baby.

On a deeper level, I believe that our medicalized design of childbirth and prenatal care generally violates women. Living in a society that already violates women for any choice they make, a society that sexualizes everything a woman does or does not do, I could see that such phenomena are present in our institutions—including our medical care. The thought of being under medical care that does not allow a woman to make her own decisions about her own body made me very uncomfortable. I am deeply saddened by the fact that women are continually discouraged and even restrained from coming to full acceptance and love of the power and beauty of their womanhood; we have believed the lies about what and who a woman should be for far too long.

That being said, I believe it is valid to equate the way most women are treated during birth with sexual violence. From placing judgment on her progress/dilation, from offering her an escape from her body, from cutting her during delivery, from setting timelines and restrictions on her body, from denying her food and water during labor, from frequent invasive internal checks, from denying her movement, and most importantly from denying her the opportunity to dive into the deepest layers of her womanhood through the process of natural birth are perhaps the deepest sexual violations our society practices. We have effectively made women believe that they aren't strong enough, that their bodies aren't good enough, that they cannot birth without the assistance of the patriarchal medical system. While I understand there are occasions where such practices may be safer and perhaps necessary for the laboring woman, overall, I do not believe this to be the case for most women.

Our medical system routinely prevents women from experiencing their full capacity. This deeply saddens me. I also cannot help but think of the implications this has for the over 25 percent of women who have experienced sexual abuse at some point in their lifetimes. Such medicalized and invasive birth experiences, it seems, would exacerbate and revitalize their sexual trauma. So, even though I had to return to the birth center at eight in the evening for my third round of antibiotics, I was happy to be walking into a space that would respect and encourage my capacity as a woman—a woman exploring new depths of her body, mind and spirit.

At about nine in the evening, my contractions were still more than five minutes apart. The midwife was going to send us home, and she communicated this to us. She decided first to do a cervical check to see how far I had progressed. I thought perhaps I would be at six centimeters or so. To my disappointment, she said that I was three centimeters and could stretch to four centimeters. The back lip of my cervix was gone, but the front remained. This was about twenty-two hours into labor, and I had progressed to a three. The midwife wanted to send me home for the night because she didn't think that I was in active labor. I cried to my husband, my mom, my doulas that I was ready to hunker down and that moving around from place to place was delaying me. One of my doulas encouraged me to communicate this to the midwife. When she came back into the room, I told my midwife I wanted to stay. She said that it didn't look like anything was going to happen tonight and I should take a sleeping pill and get some rest at home. I was really discouraged and frustrated. My doula, again, said, "Alex, now is the time to use your voice. You need to communicate what you want." So, I again told the midwife I wanted to stay and asked her to just be flexible with us. She said she would think about it.

This was my first exercise of using my voice in labor. Speaking my truth has been something that is hard for me. In life, we all want to be liked and no one wants to be abandoned, so we often choose to be nice over choosing our truth. The damage that this does to our souls over the weeks, years and months is indescribable. It's as if we are cutting our inner selves down to pieces so that we can no longer speak for ourselves—we can no longer advocate for who and what we are. We are left to the whims of other people's desires when we do this. We are also left scattered, scared and alone. We choose to be nice so that we aren't abandoned. We choose to appease the other so that we don't face our own truths. But the truth is, we are afraid of our own power and courage because it is so great. This particular evening taught me to speak my truth. When I did, I felt proud of myself. I felt powerful! And, even though the midwife had to follow a certain policy, eventually, with the help of my husband's great compassion for me and his charm, he convinced her to let us stay.

I felt so relieved. The midwife said that only my husband and I could stay because we needed rest and quiet time together. The doulas and my mom and sister left us for the evening. I was given an ultimatum, though—take the Unisom tablet (a sleeping aid) or go home to labor at home. The midwife wanted me to sleep and said I must take the sleeping pill if I was to stay at the birth center. Thinking about that ultimatum now makes me upset. I believe it slowed down my labor more. And it created another layer for me of having to use my voice during a time when I was to be honored (like any birthing woman). So, I took the pill and crawled into the large, comfortable bed in the birthing suite. My husband, Henry, lay by my side, helping me breathe through each contraction. Holding me. Loving me. Telling me everything will be okay. When the pain in my back was increasing, and my contractions were wearing me down, he would stroke my back with his warm hand, he would rub my head, and he would tell me I was doing great. I wouldn't have gotten through the night without him. He was my rock.

I had another round of antibiotics at midnight. I don't remember much this time as I was so sleepy. My contractions would wake me, require me to be with them and then let me go. Once I was let go from the contraction, I would quickly drift back into sleep. It was as if they were sweeping me up, squeezing me, then letting go. They weren't like waves but more like mountains. I couldn't escape them but had to climb them and breathe while I made my way through them. In hindsight, it wasn't the contractions that were the most challenging part of my labor; instead, it was the length of time it took.

For so much of my life, I have tried to control things by making plans—controlling time essentially (or trying to, at least). My childhood was atypical in the sense that my parents divorced when I was a toddler. My mother spent the next twelve years making her way out of poverty. We moved from place to place—our cars would break down, our food would run out, our lives depended on food stamps and government housing. My father did not help when we needed him the most. He, instead, was fighting his own demons and was less than kind to us when we were most vulnerable. My mom was also busy in the world of survival, unhealthy relationships with men, and just trying to get by. Parents have their reasons for things, but as an innocent child, I learned that having plans would get me through to the next day. Having structure was something I created for myself. I could keep going if I had this.

But, now, this birth experience was challenging me to let go of all of it. I would no longer be allowed to make plans, to create my own structure. I was innocent again, I was that child again, only this time, I had to walk a different path to get through. I had to go through a river of unknowns and unforeseens to get to the other side. I didn't have my life jacket or my floatation device anymore. I had to swim it myself. I was so vulnerable. My walls were down. The currents pulled strong, the debris would come without announcement, and the depth of the water would change without indication. I had to navigate all of it—with me—only me. No plans, no structure, nothing. Just me. This was another lesson in my birth, that it is time to let go and trust myself, my true self, my naked, bare-bones, exposed self.

Four in the morning approached. Another round of antibiotics. Baby's heart rate was still great. My water was still clear, and my contractions were still coming, albeit slowly. I received another cervical check. Now, almost twenty-nine hours into labor, I was dilated to six centimeters. I needed to change positions with every contraction. They were fierce in my back and sacrum. My legs were now shaking. My husband was tired. I was tired. The midwife was tired. My doulas came back about an hour or two later. They helped me through some of the hardest times in my labor. I cried to my husband that I was too tired to go on any longer. I cried that I wanted to go to the hospital to get an epidural and Pitocin to speed things along. I wanted to give up on my desire for a natural birth. I was done.

I soon realized that this was another layer of myself needing to peel away. My doubt. My lack of faith. My fear. It all needed to melt away, and the next four hours taught me how to let go. The midwife was now convinced I was in active labor (although my contractions were still five to six minutes apart). My back was increasingly terrorized by the contractions, so we tried to have a few contractions in the birthing tub. The water was relieving, and my doulas placed a candle by the tub (a candle that had been burning since the evening before). They turned on soft music. They held the space for my husband and me. Henry was so strong throughout the labor. He was scared for me, but he always reassured me that I was strong and I could do it. He didn't let me doubt my own body and my own decisions. He kept telling me how strong I was. He looked up to me in a way that I'd never seen before. I felt like a queen when he looked at me.

I begged to him that I "just want our baby." I asked him, "Where is our baby? Why isn't she coming to us?"

"Baby, please come out," I would cry. Henry loved me through all of this. It made my heart weep and melt to know how much love he had for me.

As the sun came up, I wondered how much longer it would take. I was frustrated again. Another layer was about to peel off. I told my doulas that I thought my baby wouldn't come out until I gave up some things. Before my labor began, I was afraid of the baby coming because I felt it would start the countdown until I had to leave her to go back to my full-time job. I was terrified of the ticking clock counting down the days and minutes of my maternity leave. It was only a matter of time before I would have to leave her. I felt like a terrible mother. I wanted my baby as long as I could, and if that meant she stayed in my stomach longer, then I was okay with it. But, at this point in the labor, I just wanted my baby. I didn't care anymore about the clock, about my job, about my maternity leave. I made a promise to my baby that I would stay with her. I wouldn't leave her to go back to work full-time. I would be her mother. I would take care of her.

I looked to my doulas, surrounding me with their love and their presence. They had tears in their eyes. They felt my pain. They felt my deepest fears and desires. They could see me for who I am. They loved me anyway. Another layer peeled away. I got up and was determined again to birth my baby. The midwife came to check on me. She knew I was having back labor, and when she checked on me, she said she had an inkling that my baby was posterior (head facing front). This may have been the cause of my back labor. She encouraged me to have three contractions lying on my right side, three on my hands and knees, and three laying on my left side. And then repeat the sequence once more. These were some of the most painful contractions of all my labor. They took my energy again and tried to discourage me. I felt weak once more. My doulas and my husband came to the rescue. They supported me and encouraged me to change my reaction to my contractions.

Once the sequence was over, I was checked again. I dilated to seven centimeters. It was happening… finally! My doulas suggested I respond to my contractions with an emotion. So, we laughed at them. We all laughed at them. We told them they cannot take me down. We walked around. We moved our hips to belly dance music. We worked together. We laughed some more. We made snarky comments about the contractions. We swore at them. We told them off. And we laughed. And we danced. I felt empowered!

To get things moving even more quickly, I was encouraged to do lunges and walk up stairs two at a time. We walked out of the birth suite and into the lobby of the birth center. I used that space to move more and go up and down the stairs. Another layer was beginning to peel off. This time, it came in the form of anger. My doulas told me it was time to get pissed at the contractions. Get pissed at how long it was taking. Get pissed and roar. So, we all yelled together. We roared together! I got angry and loud. I was able to express anger in a way I never had before. I let years of anger and frustration finally release out of my mouth with screams and roaring and yelling. I yelled at my parents for their faults—for making me be the one to take care of their feelings. I yelled at my dad for not being there. I yelled at him for all the mental, emotional and spiritual games he played. All of the abuse and guilt and shame he put on me. I yelled it out. I yelled at my mom for the struggles she put us through. I yelled at her for making me take care of her feelings throughout the years. I yelled at my parents to release me and let me take care of my baby now. I told them it is my time now. My time. Not theirs. I reclaimed my identity and my strength. After so many years of compromising myself and storing guilt, I finally let it out and showed anger toward them. At the end of every contraction, all I could say was, "Wow!" I surprised myself with how open and vulnerable and expressive I was. I never showed these feelings before. Not even to myself—although I knew they were ever lurking just under the surface every day of my life. I gave myself permission to feel the good, the bad and the ugly emotions without worrying about being nice or kind. I just was. This was me.

That layer peeled off, not without a fight, but it was finally gone. I felt naked and relieved and open and free. I was one step closer to my baby. It was 8:00 a.m. now, on Tuesday, May 20, 2014. It was time for another round of antibiotics. Another midwife came in the morning. The new energy felt great in the birthing suite. She came in with confidence, sunshine, homeopathies that helped to speed up labor, and great wisdom. When I asked her if my baby would finally come to me, she said without doubt or hesitation that the baby is coming today. She checked me. I was finally at seven centimeters. The front of my cervix still had a lip on it, and baby was posterior (sunny side up). I had excruciating back labor for so long because of this. The midwife suggested we do some new positions to get baby to face the correct way for pushing.

The next few hours were so difficult. My contractions were so strong. After letting go of layers of emotional baggage, I was exposed. This was freeing but also exhausting. The contractions were now so powerful, although they were still five minutes apart. At the suggestion of my midwife, I endured some contractions in an inverted position with my knees on the couch and my elbows on the ground. We needed to move baby out of the pelvis so she could face the correct way. These were the most painful contractions of my entire labor. I felt stabbing in my sacrum. I screamed and cried. I begged my husband to tell me when it would be over. My doulas cried with me through the pain. I finally stood back up and endured more while holding onto my husband. I cried through each one. My arms draped around his neck, and him holding me throughout. I cried to him that I loved him so much. That I want to see our baby, but that I would go through ten more days of contractions for him. That is how much I love him. Contrary to the popular belief that women hate their husbands during labor and say all the unspeakables to them, my labor made me feel closer and more in love with my husband. I never knew I could feel so much love. I never knew the depth of my love for him until we went through this together. I will never forget those sweet moments as we continue our relationship into the future.

I then went to the shower. The hot water on my back was so relieving. My husband stood with me in the shower as I was weak. My legs were shaking uncontrollably. My back was so full of pain—now constant. "Where is my baby?" I cried. "I want my baby. Come out, baby. Please, baby, come out," I whimpered. I was so shaky, so my doulas offered me the birth ball. I bounced on it in the shower. Feeling relief in my pelvis and back. I was starting to feel my body open up. Still, the contractions squeezed my back with full force. My husband, hearing my cries, held me and looked at me with such loving eyes. He felt bad that I had been through so many hours of pain. He felt my exhaustion. He felt my frustration. He was with me physically, emotionally, mentally and spiritually the whole time. He cried with me and felt my pain. He was my partner through and through.

I was checked again at 10:00 a.m. I was at ten centimeters. Finally, after thirty-five hours, I reached ten centimeters. I felt wide. I felt ready to push. But there was still a lip on the front part of my cervix. One more challenge to work through before I would start active pushing. My doulas quickly swept in and helped me with another inversion. They also used the rebozo on me to get baby to wiggle into place and to work down the lip. My midwife tried to push the lip back as I pushed, hoping baby's head would move past it. When she attempted to move it out of the way, I felt so much pain. I looked at her with all my soul and asked her if my baby was coming today.

"Alex, your baby will be here soon. You are doing so well. She will be born today!"

The words I longed to hear finally reached my ears. Even though the pain was so intense, I felt so relieved. The next four or five hours were the most blurred, yet were the clearest hours of my life. I was able to push now with each contraction. Since my contractions were still five minutes apart, I had to make the most of each one by pushing hard and with full attention. I started to push. At first, it felt so good to push. My back was still hurting, but I felt relief in my pelvis as I birthed the baby down. After so many pushes, I got tired, though. I was getting worn down. I was coming to another breaking point, or so I thought. But, just like the other breaking points, I never broke. I never gave up. This time, I thought I didn't have enough energy. But my birth team hydrated me, they gave me teaspoons of honey, they encouraged me to snack between pushes. The room felt so warm. My body was flushed and hot. I glanced at the burning candle by the tub, still going just like me. Still burning. Still enduring.

I spent at least an hour pushing on the birth stool. And then, we moved to the bed, where I curled up my knees and pushed more. These pushes didn't feel productive to me, but when the midwife asked me to place my finger inside of me to feel the baby, I felt her! I felt her head. It was soft and squishy. I could feel the moisture, and I could feel her hair. What a miracle! I was getting closer. We then transitioned back to the birth stool. I felt so tired. I told my husband I was tired again. He encouraged me. I was instructed to push harder. As our baby came down, millimeter by millimeter, her head finally peaked out. I used a mirror to see her beautiful head. I could see her coming. This was real. I couldn't believe my baby was almost here! They gave me more honey to help me keep going. I drank more water. They placed a cold washcloth on my head. They turned on Beats Antique, my favorite band, for extra motivation. This was really happening. With my husband behind me, my doulas near me, my midwife in front of me, I pushed so hard. Over and over again, I pushed. They encouraged me through the pushes, through the contractions, through the hours. When my baby's head was crowning, I looked at the mirror. They all told me she is almost here. Then, I felt the most pain of all. My midwife helped make room for the baby's head to come down fully. I felt her fingers stretch me, and then I pushed so hard. I felt my skin opening, I felt so much pressure, I felt myself tearing in places. I felt her head come out. They all cheered!

I don't know what happened next. All I know is that I had a baby in my arms. I felt no pain anymore. I was ecstatic! She was warm, slippery, bloody, and I heard her cry. I heard my baby cry! She was perfect. I held her and cried. She is here now! I couldn't believe it. I just couldn't believe it. I could feel the umbilical cord still connecting us. And her little toes were tickling me. I felt her head on my chest and her breath on me. I felt my husband behind me, holding me, kissing me, telling me how I did a good job. "That's our baby!" he said. I held my baby. I came out alive, and so did she. We birthed together. We did it.

Most birth stories stop there, but to add to an already lengthy journey, I need to make two more notes. One, about the delivery of the placenta and the afterbirth process, and another, about the birth process itself. I moved to the bed to deliver the placenta, but first, my husband helped cut the umbilical cord. I watched him cut it, and then suddenly, my baby was free. She was officially birthed, and she was now her own person. My husband then made skin-to-skin contact with the baby as I delivered the placenta. I was encouraged to cough it out. I felt so much warm blood coming out. And then, a prick in my thigh. They gave me a shot of Pitocin to help control the bleeding. And then more coughing, more blood, more warmth spilling out of me. I was given another medication to control the bleeding. Some tabs to bite on and let dissolve in my mouth. They were bitter, but I didn't care. I just stared at my husband holding our baby, feeling so blessed. I coughed some more, and the placenta came out. They massaged my uterus down to help control the bleeding. After some time passed, I got sutures as my midwife needed to repair some tearing. I had internal tearing between first and second degree, and I also had some external tears. They weren't bad, though, and I didn't feel any pain as she stitched me. They provided a local anesthetic to help, but even the shot of the local anesthetic didn't hurt. Nothing hurt anymore. I had my baby.

It took nine months of pregnancy and forty hours of labor for my baby to come to me. On another level, it took so much more. It took all the things that happened for us to come together—from all the things that brought me life, that brought my husband life, that brought him all the way from Uganda to Minnesota. All of it. This is how I know Isabella existed long before I got a positive result on that pregnancy test. She is and always has been. Just as we are and always have been.

Birth is something unexplainable. There are physical measurements, maybe even emotional ones, but the birth experience I had was spiritual and unexplainable. For anyone who is familiar with rolfing, this was an extremely intimate and internal session. I felt my being come alive. I felt challenged beyond anything I had ever endured. I felt both connected and disconnected to reality—connected to the source, disconnected from anything mundane. I felt part of an entirely different realm of existence. I felt elation. I felt I had experienced something incredibly visceral. I felt safe and warm, fragile and scared, pain and relief. I felt everything—the whole spectrum of human experience. Just as my cervix opened, I, too, opened. I expanded. My daughter gave me all these blessings. She saved me. She helped me to let go. She helped me to open up. She freed me from all the bonds and baggage I was carrying. She gave me life again. In so many ways, she is truly the one who birthed me. Thank you, Isabella Justine Kisitu. Thank you, my baby.

***

After Isabella's birth, I knew I had to continue learning about birth and sharing the knowledge that was taken from me about how powerful women are. I decided I would train to be a doula and started that program about two months after Bella was born. I also was applying for PhD programs at the time as well. I applied to some universities in Australia and the University of Hawai'i at Mānoa. When Bella was about eight months old, I was accepted into the program. We just had a baby and were about to start on a huge adventure in Hawai'i. When we arrived there, Bella was just a year old.

I started my PhD program in sociology in August 2015, and in October 2015, I found out I was pregnant with my son, Noah. I was committed to writing my dissertation with some focus on birth, but my own experience with Noah really solidified how I was to go about it. At the time, I had insurance that would have fully covered a hospital birth, but I intuitively knew that I did not want to go that route. My husband and I decided to interview home birth midwives to see if that might be a better option for us. There are no freestanding birth centers on O'ahu, so that was not an option. And, I really, really did not want to birth in the hospital even if it was fully covered by insurance, and even if it would be expensive for us to hire a home birth midwife. We interviewed Jaymie Lewis, a midwife in O'ahu.

I loved Jaymie's energy from the moment I met her. She was like a unicorn fairy of happiness and love who made me feel so honored and beautiful. She did not pressure us. She offered a lot of education and brought happiness to us from the moment we met her. We immediately decided to hire her, and she was kind enough to let us pay her in installments, so it was affordable for us. I did have tandem care, meaning that I saw the hospital midwives for labs and ultrasounds and also had Jaymie's care. If I were to have another baby, I think I might forgo the tandem care as I felt really held and supported by Jaymie. Our appointments lasted one to two hours, and she came to me, which was a tremendous help as our Bella was a year and a half old. The clinic appointments I had with the hospital midwives were so difficult in comparison. I would have to sit in Honolulu traffic, find parking, sit in the waiting room with our toddler for up to forty-five minutes and then be seen for fifteen minutes. My appointments with Jaymie were so much more humane and loving. She would talk with me about things going on in my life; she would involve my daughter in checking my belly; she would talk to my baby when she baby-mapped my belly. She would help me to feel calm and prepared, and she made me feel beautiful.

I am sure people thought I was crazy for getting pregnant my first semester of my PhD program and then having my son that summer. But he just had to be here. My pregnancy with our son was relatively easy. I never had any morning sickness with any of my babies, just a little nausea in the first weeks. My pregnancies were otherwise easy, but while Bella's labor lasted a long time (forty hours), the pregnancy with my son lasted what felt like an eternity. He was "due" to be born on July 3, 2016. As you might suspect, due dates are really guesses. He did not arrive until ten days later, on the thirteenth. My hips and back were so sore those last two weeks, and I spent a lot of time crying at night, feeling impatient for his arrival. Despite all the waiting, I was never scared to give birth to him, though.

A couple of days before he was born, my husband had a dream that he should change the direction of the bed. As it turns out, I gave birth in the space opened up in the bedroom by moving the bed. Sometimes, things happen that we don't understand, and then later, the reasons reveal themselves to us. So, without further ado, here is Noah's birth story. I do have to admit that this is the first time I am writing it. When you have two little children to take care of plus a PhD program to finish, it is quite difficult to write a birth story that pays enough homage to such a beautiful birth.

On July 12, we took another hike up Wilhelmina Rise, one of the steepest roads on O'ahu. At a 15 percent incline, it's the perfect hill to climb to induce labor. And I wasn't the first mama to hike it. I had been walking the hill every evening for about a week and a half, hoping it would start my labor. On the evening of July 12, I felt things had shifted. I felt wider and my hips looser. My back was tightening around my sacrum. I was ready to have this baby! My mom had flown into town on the third to help us with our daughter, and we had waited ten days for this baby to come. She spoke to my belly to tell baby to hurry up as she had to fly out on the fourteenth. That night, I slept for about five hours, then woke up at one-thirty in the morning with my first contraction. I was so happy that labor started. I laid next to my husband and told him that my labor was starting. My mom woke up, too, and we all decided to go back to sleep to rest up for labor.

We were living in an apartment right at the bottom of Manoa Valley at the time, and the only thing that worried me about an apartment birth was that I might disturb my neighbors with birth sounds (i.e., screaming!). I also wondered how we were going to fit my midwife, her assistant, all the birth equipment, my mom, husband, daughter, and the birth pool all in the tiny space we had. But I quickly learned that midwives know how to navigate any space, however tiny or hot or cold or hard to get to. Midwives know how to support birth, which is taking into account all the people and things in a space.

Around six thirty in the morning, we all woke up to start the day. I was relieved that my contractions weren't too powerful up until now, as I was able to get some rest. I texted my midwife to let her know labor had started. My contractions were consistently five minutes apart and slowly picking up in intensity. She told me to let her know when things start to get more intense. So, I ate breakfast and spent time with our daughter, feeling mixed feelings about the fact that we were spending our last couple of hours together as just us—her as an only child one last time—knowing that her life was about to change just as much as mine and my husband's. After we finished eating, my husband pumped up the birth pool in our living room.

My mom kept my daughter busy while I was walking around the apartment. My husband and I decided to walk to a nearby grocery store to keep labor going and to distract myself—and to grab some snacks for the day. I remember walking down the aisle and pausing to focus on a contraction. One of the store clerks asked if I was okay and if I should go to the hospital. Their concern for me was humorous as I did not need any assistance and was about to walk home to push a baby out in just a few short hours from then. After we paid for our snacks and refreshments, we started our ten-minute walk back home.

We had to cross a busy road, and as we crossed the street, a strong contraction started. I had to pause in the middle of the crosswalk to manage a contraction. My husband turned around to tell me to hurry up as the light was about to turn and allow cars to go. I shouted back to him that I couldn't hurry up my contraction. I was hoping the cars wouldn't run me over, but what could I do? Once the gripping lightened up, a.k.a. the contraction "peaked," I was able to run the rest of the way across the street. If you have never felt contractions before, they feel like a mountain and a vice at the same time. It feels like a vice that increases in intensity until it peaks, then slowly lets up, and the feeling of release as it loosens its grip is so relieving. Another contraction was behind me.

We were back at our apartment at about nine-thirty that morning, and I decided to climb the stairwell and then take a hot shower to relieve the pain. We decided to call Jaymie to let her know we wanted her to be here soon. I was already starting to feel wide and wanting to push. My voice became deeper, and I started to grunt. I felt more pressure on my cervix. I was able to feel calm until my midwife showed up. Once she arrived, it finally settled in my soul that a whole new person was going to come through me, and I just fell to tears. She lovingly held me and touched my belly, connecting with my baby as she had done so sweetly each time I had seen her during my pregnancy. She spoke words of love and encouragement into me. It was about eleven thirty in the morning. I asked her to check how dilated my cervix was as I felt like things were moving quickly. I prayed that I was more than two centimeters, and it turned out I was at a five. Halfway there. I could do this!

I decided to go into the birth pool. I felt so buoyant and ungrounded, so Jaymie put a couple of drops of frankincense oil into the pool. I enjoyed the smell but still felt ungrounded. The water was warm, and my husband and midwife took turns pouring water down my back. I felt like I was traveling to a place—one that all birthing women go to. It is unexplainable. But I was on my way there. I was oscillating between this space and what was in front of me. The water cooled off and became uncomfortable without heat. So, they heated up water and added it to the birth pool. As that happened, I became too relaxed, and my contractions slowed. It was a nice break, but I was ready to have our baby. Labor is such a dance between movement and moments of stillness. This labor, unlike my daughter's, felt different. I could intensify the labor by moving around and doing lunges. If I were still, the contractions would be less intense and further apart. I was working with my body and its timing. So, I climbed out of the birth pool and made my way to our bedroom to lay on the bed. I needed to rest a little more on the bed as I was getting closer to birthing our son. Soon, I couldn't control the timing or intensity of the surges. Birth overcame me. I had to surrender.

I knew the time was getting closer, and my midwife and her assistant (named Madeleine, who was a wonderful naturopathic doctor and midwife) started laying down chucks pads, getting blankets ready, turning the fan off so baby wouldn't be cold, and much to my dismay, they pulled out the birthing stool. I had a love-hate relationship with that thing. A birthing stool is a backless stool, typically in a U-shape. There is a cutout, in other words, in the middle of the seat. Usually, a support person (doula, partner or midwife) will sit behind the woman for support while she uses the birthing stool for support as she squats and pushes her baby out.

Birthing stools have been used globally for millennia and are used in many cultures today, including in my husband's home country of Uganda. Birthing stools can improve maternal and fetal outcomes, help open the pelvis, and take pressure off the spine. When obstetrics assumed power over birth, women were made to lie down during birth. This can intensify the pain and delay labor, especially in the pushing phase. For me, the birth stool meant business. It meant baby time! And it meant that I had to go to that place of full surrender. So, reluctantly, I squatted down on the birth stool. Fully naked. Fully vulnerable. Fully loved. I was there, but I was gone – off to the rainbow bridge to get my baby.

I pushed every time I felt a contraction, on and off for about forty-five minutes, I would give all my might, my energy, my strength, my breath to each push. I was so winded and sweaty. I felt my baby's head open my pelvis and press against my tailbone. I knew I was opening, not just physically, but in all ways. I was surrounded by the love of my midwife, her assistant and my husband. But, even when surrounded by all the love, birth is a woman's individual work to do. It is her journey through pain, elation, doubt, tears and triumph (if all goes well).

My midwife noticed I was starting to doubt myself. I felt I would split into a million pieces and dissolve. I felt that I couldn't expand anymore. "Infinite expansions," my midwife spoke as she stared into my eyes. I knew I was capable of expanding, of experiencing all the pain and doubt, of overcoming and transcending all of the fear and anguish, of transmuting all of this into a miracle, and of bringing this baby into the world. I went to that place within. And I was able to come closer and closer to my baby. He was almost here.

My mother had taken my daughter down to the swimming pool to swim and nap. She woke up around this time and said to my mom, "Happy Birthday." A few minutes later, my baby boy emerged from my womb. My water broke as he came out. He was almost born *en caul* (in the birthing sac). He was finally here. My sweet boy. We named him Noah. And, just as he was born, it started raining in the valley, making a rainbow over the mountains. His energy was so sweet and calm. He still is the sweetest, kindest, most thoughtful child I've ever met. His sister held him. We all loved on him. And my womb, once again, brought life into the world. What a blessing and an honor to be that vessel. It was two-thirty-one in the afternoon on July 13, 2016.

***

The birth of my daughter led me to pursue a PhD in sociology at the University of Hawaiʻi at Mānoa. And, when we got to Hawaiʻi and birthed our son in 2016, I knew that I had to focus my research on home birth. No topic was as important to me as this one. I interviewed home birth mothers and heard their stories of physical and spiritual transformations. I had never felt so connected to a group of women as I did through this process, knowing that they had gone through the same initiation as I had. This collective means the world to me even now. These are the women and midwives who honor life. I am here to tell my story, their stories, and ultimately the story of the womb. It's a story of struggle, disruption, pain, triumph, loss, spirituality, geneology and expansion.

Chapter 1:
The History of Childbirth

When we are taught sex-ed in school, we are taught how women become pregnant. But they fail to mention how to prep women for pregnancy and birth; and, further, they fail to also mention the history of childbirth in America. This history may surprise you; it may even irritate you. One question that always perplexes me is why we don't know more about the history of birth. Why are we not teaching our youth about this history? Why are we not teaching young women about the capacity of their bodies and their spirits? Why are we not teaching everyone about the processes that perpetuate our human existence? This book will unravel these questions and hopefully provide some answers and direction for those who believe and know that birth is perhaps the most important topic of our time.

Birth took place at home for much of our human history. It was only in the early 1900's when some women began birthing in a medical setting. By 1940, almost half of all births were in the hospital, and by 1969, home birth was down to just one percent of births. Unless you have explored this topic of birth diligently and unbiasedly, I am sure by now you have been conditioned to believe that home birth is absolutely dangerous and that mothers and babies died by droves before hospital birth. Hospital birth was our savior. But what is left out of this conversation is the fact that there might have been a multitude of variables and factors affecting birth outcomes during that time (including unsanitary water and living conditions), the least of which may have been the location of the childbirth. Yet, our conditionings and our collective and cultural beliefs around childbirth have been meticulously designed by elites, not by birthing women themselves.

As hard as it might be to hear, you have been molded to think that birth is unsafe. You have been conditioned to believe that women aren't strong enough to birth on their own; you have been conditioned to run away from pain rather than let it transform and strengthen you; you have been conditioned to believe birth was so very dangerous before hospitals and doctors intervened. You've been lied to. And, of course, birth is just the tip of the iceberg on our conditioning. If women were not designed to birth naturally, why have we survived so long? Why are home birth midwives snubbed as being less educated and "woo woo"? What kind of power did women possess before it was taken away from us through mental conditionings that infected us with insecurity and fear? These are questions that I have always pondered. I don't mean to say every woman can birth without assistance or that it is always safe for every woman and baby, but the vast majority of births happen naturally and without issue. I started asking more and more questions during my pregnancies and birth experiences.

When you ask questions, sometimes you end up opening Pandora's box. And your conditionings begin to unravel, and you may start to see where you give away your own power and responsibilities to others and to systems. Birth is such a metaphor for this process—where you begin to see new truths and possibilities. Still, it's been a challenge to consider my own conditionings, my own fears, my own aversion to pain, and the ways in which I have so often given away my own power and sovereignty as a woman and mother. Reclamation is an ongoing process and sometimes a painful one. No one is perfect at this. But it is work that must be done. I believe that one day birth will be reclaimed. It is in our bones, in our cells, and in our wombs.

There is an untold history of how and why birth moved from home to hospital, and what is often left out of the picture is how powerful women are and how much the power-stealers then and now continue to stigmatize home birth. I wanted to know who erased our histories and replaced them with stringent cultural rules about what to do with our births. So, I set out to understand more about the history of childbirth. The medical-industrial complex was introduced by wealthy elites in the early 1900s. They essentially wished to assume control over "healthcare" (including birth, life and death) through codifying medical practices, funding and establishing medical schools, and building hospitals. Anyone who wasn't trained in their system (which was essentially rich men at the time) was guilty of illegal activities under the guise of "practicing medicine without a license." They—and I mean the Rockefeller, Rothschild and Carnegie families specifically—were funding this all. They were assuming the power over medicine, the power over healing, and the power over birth.

They fiercely protected their business—the business of power—by initiating smear campaigns against midwives, home births and healers. They aimed for more and more clients. So, they marketed hospital birth as superior and safer than home birth (a brilliant strategy to obtain a never-ending flow of dollars and clients). Although some of the earlier hospital birth practices were quite unsafe and even barbaric (like strapping women to a table and putting them to sleep), their campaign to move birth to the hospital and into the hands of doctors was very successful. Nowadays, most births in the United States take place in the hospital, yet there is a small percentage of women who still choose to birth at home with midwives and/or unassisted. They choose to question the narrative given to them and instead may choose to trust their own research, their own bodies, and their own intuitions. In recent years, out-of-hospital births have even been on the rise, perhaps as a response to sociocultural factors or perhaps as a spiritual inclination toward a reclamation of our innate intuition. While out-of-hospital births account for a tiny percentage of all births, women continued to be vilified for choosing home birth. But why? Why is this choice so very controversial? Who made it so? How does this impact our births and our babies?

Let's dive in and start with the American College of Obstetrics and Gynecologists (ACOG), a large, well-funded organization that shapes policies around birth and practices used in hospital birth. It's not surprising that ACOG has continuously expressed its negative stance against home birth, citing studies that conclude that home birth is less safe than hospital birth (Committee Opinion 697). While ACOG is involved in producing guidelines for providers and educating patients, they are also actively involved in lobbying against and providing statements on legislation related to birth and midwifery. Isn't it amazing the lengths that particular industries go to in order to protect their profit? ACOG commonly cites studies (which are often sponsored by some arm of ACOG or similar organizations) indicating that home birth is risky and unsafe for mothers and babies. Yet, there is mounting evidence suggesting otherwise, particularly for low-risk mothers and babies. And there is also mounting evidence that hospital birth in America is increasingly unsafe.

ACOG's stance connects directly to the history of birth and medical authority in the United States. As mentioned, when the American medical establishment began gaining power and rapport in the early 1900s, midwives were routinely criminalized, and their reputations were smeared for "practicing medicine without a license." They were also seen as a threat to the larger aims of the biomedical field, which include medical dominance, physician authority and financial gain. The medicalization of birth became a process through which physicians assumed the authority to view pregnancy and childbirth as pathological (i.e., a condition to be managed). So, not only did this medical establishment take away the innate ability of healers to practice their healing modalities, but it also assumed authority over instances of birth and death. When childbirth and pregnancy were medicalized, only the medical institution had the authority to oversee these natural life processes.

Medicalization, put briefly, is the process by which normal, nonmedical problems and even life processes (such as childbirth, menstruation and menopause) are defined and treated as medical issues (Bird, Conrad and Fremont, 2010). The medicalization of birth also, not surprisingly, happened during the same time that indigenous healing modalities on the US mainland and in Hawai'i were being banned as well. The criminalization of home birth (especially for indigenous women and women of color) and the larger colonial project of Western biomedical dominance all contributed to the medicalization of birth as well as the move from home to hospital (Oparah and Bonaparte, 2016). The stigmatization of home birth and home birth mothers is connected to the proliferation of scientific thinking and the dismissal of other ways of knowing as well. Essentially, medicalization has stigmatized home birth mothers and healers in this way.

Other ways of healing and knowing beyond the scientific realm are sacred to many. These ways of healing are often intuitive, meticulous, refined, ancestral and spiritual. Western biomedical dominance completely wipes these other methods of healing off the map. It is not just medical warfare in this sense, but it is also a spiritual war against our most innate, intimate, spiritual, ancestral and familial ways of healing.

Who Are Home Birth Mothers?

While all of us have been conditioned to birth in the hospital, there are a select few (less than two percent in the US) who choose to birth at home instead. I understand why I chose to birth at home, but I wanted to understand why other women did as well. I also wanted to know more about who these women were, what values they had, how they lived their lives, and how they viewed the world. Rather than be led by some idea or trope that has been propagated to us by the medical-industrial complex, the best way to understand who home-birth moms actually are is to ask them. I've found that the best way to know anything is to go to the source, anyhow. Want to know who someone is? Spend time with them. So, I did. I sat with the stigmas, the ideas, the rumors about who home-birth mothers are, threw them out the window, and decided to ask them to describe themselves. Throughout my pregnancy, I became closer to the home-birth community, and when I finally decided to focus my dissertation on the topic of home-birth mothers, I decided to interview fifty-nine of them.

Before I explain more about these mothers, I also want to provide some context around the histories of Hawai'i. Hawai'i has complex histories, rich cultures, and has been subjected to colonization, violence and disease due to the American occupation of the Islands. These histories shape women's home birth experiences as well as the mothers' worldviews and lifestyles. These histories also shape birth. In 2019, 16,649 babies were born in Hawai'i. Of those births, 302 (1.77 percent) babies were born outside the hospital through planned home births, and seven babies were transferred to the hospital for further care (The Hawai'i Home Birth Task Force, 2019). This is a relatively small number of babies born at home and a small number of women who make this choice. Today, only about one percent of babies are born at home in the United States each year. While home births happen all across the continental United States, Hawai'i is a particularly unique place given its history, location in the middle of the Pacific, diversity, climate, topography, culture, politics and values.

As someone who birthed my son at home in Hawai'i, I am particularly interested in this place, its spirit, and its people. This place also offers an opportunity to explore how home birth is deeply entangled in social interactions and experiences that connect to settler-colonialism, medical authority, midwifery, neoliberalism, medical individualism, spiritual practices, culture and sovereignty. For instance, many people in the home birth community in Hawai'i have strong connections with their midwives, their spiritual practices, the Hawaiian sovereignty movement, and their respective cultures. Many people in the community value health practices and aim to reduce reliance on paternalistic medical systems.

As with anything in life, nothing is cut and dry. Everything flows and overlaps, and if you can open your mind and spirit, you will see that everything is interconnected. When I set out to understand who home birth mothers are and what their lives are like, I found out how interconnected all their lives were, from their value systems to their lifestyles. I needed to have some sort of visual to understand all that goes into deciding to home birth and all its interconnections and overlaps. So, I developed a conceptual model in an attempt to capture the experiences of home birth mothers, including not just their physical experience of birth but all its spiritual, ancestral, intuitive and expansive facets as well. Likewise, the importance of spirituality, the microbiome, family connections, and indigenous identity are vital to many of the home birth moms. To give you more insight into how these all connect, this conceptual framework could be used to understand the linkages and connections between a variety of physical, emotional, and spiritual experiences shared by home-birth moms in Hawai'i. For instance, many mothers viewed family-centeredness as a place to incorporate their spirituality and ancestral strength.

I hope that the following conceptual model helps you to see that home birth is connected to so many seemingly unrelated topics and ways of living (while some may be obvious as well). These topics will be addressed throughout this book and will hopefully help you to see that home birth isn't some crazy, unsafe choice. Or perhaps you bought this book because you are a home-birth mother, or maybe you are considering having a home birth. In this case, I hope this book brings you the strength, inspiration and encouragement to birth on your own terms and helps you connect to other home-birth moms throughout the world.

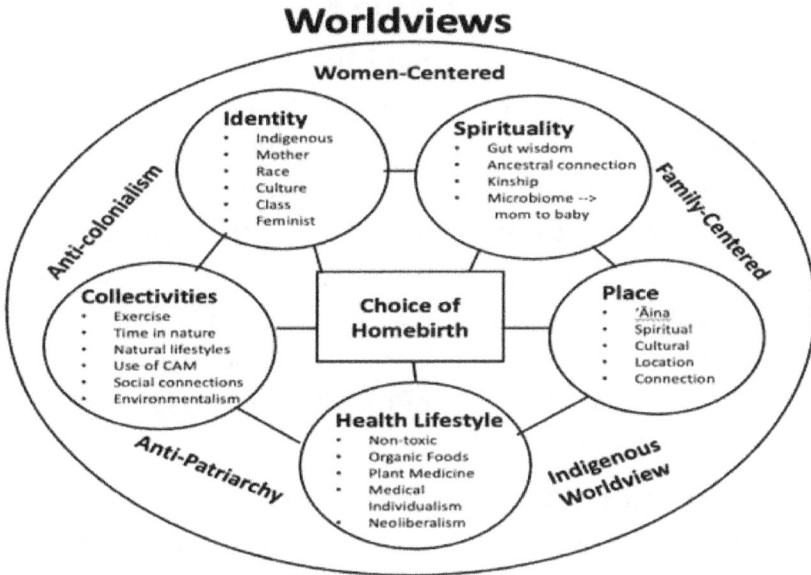

Worldviews

Women-Centered

Anti-colonialism

Family-Centered

Identity
- Indigenous
- Mother
- Race
- Culture
- Class
- Feminist

Spirituality
- Gut wisdom
- Ancestral connection
- Kinship
- Microbiome -->
  mom to baby

Collectivities
- Exercise
- Time in nature
- Natural lifestyles
- Use of CAM
- Social connections
- Environmentalism

Choice of Homebirth

Place
- 'Āina
- Spiritual
- Cultural
- Location
- Connection

Health Lifestyle
- Non-toxic
- Organic Foods
- Plant Medicine
- Medical Individualism
- Neoliberalism

Anti-Patriarchy

Indigenous Worldview

I would also like to make a note that particular terms are used interchangably. I use the terms home birth and out-of-hospital birth interchangeably. All of the births referred to are planned home births. Home birth essentially means any birth occurring at home (one's own home or another's home). Out-of-hospital birth can include birthing anywhere outside the hospital, including outdoors, indoors, at a free-standing birthing center, or at home. Additionally, I may use the terms "freebirth" and "unassisted birth" to refer to any mothers who intentionally birthed their baby(ies) without a midwife or a doctor present. I would like to offer definitions of various forms of birth workers:

Certified Nurse Midwives (CNM): Certified nurse-midwives are trained in both nursing and midwifery. Their training is hospital-based, and the vast majority of CNMs practice in clinics and hospitals. Although their training occurs in medical settings, the CMN/CM scope of practice allows them to provide care in any birth setting (Midwives Alliance North America).

Cultural, Lay, Traditional Midwives: There are midwives who—for religious, personal and philosophical reasons—choose not to become certified or licensed. Typically, they are called traditional midwives. They believe that they are ultimately accountable to the communities they serve, that midwifery is a social contract between the midwife and client/patient and should not be legislated at all, and that women have a right to choose qualified care providers regardless of their legal status (Midwives Alliance North America).

Direct-Entry Midwife: Direct-entry midwives are trained to provide the midwifery model of care to healthy women and newborns, primarily in out-of-hospital settings. They do not have a nursing education as a prerequisite for midwifery education (Midwives Alliance North America).

Certified Midwife (CM): Certified midwives have a background in a health-related field other than nursing and then graduate from a master's level midwifery education program. They have similar training to CNMs and conform to the same standards as CNMs but are not required to have the nursing component (Midwives Alliance North America).

Certified Professional Midwife (CPM): The vast majority of direct-entry midwives in the United States are certified professional midwives. The CPM is the only midwifery credential that requires knowledge about and experience in out-of-hospital settings. Their education and clinical training focus on providing midwifery model care in homes and freestanding birth centers. In some states, CPMs may also practice in clinics and doctor's offices, providing well-woman and maternity care (Midwives Alliance North America).

Obstetrician: A physician or surgeon qualified to practice obstetrics, which deals with all aspects of pregnancy, from prenatal care to post-natal care. An obstetrician delivers babies (a gynecologist does not).

Gynecologist: A physician or surgeon qualified in the care of women during pregnancy and childbirth and in the diagnosis and treatment of diseases of the female reproductive organs.

Doula: A person, typically a woman, who provides continuous physical, emotional and informational support to a mother before, during and shortly after childbirth.

Childbirth in America and Hawai'i

Birth workers, family members and midwives oversaw most pregnancies and births from time immemorial up until birth was moved from home to hospital in the early 1900s. Throughout history, birth workers have helped families usher in new generations. Beginning in the 1800s, midwives and the practice of midwifery were snubbed by elitists as the biomedical establishment asserted more power and authority over pregnancy and birth. During the early 1900s, some women, especially upper-middle-class White women, advocated for physician care and pain relief during labor (perhaps somewhat in response to the idea that women deserve pain during childbirth as a punishment for original sin). Others were opposed to taking birth out of the home and into hospitals. With the advancement of university hospitals and scientific research (funded by the Rockefeller family and other financial moguls), ideas about birth and pregnancy began shifting. Accordingly, Dye (1980:97) writes:

> Virtually all histories of obstetrics conceptualize the development of modern obstetrical practices in a linear, progressive fashion: a handful of dedicated men in the late eighteenth and nineteenth centuries brought birth out of the realm of ignorance and superstition and laid the foundation for a scientific understanding of the birth process.

As male physicians aimed to develop autonomy and authority, and indeed more clientele, the campaign against midwives and "superstitions" (i.e., natural medicine, healers, metaphysical healing) turned repressive. Despite generations of healing knowledge and birth work, midwives were criminalized for practicing medicine without a license and, indeed, for being seen as a threat to medical dominance, authority, and financial gain (Ehrenreich and English, 2010).

For example, Granny Midwives, descendants of enslaved Africans, carried on birth traditions and midwifery practices from their African ancestors. Granny Midwives assisted both Black and White mothers in the birth of their children during slavery and the mass settlement of the landmass that today is called the United States of America. Granny Midwives were once revered and used by slave owners for their healing powers and birth knowledge. Yet, in November of 1921, the Sheppard–Towner Maternity and Infancy Act was passed into law, making the practice of midwifery illegal for Granny Midwives unless they attended expensive schools for training and paid for licensure (History, Art and Archives). Of course, the Granny Midwives often did not have the funds for or access to such "schooling" and licensure. The Sheppard–Towner Maternity and Infancy Act did supply some funding for midwifery training for in-hospital births; however, many Black mothers "preferred home births to hospital deliveries because they could avoid the prejudice and discrimination they often experienced in White society" (Morrison and Fee, 2010:238).

Despite the attempts to advertise hospital birth as a safer alternative, there was not a full assessment of the dangers of new medical practices during this time. It was widely argued that hospital birth was safer and based on reliable science, and yet there is still little known about how social class and race affected the medical treatment and maternal and neonatal outcomes during the early 1900s. Although midwifery was described as unsafe, unsanitary and perhaps even deadly for mothers and babies, there was a lack of data to support this statement. In fact, hospital birth did not initially result in lower mortality rates, and mortality rates *actually increased* after midwives were run out of their practices. Rumor has it that the midwives had to train the doctors to wash their hands, as many women were dying of childbed fever during hospital births.

The US has a long history when it comes to home birth. In fact, Hawai'i has had its own unique history with midwives and childbirth choices. Native Hawaiian and cultural midwives in Hawai'i existed long before the United States occupied the Islands and overthrew Queen Lili'uokalani. Birth traditions were passed down from generation to generation through the family, but in 1883, when Lili'uokalani was overthrown by elite American businessmen and the US military, Hawaiian cultural and healing practices were banned (Trask, 1999).

The Department of Health (now the State of Hawai'i's Department of Health) passed a law in 1931 to regulate midwives. Many midwives who did not fall under the scope of state regulations became illegal, including Hawaiian midwives and birthworkers, despite generations of practice and training. In 1998, the midwifery regulation bill was repealed when nurse midwives, the vast majority of whom worked in hospitals and did not attend home births, were placed under the board of nursing (Blair, 2019). Following the repeal of the bill, midwifery was no longer regulated in Hawai'i, and home-birth midwives were able to practice in a sort of legal grey zone. As of July 2023, only midwives trained on the mainland are allowed to practice home birth midwifery, leaving out dozens of culturally trained midwives with ancient knowledge and decades of experience.

During the 1960s and 70s, when lay midwifery was illegal in Hawai'i, the Hawaiian Cultural Renaissance was underway, and Hawaiians were beginning to reclaim traditions, language, hula, chants and cultural and birth practices that were previously banned by American settlers and cultural forces (Pacific Birth Collective).

> Once at the brink of extinction, the language is taught widely in immersion schools around the Islands. However, generational trauma still exists, and the traumas of the past are not viewed as distant historical events but run as an undercurrent to modern culture, politics, and society. (Pacific Birth Collective 2020)

The Hawaiian renaissance in the 1960s and 1970s also coincided with the midwifery/home-birth renaissance and women's health movement on the mainland. An exciting new energy of reclaiming power over the female body and making informed health decisions proliferated US culture. And in Hawai'i, this went deeper into reviving cultural birthing practices. Still, the reclamation continues as cultural practices have become Westernized in Hawai'i. The Pacific Birth Collective (2020) writes:

> Many of the traditional birthing practices have been replaced, indoctrinated, or wiped out by Western models of health care, education, and standards. Despite these challenges, we still have a growing number of Native Hawaiian birth keepers, ko'okua (doulas), advocates, kumu (educators), and pale keiki (midwives) who are nurturing, revitalizing, and bringing back the traditions around pregnancy, birth, and postpartum. They are planting the seeds of change for this generation and for all future generations.

The reclamation of birth practices and the increase of women choosing home birth during this time seems to signify not only a resistance to colonization and reclamation of culture but also changing ideas of women's roles and reproductive choices in society. These ideas of who should have (and even who is allowed to have) a home birth, who is equipped to be a good mother, who should manage their fertility and who shouldn't, however, continued to differ depending on a woman's race, class, sexual practices, culture, indigenous identity, etc.

Despite the rise of the women's health movement and the Hawaiian cultural renaissance, midwifery and home birth continue to be under threat in Hawai'i. Bills have been annually proposed to the Hawai'i State Legislature that seek to regulate midwives and ensure they are educated by accredited Midwifery Education Accreditation Council (MEAC) schools on the mainland. Since its establishment in 1991, MEAC and its accredited midwifery schools are, by and large, considered the "gold standard" for midwifery education. This standardization of midwifery practice, and indeed some midwifery schools, have been criticized for being exclusionary to BIPOC midwives and cultural birth practices (Hawai'i State Legislature: Testimony in response to SB1033). Additionally, there are no MEAC-accredited midwifery schools in Hawai'i, so the midwives who would be allowed to practice in the Islands have to leave home to get educated.

Despite such hurdles, year after year, midwifery regulation bills are proposed, and year after year home-birth mothers, midwives, doulas, naturopathic doctors, some medical professionals, and other community members of all racial, ethnic and economic backgrounds spend time, energy and money fighting regulatory bills. Yet, in April of 2019, SB 1033 SD2 HD2, a bill to regulate midwifery, was passed, legislating that midwives in the Islands must be educated through a mainland MEAC-accredited school and must pay for yearly licensure (Hawai'i State Legislature). There is a section in the bill that may or may not allow for lay and cultural midwives to practice. The Hawai'i Home Birth Task Force, comprised of midwives and birth workers, have tried to convince the State of Hawai'i and its regulatory bodies to agree that lay and cultural midwives should have the legal right to practice in Hawaiʻi if they are to continue practicing in the ways that are most spiritually and culturally aligned (Hawaiʻi State Legislature). Unfortunately, as of July 2023, lay and cultural midwives are no longer allowed to practice midwifery without Western midwifery training through a MEAC-accredited mainland school.

So, we see that midwifery and home birth continue to be regulated, scrutinized and stigmatized in many complex ways. Midwifery and home birth are deeply enmeshed in histories; regulations; laws; state power; medical power; paradigms on women; views on birth, safety, access and location; indigenous histories and practices; and race, class and gender. Mack (2016:48) argues that:

> Home birth is still socially stigmatized as unsafe;
> many insurance companies do not cover costs
> associated with home births, and the legal status
> of midwifery is continuously contested.

The result is that the medicalization of pregnancy and childbirth continues to be the dominant culture's idea of the "acceptable" way to birth. And ACOG and other organizations continue to push midwifery and home birth to the margins.

What is *Medicalization*?

I think it's important to understand the concept of medicalization as it relates to birth and pregnancy. You may have picked up on some of the processes of medicalization I went through in my own pregnancy experiences shared earlier. Medicalization is defined as "a process by which nonmedical problems become defined and treated as medical problems, usually in terms of illnesses or disorders." (Bird, Conrad, and Fremont, 2010:322). A normal process, like childbirth, is medicalized when it becomes defined in medical terms using medical language to describe the process, and then medical interventions are utilized to treat or manage the process, especially in hospital settings. Sometimes, this language ends up dehumanizing the mother, however, as it is purely pathological terminology that does not acknowledge the spiritual, emotional and mental aspects of pregnancy and birth.

Medicalization and de-medicalization fall on a dynamic spectrum in both biomedical and alternative medicine spaces. A midwife, for example, may prescribe pharmaceutical medications, treatments or interventions for a pregnant mother. A midwife may also use diagnostic tools and screenings, even though she does not view childbirth as pathological or as a medical event. An obstetrician, likewise, may advocate for a low-intervention birth and may steer away from prescribing certain unnecessary medical interventions and medications. The concept of medicalization is, therefore, dynamic and falls on a spectrum, particularly when it's applied to pregnancy and childbirth.

Midwives and home-birth mothers have critiqued the idea that childbirth should be medicalized. The profession of medicine, which male physicians have historically controlled, utilized the powers of professionalization and support of the state to become *the* occupation that assumes autonomy over what is a disease, who is allowed to diagnose and treat diseases, and who is allowed to produce certain kinds of knowledge (in this case medical and scientific knowledge). Professionalization of the medical field and what constituted the *right kind of knowledge*, according to Freidson (1970), allowed physicians (male) to assume social control and monopolize the right to define and treat illness.

Other healing practices, often called quackery or witchcraft and often practiced by female practitioners, were discredited, as were female knowledge and "superstition" (Ehrenreich and English, 2010). The field of medicine has simultaneously pathologized pregnancy and birth while discrediting female wisdom. And, while there are, of course, wonderful, lifesaving advancements, procedures and medications that have come out of the medical field (and there are many wonderful, compassionate people in the field as well), the medical system itself exerts power over birth, death and life in many ways. The medical field is intrinsically connected to social control and the dismantling of healing power and has historically had vast benefits for upper-class men as well. Medicine, therefore, is also often utilized as a social process or means of social control rather than *just* for treating disease. Dare I say that the field of medicine has also been utilized as a tool for spiritual control. We become separated from our intuition, innate sovereignty, spiritual knowledge and inclinations when such industries assume control over the very essence of life itself.

Still, I think it's important to tell both sides of the story, and the truth is that many medical professionals, women and feminists have called for the medicalization of pregnancy and childbirth, believing that hospital birth is safer and far more painless for mothers and babies. Many women were on the front lines of advocating for pain medication and relief during labor, as well as advocating for prenatal care, insurance coverage and better OBGYN care. Indeed, there is good that comes from this, as many women who don't receive prenatal care during pregnancy end up having poor birth outcomes (though this might be attributed to poverty).

Additionally, there are emergencies that may unexpectedly arise in childbirth, such as oxygen deprivation to the baby, shoulder dystocia, retained placenta, hemorrhage, prolonged labors, placenta abruption, placenta previa, preeclampsia, pulmonary embolism, etc., which increase the risk profile for both mothers and babies. While midwives are trained to manage some of these emergencies, sometimes particular emergencies do require immediate medical attention and medical tools. This book is not written to shun the medical system altogether or to judge mothers who need to or choose to birth at the hospital. Rather, I wish to critique the medical approach to birth that tends to silence mothers' needs and voices—you know, the model that puts profits over people and the medical conditionings that strip us away from our sovereignty, ancestral wisdom and female intuition.

Why do female and indigenous knowledge, especially in terms of pregnancy, birth and healing, continue to be discredited by medical authority? For example, in the birth room, female intuitiveness might be discredited if a woman feels her birth is progressing nicely and decides to decline Pitocin (a medication given to induce and speed up labor). The power dynamics in the medical setting often silence these inclinations and intuitions that mothers have, where doctors remind mothers of the importance of following directions for the safety of their babies.

Unfortunately, this also constitutes a huge disruption in her confidence and ability to listen to her body and her intuition. At its worst, such medical paradigms and disruptions signal to the mother that she should not trust in her body, should reject its knowledge, should reject her own inner knowingness, and perhaps even question her connection to her baby. In this way, it is a sort of spiritual disruption that can traumatize a woman for years to come. Imagine, though, a world where intuition, connection and love are at the center of birth, where doctors take the mother's lead, and where this might give the mother immense confidence in herself and her mothering abilities. Perhaps it would change our world in profound ways.

We know that the medical field views birth purely as a physical event. Yet, birth is much more complex and deeper than that. Birth *means* something. It is not just a physical event. The meaning of birth can shape a woman's perception of herself and her baby as well. Oftentimes, home-birth mothers pay special attention to their health and appreciate making choices that promote optimal functioning in the mind, body and spirit. Having control over one's life and health is actually one of the most important determinants of well-being. In my research on home birth, my own home birth experiences, and the conversations with home birth mothers, it became clear that there was a journey to regaining control over one's health and health-related decisions. But these decisions weren't purely for the optimization of physical well-being. These choices and decisions were also quite spiritual. This was particularly highlighted by the indigenous Hawaiians I interviewed.

Indigenous communities have asserted their rights to healing modalities, herbal remedies and plant medicines. And these healing modalities are vital to their communities. Yet, the medical field demonizes indigenous people for any poor health conditions without taking a structural analysis of the effects of colonization and dispossession. Furthermore, when indigenous herbal remedies are effective and/or become more widely used, we often see that such healing modalities are co-opted and marketed by wealthy investors and elites. This "marketing" of plant medicines is a disgrace to the spiritual connections many people have with plant medicine and healing practices.

Colonization, Sovereignty, Birth

It is important here to briefly mention the history of Hawai'i and the anti-colonial struggle to which many Hawaiians and others align themselves. The mothers I interviewed birthed their babies in Hawai'i, after all, and many of them are Hawaiian themselves. The history of Hawai'i is both unique and common in terms of indigenous struggles. While Hawai'i's location in the middle of the Pacific Ocean makes it a unique and perhaps difficult site for settler-colonialism, Hawaiians were, nevertheless, colonized by Westerners (a commonality among many indigenous peoples).

The Hawaiian monarchy was overthrown in 1893 by American businessmen and the US military (Trask, 1999). Hawaiians have since endured language bans, bans on cultural practices, land and resource theft, environmental pollution, disease (including Westerners deliberately giving Hawaiians deadly diseases), cultural loss, loss of indigenous ways of knowing and being, and criminalization (Trask, 1999). In response, Hawaiians have led sovereignty movements, advocating for recognition from the United Nations as a sovereign nation, engaging in language revitalization, revitalizing hula, utilizing traditional healing modalities (e.g., use of herbs, medicinal foods, and lomi lomi), fighting for land reclamation and personal and communal anti-colonial practices (Trask, 1999).

The fight for reclamation extends beyond just land and nationhood. This reclamation also includes birth. And this is not just a Hawaiian-based process. Women all over the world have viewed home birth as a process by which one reclaims sovereignty over their body, their families and/or their birth practices. The birth community to which I belong seems to view the American medicalization of birth as colonization over women's bodies as well. Various efforts to resist medicalization and colonization over the body include revitalizing traditional healing and birthing practices. These practices include but are not limited to allowing a woman to labor for as long as she needs, birthing in an upright or squatting position, burying or consuming the placenta, using a rebozo, using herbs, eating and drinking during labor, using plant medicine, etc. Oftentimes, these practices are not allowed in hospital birth. For instance, in American hospitals, women are generally not allowed to eat during labor (despite how long her labor lasts or how tired or hungry she is). Women are often told to follow the directions of the doctor rather than follow their intuition during childbirth. She is generally not allowed to use a birth pool/tub or birth in any other position besides laying down on her back. These rules are an extension of both the medicalization of and the colonization of women's bodies.

The colonization of birth also extends to belief systems about the body, about women's roles and about women's power. Over time, collective beliefs formed through science and dominant knowledge began to impact how doctors and the rest of society view birth. Other ways of being, other ways of birthing, other ways of doing healing work, other ways of living, etc., are often stigmatized and criticized as being unscientific, superstitious, unproven and even irresponsible. This way of thinking ensured that indigenous ways of knowing and being would be discredited, co-opted and appropriated by the field of medical science. In the context of Hawai'i, dominant ideas of science and medicalization may conflict with some mothers' worldviews, cultural ways of viewing birth, use of plant medicine, healing modalities and even cultural practices around home birth. In the next chapters, I share stories of many births, experiences and viewpoints that touch on these issues in deeply profound ways.

Chapter 2:
The Birth of a Mother

As you now know, the birth of my daughter transformed me, and I became obsessed with birth. This happens to so many women once they have babies. Their first babies transform them in ways they never thought imaginable. I spent a lot of time reflecting on how birth had been presented to me as a young woman. I was indoctrinated by the media, by culture, by stories and by people who told me that birth was the most painful, horrible experience ever. To be sure, birth was painful, but the pain was maybe two percent of the experience. They had left out that birth is amazing, transformative and spiritual. They didn't teach me that I had the power to bring in another soul and to feed a child with my body and my love. They didn't teach me about how much I could expand— from my cervix to my heart. I spent a lot of time wondering why I wasn't taught these things, and sometimes became frustrated and angry. Like, why was I told my body couldn't handle the contractions when it was my body producing the contractions?! I began questioning so much during that time. I suppose I have always been this way—a natural divergent, a person who doesn't accept what is at face value, a natural researcher—but having such a somatic experience as childbirth sent me into overdrive.

I know I am certainly not the first to talk about home birth or home-birth mothers. Nor am I the first person to critique the reasons why our birthing and creative power was taken from us. I suppose the best way to bring the truth about birth forward is to share stories and powerful testimonials of women who gave birth at home. I wanted to share more about who home-birth mothers are beyond the stigmas placed upon them. Maybe, then, people would see them as thoughtful, well-educated and loving mothers capable of following their intuition and honoring their cultural traditions. People might finally realize the incredible responsibility we have to our children and mothers to teach them about the power of birth.

The women I got to know were multifaceted, varied in their backgrounds and were reflexive, thoughtful and mindful about their choices. They smashed any stigmas or preconceived notions about who they were and why they chose home birth. They shared incredibly transformational, spiritual and beautiful stories about their births and their lives with their children. After I finished interviewing all the mothers, listened to their stories several times on my audio recorder, and typed up and read through transcripts of all the stories, I found so many insights, themes and nuggets of wisdom that should be shared with the world—or at least the readers of this book.

I was encouraged by my university committee at the time to reflect on my personal experiences and my background among the stories of the woman I interviewed. The humanities generally push students to reflect on their positionality, and sometimes, this is a good thing. Sometimes, however, it can place students and writers into boxes whereby they must play the game of identity politics and cancel culture before they are able to write anything remotely meaningful, authentic or truthful for humanity. I was troubled by this many times, especially in this politically correct, cancel culture full of wokeism and lacking empathy for alternating viewpoints.

As a home-birth mum, sovereignty (especially with things I create) is particularly important to me. Sovereignty over my words and my perceptions during my PhD program were often challenged, and that felt wrong to me. As a writer, I want sovereignty over my words without the latest hammering by social justice warriors. I want to sit with my words and want others to do the same (even if they disagree). I want an open heart to do the same for others I disagree with as well. I don't want to pander to any one group, but I wish for respectful discourse that moves everyone forward. I don't say this to relieve myself of reflexivity or thoughtfulness regarding our current social climate; I say this as I believe it is important to present one's experience without tallying all the ways in which it might be offensive to someone and quieting one's truth and sovereignty as a result.

That being said, the next section describes some of that "reflexive" process whereby I had to walk on eggshells at times not to be judged for my truths and my identity in the university setting. That is not to say that I don't understand that we are living in a world where people's backgrounds shape their realities, identities and experiences. Yet, being able to express oneself and one's point of view creatively is becoming increasingly more policed and surveilled. As a home-birth mum, this was a huge dilemma for me. Even in our current political and social temperature, I often resist the pressures of being politically correct. I choose authenticity when I can and hopefully in inspiring and non-offensive ways. But words offend. And, apparently, having a birth at home offends as well. Maybe you are also a disrupter of the status quo. If so, welcome! Nevertheless, I am keeping the next section in this book as it was my way of responding to the idea that I needed to categorically separate myself from others because of social constructs and identity politics. I make the point that we can overcome such a notion by returning to the wisdom of the womb, which is a place that connects us all. After all, we are all human, and we all came from the womb.

Reflexivity and the Womb Space

Perhaps all of creation traces its way back to the womb. The womb as a place to start, ponder, connect, diverge and create resonates with me deeply. When I think about what it means to be me, to create from my womb, to have home births, to be a mother, to be a wife, etc., I know I can trace my beginnings back to the womb. Without my womb, I would not be writing this, as my babies have paved the way physically, intellectually, emotionally and spiritually for this work. My existence is traced to my mother's womb, and hers to my grandmother, and finally back to the first grandmother. This great power of the womb to create humans and to make mothers continues.

Before I knew of the power of my own womb, I knew of the power of creation. I connected to it. I learned about what this meant through adventures in the woods and on the lakes of Minnesota and Wisconsin with my stepfather; through my husband, a Ugandan man, who grew up with healers and midwives and now experiences living in the United States, and through my childhood babysitter who is a medicine man, a pipe keeper, and who taught us what it meant to listen to the animals and to the spirit of creation. I learned about what this meant as I watched mothers, and my own mother, bear the weight of what it means to have a womb—the responsibility of creating life. I learned about what this meant when I saw other humans suffer and when I also suffered. It all comes back to the womb.

I know in the social context today, being able to enjoy one's womb and the fruits of it comes from a privileged place. "Privileged" is such a relative term, and I tend to reject its oversimplification, though. Some might view me as privileged because I had birth at home. And, yes, I am highly educated. I have some resources. I have some peace that is inaccessible to many due to a variety of factors. I have access to home birth. I have the ability to write this book. I understand this. I feel a heavy responsibility to do no harm, to learn and to help change things for the better, at least in terms of home birth. But, I also know that the womb can bear the weight of this tough responsibility, and yet it is soft and forgiving. As a child seeks out their mother in times of need, I returned to this womb space when my writing became difficult and when I didn't know how to reconcile conflicting realities and challenges during this time of social strife.

I returned to the womb when I questioned what it meant to do research in Hawai'i, to be a mainlander, to be a woman, and to be a graduate student at the University of Hawai'i. My first experience coming to the Islands was in 2008 as an undergraduate student at the University of St. Thomas in Saint Paul, Minnesota. I took a January-term course in Hawai'i. The course was called Multicultural Communications in Organizational Settings. Our class spent the first part of the course on O'ahu, visiting Iolani Palace and learning about the American occupation of Hawai'i and the overthrow of Queen Lili'uokalani, visiting the Honolulu Museum of Art, "Diamond Head" and taking "The Bus" around town. I had never seen such beauty as I have in Hawai'i. The air smells and feels like a flower's kiss. The sky is a new portrait of heaven every night. The earth felt so alive there and so grounding. I had never experienced being somewhere so beautiful.

We had the opportunity one weekend to leave Honolulu and visit the North Shore. When some classmates and I arrived, we sat at Sunset Beach, where surfers caught huge winter swells. The waves let off a magical mist that left thousands of rainbows dancing as the water curled over and crashed onto the shore break. The sunset there felt like a dream as it painted colors of orange, red and purple on its descent over the ocean horizon. The green mountains throwing more splashes of color onto the most beautiful canvas God could ever create. My soul ached at such beauty. I was already so connected to this place. And yet, even amongst the beauty, there was great sadness and trauma. On our drive that day, we also stopped at the Dole Pineapple Plantation, where I saw many tourists excited about the novelty of being at the "source" of tropical fantasy. I wondered why they weren't as excited to see the sunset, the ocean or the mountains. That always left me confused.

I vividly remember learning that day about Sanford Dole, former owner of many plantations in Hawai'i, who had committed atrocious acts of trauma on Hawaiians. How could anyone be here and want to hurt anyone else, I thought to myself. And while everyone was enchanted with the plantation, I did not see the pineapples so much as I saw disconnection from the source, the womb. I frequently walked Dole Street (a road in Honolulu named after Sanford Dole) during my years as a graduate student at the University of Hawai'i at Mānoa (UH). I later learned about the history of the university from friends and scholars there and how the valley used to be taro fields extending down to what is called Waikīkī before it was taken from Hawaiian families. I learned that UH developed genetically modified kalo, and it helped develop Agent Orange. I kept learning that even amongst beauty, there was so much pain and destruction. What a metaphor for our female bodies and our wombs.

The second part of that January-term class in 2008 was spent on Kauai, where we hiked part of the stunning Napali Coast, visited the lo'i (kalo garden) at Kauai Community College (KCC), and learned a little about Hawaiian history and the experience of American colonization from KCC students. We also spent several days at the Ke Kula Ni'ihau O Kekaha (KKNOK) charter school in Kekeha. KKNOK is a public charter school on the west side of Kauai that serves families of the Ni'ihau community living on Kauai. The school teaches the Ni'ihau dialect of 'Ōlelo Hawai'i as well as English. We worked on a language project while we were there, and we did a beach clean-up at Salt Pond, where we collected trash and turned it into art.

Several years later, I returned to KKNOK for my master's research on indigenous revitalization through cultural-based education. My husband also joined me and did his master's research on leadership at the school. We were blessed to hear stories about the school and the Ni'ihau culture from the leaders. These stories included many challenges stemming from colonization, limited resources, state regulations, etc. We heard stories from another teacher about his involvement in the Hawaiian language revitalization movement from the 1970s until the present-day. He gifted us our first Hawaiian language dictionary, which he helped write and publish alongside other Hawaiian language activists. This was important, as the Hawaiian language was almost extinct due to the American government banning it.

I also spoke with school staff, who are not only teachers but family and community members. They told us stories about Hawai'i, from the days of leprosy to the way life is lived on Ni'ihau (this is one of the Hawaiian Islands that is privately owned and highly regulated as to who can be on the island). They reminded us of the importance of 'Ōlelo Hawai'i (the Hawaiian language) to the cultural and literal survival of the Hawaiian people. We visited the Kauai Botanical Gardens in Poipu with the school and helped construct a traditional Hawaiian hale (house) with members of the US Navy. I also had the chance to talk with Dr. Denis Chun at Kauai Community College and hear his story of the resistance against the Superferry, where he detailed how he and other surfers blocked it from docking on Kauai in an attempt to protect the 'āina (land) and the people of Kauai from further environmental and cultural degradation. I also spent time on the Big Island, visiting several times to participate in dance retreats. There, I connected with other women and carried on legacies of feminine dance knowledge and movements.

My daughter, Bella, was in my womb during one of the return visits to KKNOK and at these dance retreats. I later birthed her in a bedroom at the freestanding birth center in Saint Paul, after laboring for forty hours and traveling to the place where souls are retrieved, as I told earlier in this book. I wrote her birth story when she was three days old, during a warm May morning when the sunlight was shining on us through our living room window. It was then that I knew the importance of the womb and that I had to do work centered on birth.

When we moved to Hawai'i, I continued learning about birth and became pregnant with my son just months into my first year of the PhD program. My womb was full again, as you know. I spent the first semester growing my baby and doing other things that never measured to the importance of creating life. During my pregnancy with Noah, I also met many home-birth mothers and was already dancing weekly with many of them. I met my midwife and other birthkeepers as well. I learned so much from them. In the summer of 2016, I traveled again to the space where souls came from and birthed my son in our apartment bedroom in Honolulu.

I did not grow up in Hawai'i, but the time I have spent on the Islands, visiting and living there, has impacted me significantly and has reaffirmed much of what I was taught in childhood about life, land and existence. I am compelled by heart and mind to honor the histories, the mana, the 'āina, and the people of the Islands through learning more, supporting access to home birth and cultural/lay midwives, and through connecting with mothers. Like all of us, I come from the womb. I come from many grandmothers, some of whom come from the Middle East, some from Europe, and some from the First Nations in America, all of whom are descendants of the first womb, that which/who connects us all. I can only hope this womb space continues to give me the strength to hold these mother's stories and to present them as they would. The womb endures it all.

The Mothers

My experience birthing my son at home in Hawai'i connected me to a network of women who also had given birth outside the hospital. My social circle included many mothers who had given birth at their homes. I spent time with many of these women, at mother-baby classes, at the beach, at Paki Park, at the Honolulu Zoo, at our children's birthday parties, and even through a dance group I was a part of on O'ahu. Because of this proximity to the birth community, my midwife and political activism, I was involved in fighting midwifery regulation bills at the Hawai'i State Legislature.

I was connected with many individuals in the birth community in Hawai'i. When I talked with the mothers, I wanted to understand their lifestyles and worldviews to help destigmatize the perception of home-birth mothers and home birth in general. I asked them about their lives, their values, their worldviews, their birth experiences, what they eat, how they live, etc. The women graciously and openly shared their stories and accounted for the cultural and historical nuances in birth and the fight for midwifery. Because birth is very personal, and relationships with midwives can be deep, close and complex, speaking about such experiences evoked tearful responses from many mums. When I talked with them, I also shared my own home birth experiences, and I believe they were able to talk to me about things they knew I would understand without having to overly explain or defend their experiences because of this shared connection. They also seemed quite aware that I did not feel uncomfortable discussing topics such as placentas, blood, birth plans, pain, death, colonization, informed consent with vaccines, birth, midwifery, feelings about Western medicine, medical authority, etc.

It is often said that childbirth is a rite of passage, and there comes a deep understanding and, oftentimes, comradery with other mothers once a woman experiences birth. For home-birth mamas who choose to have the unique experience of birthing outside the hospital, which accounts for just over one percent of births each year in the US, the understanding of these topics takes on an even deeper form and conversation. Having had that experience myself, I believe this connection was vital to the conversation. Although, I do have to add that most women do love sharing their birth experiences.

Another note to make is that home birth is not accessible nor desired by many people. Many women cannot have a home birth due to conditions such as pre-eclampsia, placenta previa, delayed or stalled labor, failure to begin labor, and even premature labor and birth. The mothers I talked with did not communicate any significant risk factors during their pregnancies, however. That doesn't mean that they were all in perfect health according to biomedical standards, however, as at least two mothers had had histories of physical trauma and serious illness. Two other mothers also explained that they might have been considered high-risk as their weight was higher than what was "biomedically acceptable" for a low-risk pregnancy and birth. Several mothers had GBS (group-B strep), which is a common bacterium that poses a small risk to the infant if left untreated. Several mamas also went past the forty-week pregnancy threshold typically allowed in hospital birth models or gave birth before thirty-seven weeks (another risk factor for potentially adverse neonatal outcomes). Yet, the mothers who may have risked out of home birth were able to navigate their health and their decision-making process with their midwives.

I met with a total of fifty-nine women who had one or more births outside the hospital in Hawai'i. Most of the mothers lived on O'ahu, and several others lived on Hawai'i Island, Maui, and Kauai at the time of their birth(s). I only included mothers who had a planned out-of-hospital birth and did not include mothers who had accidental home births or car births due to fast labors. Most of the home-birth mamas were around twenty-eight to forty years old at the time of the interviews. Most were women from the mainland USA, many were born and raised in Hawai'i (some who would identify themselves as locals), and some had moved to Hawai'i from other countries. As a note, the term local in Hawai'i is a contested, nuanced, complex identity category. Local generally means being born and raised in Hawai'i but also having an appreciation for Hawaiian customs, the culture and the land (Okamura, 1980).

The mothers had varying backgrounds in terms of race, ethnicity, culture, homeownership, education, social class, etc. While their backgrounds impacted their worldviews to an extent, there was so much more in common between the mothers. They all were open-minded individuals, loving, at times fierce, thoughtful, skeptical, well-spoken, mindful, caring and smart. They all had a deep love of family, a deep love and reverence for the capacity of the female body and for other mothers, and they had a deep knowingness and intuition that allowed them to follow their own path and not necessarily the one laid out for them. They were keepers of their wombs in the most magical ways possible. They were incredibly resilient and committed to living life in the way they deemed most authentic. In the next couple of chapters, I am going to share their stories and pay homage to the power of their wombs.

Chapter 3:
Home Birth in Hawai'i

They say birth changes women forever. But in what ways? Birth is different for each labor, each woman and each baby. Birth is not just pushing a baby out; it is many things—it is our connection to the past, present and future, and it is cultural and social. Birth shapes how we see the world and how we measure our lives.

When I asked mothers about their worldviews and how they see birth, I was met with a variety of responses that were rooted in their respective identities, experiences and backgrounds. Sometimes, I did not have to ask about how these mothers saw the world and birth because they often brought up these topics before I could ask the question. Our conversations were so candid and open. Most notable were those women who reported that birthing at home was a choice made in response to colonization, in response to the need to reconnect to 'āina (land) and to reclaim their identity and their culture amongst continued American occupation of the Hawaiian Islands. Women also explained that this related to their need to connect with their innermost knowingness about how they are supposed to birth. So, what has removed women from their connection to land, self and feminine power, and why do some women feel so intuitively compelled to birth at home and reconnect with their inner knowingness?

I continued to have more and more questions as I interviewed the mothers. I needed to know how colonization impacted Hawaiian birth traditions and how Hawaiian moms especially mitigate the impacts of colonization. Hawaiian birth practices can still be understood through the Historical Hawaiian Language Repository, according to Pinto (2019). In her thesis, Pinto describes how pre-colonial birth practices were passed down through oral traditions and stories as well as through the *ohana* (family) systems.

Birth practices weren't limited to labor and delivery, either, as there were intricate protocols, ceremony and methods that pregnant women followed. Relatedly, illnesses, cravings, the child's demeanor, diet choices (i.e., not consuming coconut and certain types of seafood during pregnancy), labor (utilizing different birthing positions that aren't typically allowed in hospitals), postpartum (rest, warmth, soups, plant medicine), care of the afterbirth (placenta), naming customs, umbilical cord care using plant medicine, extended breastfeeding, and weaning all had specific protocols in Hawaiian culture (Green and Beckwith, 1924). For instance, if a mama is craving a particular food, it might mean that her child will have some demeanor related to that food, or if the mom has a longing to see a friend, it means that her child will have a special connection with that friend (Green and Beckwith, 1924). However, such practices and knowledge were essentially undone and banned through the colonization of the Islands. According to Pinto (2019:86):

> Colonization disrupted the intimate relationships
> people have to each other and the environment. It
> disrupted the value of sharing family stories to help
> us navigate current problems because sometimes
> those stories are contradictory to that of Western
> Medicine or Capitalistic models. To be told by West-
> ern Medicine doctors that your culture doesn't work
> rather than to look at the displacement of people, of
> their land, their food source, their medicine, their

trust is a broken model of a health care system, broken land tenure strategies, and broken trust.

Birthing at home and reclaiming traditions and protocols become a sort of decolonial project whereby women, particularly Hawaiian women, might reclaim elements of themselves and their culture that have been taken from them. The following stories dive deeply into the pain of colonization as well as the idea that home birth can be a decolonial practice that invites love, connection, cultural healing, reclaimed identity, sovereignty and kinship.

Journey Toward Reclamation

I first met her at the midwifery bill hearing on Valentine's Day in 2018 at the Hawai'i State Capitol, where we home-birth mothers were fighting against a midwifery regulation bill that would have the potential to outlaw traditional midwives. The hustle and bustle of the capitol building was invigorating and nerve-wracking. Lawmakers, administrators, home birth mums, babies, children, representatives from ACOG and other anti-home birth organizations were all in attendance. It was a mix of sounds—heels clicking on the tile floor, legislators calling off bills to be heard, sounds of babies and children. There were many people there, but one woman stood out the most to me.

She is a vital leader in the birth community and carries herself with the wisdom of a thousand ancestors. She is Hawaiian, kind and strong, and had her baby wrapped up close to her body. She spoke to the panel of legislatures with a voice that was just as quivering as much as it was erupting with strength from the ground beneath her feet. Her long hair and thoughtful words, her strong maternal energy, and her conviction that birth must be held in the hands of women and not male-dominated institutions, was so moving. We hugged at the end of the hearing, although we did not even know each other yet. Still, I was enamored by her strength and ability to articulate herself, share her peoples' stories of colonization, fiercely protect birth, and face a panel of Hawaiian state legislators (or foreign state actors/intruders, depending on how you view it) all after traveling all day with a baby. I later asked her if she would like to be interviewed about her home birth and her lifestyle. She agreed, and we talked over FaceTime as she was on Maui, and I was on Oʻahu at the time of the interview.

She is a *pale keiki* (loosely translated as midwife but means so much more) amongst all the other work she does, and she spends countless hours taking care of her family and her community making sure that Hawaiian birth traditions and healing practices continue into the future. When I asked her whether she holds any worldview that is embedded in anti-colonialism and how that connects to her home birth decisions, this is what she had to say:

> My people have lost so much to colonialism and genocide because of the oppression that comes with that, and it's still alive and well today, unfortunately. You know, looking at this is one of the things I keep reiterating in my testimonies (referring to the midwifery bill meant to regulate midwives). Even around midwifery today in our state and legislation is that it's just an extension of one more form of colonization as they look to kind of oust the traditional practitioners with no reverence for those practices which have been around a lot longer than anything that they're recommending and have been the foundational teachings for those who even created the programs that they say we need, you know, so that's really hard.
>
> I also have a kumu (teacher) who was in my life, and even her last dying words were, "You're right, baby, it's all about birth sovereignty, you know, like these guys are never going to hear you. They're never going to see you like I see you." I said, I'm going to go to nursing school and get some skills, or I'm going to

go here and do this, and she said, "The hell you are!" She was really passionate, and she opened my mind up to be excited about me pursuing these pathways. And she said, "No, but what you have is so sacred. What you have is so special, and it's been stripped of you and your people for so long. Please don't think that you have to focus so much energy, and time, and money, and whatever on being like everybody else." So, part of my practice is definitely about birth and body autonomy in general… body sovereignty, birth sovereignty…

Part of my choices in my own births have everything to do with that. I'm the only one that has to do it. Nobody can do it for me. So I need to be in a place where I feel like I can perform to the best of my ability—this task (laughs), you know, this heavy, heavy big thing. But I'll tell you first-hand the births that I've had. I can tell you the last two births being on their 'āina kūpuna (ancestral lands), not even having a fancy house or fancy anything for that matter, but just being connected to that 'āina being, connected to the rhythms, you know, just being in tune to our kūpuna out there, those births were like two I didn't even push those babies out. You know what I mean? Whereas my other births were totally different. I felt so sovereign. I felt so free. Everybody thought I was crazy, but I felt the most sane I ever felt. And everybody else was saying, "Oh, you can't stay out there, you gotta come to town," and whatever, and I'm like, hmmm, even though when we lived in town, we didn't have access to this 'āina yet.

We went to Happy Valley, out to Kepaniwai, where the first girl was born… just to be back in that home in the country because I had to get out of town.

That's just my perspective. I think it's related to my perception and my experience of feeling really over-whelmed by town, which is not—has been exploited and blown up. And it's just full of all kinds of things that aren't keeping us grounded... We actually drove an hour and a half out to Kepaniwai just to give birth down there because it was out of town, in our cous-in's house. Just to get out of the whole energy and vibration of town, you know? I mean, like getting to a place where I can put my feet on the soil and feel connected... I can hear the river flowing. I can hear the birds. I can see the sky (laughs). (Interview 57)

She went on to talk more about how important autonomy, birth and body sovereignty were to her own birth choices. One important note to make is how she brings up this idea that everybody thought she was crazy; that is, she expresses that there is a level of stigma toward the decision to home birth, particularly away from Kahului, where hospital access is close. This feeling of being stigmatized is not uncommon for home-birth mothers, and they navigate it in a variety of ways, including relying on family traditions.

It was also so very important for her to birth on her *'āina kūpuna* (the land that her ancestors lived on) and connect to the rhythms and energy of the land and tune into her kūpuna (elders/ancestors). *'Āina,* which loosely translates to land, is much more than land for Hawaiians. *'Āina* has spirit and power and is the place that sustains life, mana (power/energy), identity, culture, health, spirituality and community (Goodyear-Ka'ōpua, 2017; McMullin, 2005; Trask, 1999). The freedom this mother knew that being connected to the land, hearing the river flowing, hearing the soil under her feet, and seeing the sky allowed her to feel connected to herself and her kūpuna while disconnecting from "Babylon" (i.e., Kahului, colonial places, traffic, buildings, etc.) so to speak. 'Āina was the place where she found her grounding as a Hawaiian birthing mother; where she could disconnect from colonialism (at least to some extent). Here she describes her experience as deeply intuitive and spiritual:

> For me, just getting out of Babylon, out of this cement jungle that is connected to colonialism and all the development that's happened here in OUR home… just getting back… I think that part of me is deep in my na'au (heart/gut wisdom), that just yearns for something different so that I can feel connected again.

> As a practitioner… we have these meetings through the years where we talk about how we can obtain sovereignty as a nation and whatnot, and one of the biggest things is when we break up into our groups, and I say, okay, you guys have specialties in this area, these guys have specialties in that area. If we were to break off as a nation, how would we lift each other up? And so, one of the first conversations is, well, it starts at birth, right? Sovereignty starts at birth (laughs), so I mean, part of my practice has definitely been focused on supporting those who don't want birth certificates and actually want to be a part of the Hawaiian nation and have only Hawaiian birth certificates. Not everybody's ready to do that, you know.

> A lot of people will do dual citizenship and, at this point in time, I think that's a wise thing to do. But some people want total separation, and I totally support them. And I think I'm one of the only midwives in Maui that actually offers that option because we are bound by law to offer them a birth certificate, but at this point, they actually took that away from us. Anyway, to be able to do our own birth certificates. Now they have to go to the Department of Health, so that's kind of on them at this point anyway, and

> I guess it's kind of a blessing in disguise (laughs) on
> some level because it's taken kuleana (responsibility)
> away from us. (Interview 57)

She painted a picture of contrasts in her words: concrete and nature, sovereignty and colonization, connection and disconnection, nationhood and occupation, and following one's *na'au* (heart) versus going along with mainstream/colonial American ways of birth. Most importantly, I think she highlights the idea that sovereignty as a nation, sovereignty in her identity as a Hawaiian woman, and sovereignty over her body and her baby start at birth—from how we choose where to birth, connecting to 'āina, following and trusting your na'au (heart/gut wisdom), obtaining Hawaiian Nation birth certificates, and building community. This all is part of her identity as a Hawaiian woman, and these practices support her personal and cultural identity.

In Mary Tuti Baker's article (2021), "Gardens of Political Transformation: Indigenism, Anarchism, and Feminism Embodied," the relationship between people and land is described as vital to the concept and practice of aloha 'āina, which is a deep love and reciprocal relationship with the land. Aloha 'āina not only supports the health of land and people but serves as a way of organizing Hawaiian nation-building and political mobilization (Baker 2021). In Western traditions, sovereignty and nation-building are founded upon state formation, borders and power structures. Yet, for many Hawaiians, nation-building, self-governance and sovereignty are intimately connected to the land and to aloha 'āina .

The possibilities for connecting with 'āina that may emerge from the home birth experience may forge a sort of political project whereby home birth becomes part of nation-building. But, this nation-building differs from Western ideologies in that it is founded upon aloha 'āina and "ancestral knowledge, values, and beliefs embodied in the everyday experiences of being 'of-and-on' indigenous ancestral land" (Baker 2021:1553). The connection between home birth, 'āina/place, sovereignty, ancestral knowledge and nation-building is evidenced through many interviews with Hawaiian mothers.

Reclaiming home, 'āina, sovereignty, community and culture seem to be made possible through home birth. Perhaps the process of birthing at home surrounded by family, free from Western medical impositions, and perhaps disconnected from the artifacts of colonization all seemingly foster a sense of sovereignty and empowerment. Other mothers expressed these sentiments as well. I previously met a Hawaiian mother through home-birth friends and later connected with her through holistic living practices. She explained to me the importance of birthing on 'āina/land that is also connected to family. She explained how birth is connected to bureaucracy and militarism and how she reconciles utilization of and contact with colonial institutions amidst practices of reclamation:

> I feel like the colonization of Hawai'i by America, American culture and the institutions that are operating within that framework include hospitals, and I definitely value hospitals and all that they do. We've utilized them many times, but I felt like I could be more outside of that colonized context having a home birth, and it even gets into our birth certificates. I wasn't forced to get a birth certificate within twenty-four hours or whatever it is that you need to do before you check out of a hospital. I did it in the month, one of my children—several months later (laughs).
>
> But yeah, I felt like we could do it on our own and be at home and do it our way, obviously not the same way as my Hawaiian ancestors or as my grandparents' generation even, but having a lot more, I would say… being on our land is important, as well as my kids get to say that they're born where they live, you know, "I was born in my grandma's house." And it's very different.

A lot of other people like this talk about colonization. I was born at Tripler (a military hospital on O'ahu) because my grandfather was in the military, so I have issues with where I was born. But I don't think of my birthplace so much as the place of Tripler or as Tripler hospital as a place, but that the land has a history before Tripler came along, before the military came along, and there are important places and histories there as well. (Interview 58)

Even though spaces and places have been built on important land, there is still the possibility for an unraveling, a sort of peeling back, so to speak, of colonial structures and ideas to reveal what was there before. This strong connection to 'āina rather than to the hospital still lives on. It is then possible to return to the energy of the place. Through many of the interviews, it became clear that while hospitals are utilized and appreciated in particular situations, there is tension because hospitals and Western biomedicine are often considered colonial or at least operate within the colonial frameworks and power dynamics.

Connection to 'āina and the histories and mana (energy) of a particular place are incredibly important to home-birth mothers, particularly Hawaiian mothers. Hawai'i is unique as the island chain is in the middle of the Pacific Ocean and is a land mass that is the furthest from other land masses. Its physical beauty is stunning. Its histories are complex. And, certainly, Hawai'i has unique cultural diversity.

Understanding how places come to be is particularly important in a Hawaiian context due to colonization, migration and tourism, which all impact birth in their own ways. In Hawai'i, the concept of place can also give life and mana (power). It also shapes cultural practices through that life and mana. Land is spiritual for Native Hawaiians and many others who live in the Hawaiian Islands. Culture and spirituality, therefore, are intimately linked to 'āina . That is, place is not just the location at which certain things occur; it is in relation with people as well, it shapes culture and spirituality (and vice versa), and it impacts everyone on the 'āina. Place shapes connections, worldviews, choices and lifestyles. Think about the place where you live and how that place feels, looks and shapes your own lifestyle, your spiritual practices, your community, etc. It is significantly more powerful than you might have ever imagined before.

The significance of place and 'āina continued to erupt from the interviews; from experiences with the hospital setting and sacred temples on the 'āina, place informs peoples' experiences, challenges, and choices that mothers, particularly Hawaiian ones, made in terms of their birth decisions.

Another Hawaiian mother I interviewed, who is a community activist, artist, public health professional, and chef, among many other things, explained that her choice to have a home birth was certainly impacted by the work she has done on decolonization and anti-colonial efforts. She had been mentored for years by Dr. Kekuni Blaisdell, who worked on Hawaiian health and the decolonization of health care (he was also a medical doctor). She explained her own birth experience coming into the world, how it was overly medicalized, and that she experienced birth trauma herself when she was born. She explained her decision to birth at home, how she found her midwife, and how it was sort of wrapped in her struggle with medical control:

> I would just say I don't do well with excessive medical control environments, especially for something like birth. I definitely wanted to stay out of that, so this was when I was going to have my oldest, and I didn't know any of the birth community at all… you know, this is 1993, right? So, at that time, midwifery was totally illegal and out of hospital, none except for nurse midwives. There were no nurse midwives who were practicing out of hospital, so basically out-of-hospital birth was illegal to attend.

> I think it goes back to my own birth experience, honestly, which I can't consciously remember,

but I know that it was very, very traumatic. I have dents on the side of my head because they yanked me with forceps, and I always kind of joke that that was my first struggle with the medical system, and it hasn't stopped (laughs). So when I was pregnant with my oldest, I was looking for an alternative, knowing that at that time midwifery was illegal, and I really didn't know how I was going to do it, but I already knew I was not going to the hospital (laughs). I just didn't know how I was going to pull it off, but I already knew one way or another, I'm not going in, and so fortunately, the head of the University of Hawai'i Women's Center, she somehow came up with a list of possible midwives, and so I took her list.

The first number I called was Medra's. I just heard all these birds going off behind her, and (laughs) it was kind of a crazy conversation, but by the end, I was like, I'm not calling anybody else (laughs). So she's been really a wonderful midwife and teacher all these twenty-four years, twenty-five years now. (Interview 22)

Certainly, her worldview was formed from her very early experiences with the medical system and the trauma she experienced, as well as the resulting issues she had with the medical system. This shaped how she related to the medical system and, to some extent, the health choices she makes in her life now. She later went on to tell me how her first birth, although outside the hospital, was situated in a variety of struggles, particularly related to colonization and authority. She told me that the 'āina/land had called her to birth at a women's temple she had been taking care of, which is now paved over by the H3 Highway. This calling came from her connection to the land. She had been taking care of this place, praying with it, speaking with it, and letting herself be transformed by it.

While she wanted to birth there, the sheriff set up a roadblock and attempted to stop her from going to the temple. She was able to run the gate because their car was near a garbage truck that had to pass, so when the gate opened, they were able to get through the roadblock and drive to the temple. This all happened during the early 1990s when many Hawaiians were being arrested for protesting against repressive colonial pressures and were removed from their lands and prevented from visiting sacred sites. This mother was among those who were arrested during the protests. Such struggles have been common in the Hawaiian sovereignty movement, most recently with kūpuna being arrested on Mauna Kea for protecting it against desecration by state and corporate interests. Accordingly, her decision to birth at the temple was so entangled in colonial efforts to control Hawaiians that they literally set up roadblocks to prevent her from doing so. Yet, she was able to run the roadblock and birth her first child at the temple:

> You know, it was the place I was connected to, and it was a woman's temple. It was like, really? You're going to tell me I can't go? You're going to tell a laboring woman she cannot go to the Hale O Papa (temple)! What the hell is wrong with you people, c'mon! (laughs) So the, yeah, basically, it seemed pretty simple to me, but they did seem to have a problem with it. Oh boy, did they have a problem with it! And, particularly, the female person in charge of the Department of Transportation's decision. Oh my gosh, she was like totally on the witch hunt. Oh my gosh.

> It was interesting because I had to deal with all these men because I let them know beforehand. I went in, and I notified the... I didn't ask permission... but I notified them of what I was going do and basically told them that if they interfered with me while I was in labor, I... although lawsuits were against my

principles… I would sue them. If they… if some harm came to my child because they were going to be totally stupid… I wasn't going to just take that. I basically let them know they were going to be liable, so I think they were a little wary because of that. They didn't know how to handle that.

It was in their interest to keep the whole thing out of the media. I had no interest in calling the press, but if they were going to arrest me during labor, I sure as hell… In fact, I had a press professional, a really good one, with her finger on the red button should anything go wrong. She was prepared to totally set off the alarm, so you know, they were in a little bit of a difficult compromised situation where they had to rethink their decision a little bit. The whole thing was pretty stressful. There were complications and stuff.

It was my first baby, and it was kinda nuts (laughs). But it's not like things have gotten all that much easier, but uh (laughs), but yeah, the reason that I was there was just basically… it wasn't really to prove anything or anything like that… it was because that was a place where I could talk to the land and the land told me, "yeah, come here," (laughs) because I was a weed nik, you know.

So I was wondering where am I going to go because, at the time, we lived in this little apartment where we had very close neighbors all around, and it was like how am I going to give birth over there? It just wasn't happening. It wasn't secure, safe enough. It wasn't where I needed to be, and I didn't really have an alternative, you know, which is the same situation with my daughter, too, but I just did not have a good location, and so I was really praying on a good location,

and since I would go up there and pull weeds, of
course I would be praying at the temple to figure out
a good location. And it's like the whole land is just
like hello duh, you know (laughs), so basically it was
a very clear message: come here. That's it.
(Interview 22)

She ended up following the call, which came from the 'āina, to
birth at the Hale O Papa, and was able to successfully do so. However,
it is clear that her decision to do so was wrapped up in a myriad of
struggles with the State of Hawai'i. These colonial forces literally
aimed to remove Hawaiian mothers from their land and, therefore,
from their identities, their source of life and mana, their culture, and
their practices. She utilized the language of the oppressor, so to speak,
in order to secure the birth she was called to have by threatening
them with lawsuits. While not in line with her value system, she had
to use the pressures of litigation, liability and the threat of bad media
attention to push back against authoritative pressures and rules. She
utilized her networks, her own communication savvy, and prayer as
well.

Colonial authority placed her in the position to have to "defy
orders" so that she could answer the call the 'āina had for her. Her
birth story almost seems to be a David versus Goliath circumstance,
where she had to fight, coordinate and navigate her way to have the
birth she wanted despite insurmountable odds. Alas, the tentacles of
colonization seem to suction themselves to each birth story shared
by Hawaiian mothers.

It is important to note that the majority of Hawaiians have been
displaced from their 'āina kūpuna (ancestral lands) by the American
occupation and militarization (Trask, 1999). Land dispossession and
displacement not only disconnect Hawaiians from their land and,
therefore, their cultural practices, but land dispossession also takes
away access to growing healthy foods, fishing ponds, plant medicines
and spiritual locations (Trask, 1999; McMullin, 2005). Economic and

structural adjustments, tourism and migration also result in the high cost of land and housing as well as low wages in Hawai'i, leaving many Hawaiians without the ability to purchase land and grow their own food (Trask, 1999). This leads people to consume more processed foods as they are cheaper and more accessible, and chronic illnesses arguably increase in the Hawaiian population because of it. Further, militarization and agricultural companies have polluted the land and water in Hawai'i. This has resulted in higher rates of chronic illnesses in the Native Hawaiian and Pacific Islander (NHPI) population. For instance, in their community-based participatory research approach looking at social determinants of health in the NHPI, McElfish, et al. (2019:18-19) found that:

> NHPI community members have faced a significant nutrition transition with changes in lifestyle and food systems resulting from colonization and nuclear test-ing, which has contributed to a higher prevalence of non-communicable diseases. The loss of traditional diet has led to a reliance on imported, canned, and processed foods that are high in saturated fat, sodium, and added sugars, and void of many essential nutri-ents and dietary fiber.

As such, many mothers may not even consider home birth if they're high-risk with health issues such as obesity, diabetes, heart disease and/or cancer. It then becomes apparent that access to home birth and access to birthing on the 'āina are limited by colonial processes that negatively affect health, land access, cultural practices and traditional medicines. Some schools of thought also critique our current lifestyles as being harmful to birth in that sitting too long, not exercising enough, living modern lifestyles, etc., weaken women such that they may not physically consider home birth. Others argue that routine and generational C-sections actually affect the shape of the pelvis such that women cannot give birth naturally. Others argue that routine birth control for most young women actually changes our brains and bodies such that we are not in a natural state physically, mentally or emotionally to handle pregnancy and birth. Such arguments and notions should be talked about and hashed out as birth is the one and only thing that keeps our human race perpetuating and, therefore, is one of the most important things to be protected.

Medical Institutions as Colonial Structures?

Part of birthing outside the hospital for most of the moms meant resisting or turning away from colonial frameworks and reclaiming the power and space to birth in one's own way. This is not just turning away or resisting American culture or colonization; it is more than that. It is about turning toward 'āina, and to self, spirit, ancestors, and to one's power source, to family, to comfort, and to safety in many cases as well. This was not limited to Hawaiian mamas and was a theme that mamas of various backgrounds discussed. In many ways, it is also a turn away from the reliance on medical systems that were imposed upon people due to lifestyle changes resulting from colonization. Certainly, colonization resulted in changing birth practices for Hawaiian women through prohibitions of using plant medicine and conducting birth practices that were considered illegal or suppressed. As such:

> Written accounts of the practices relating to child-
> birth in old Hawai'i are scarce, owing, no doubt,
> to the suppression of the practice of native herbal
> medicine during the early missionary period and to
> the native practice of placing many herbal formula-
> tions under kapu' (i.e., prohibition against their being
> revealed). (Kobayashi, 1980:260)

Nevertheless, we know that Hawaiians tended to eat particular foods in certain months of pregnancy, used plant medicines in preparation for birth, often birthed in a squatting or kneeling position, practiced particular ways of tying the umbilical cord, buried the placenta and *piko* (umbilical cord) in significant places on the 'āina, and even consumed specific nourishing post-birth meals and plant medicines. But, due to colonization, land dispossession, environmental toxicity from agricultural companies and the military, and changes in diet, access to land, access to rest, leisure, cultural practices, birth support, etc., have made people, particularly indigenous people, reliant on dominant medical systems. Such reliance becomes strengthened, as well, through state-sanctioned regulations on particular practices, like midwifery and childbirth, which also reify medical power. Accordingly, several mothers explained how the midwifery regulation bill SB 1033, which passed in April of 2019, for example, is an extension of the colonization of birth:

> It is colonization that causes us to be unhealthy and
> reliant on the medical system, you know, excessively
> reliant. So, I think it's definitely been a major focus,
> and certainly with these midwifery bills that have been
> coming up. I think that has been a difficult process
> because it is an issue of colonialism. Regulation of
> an ancient practice is colonialism. That's where it's
> coming from. So it's been really challenging because
> we also want to hold our community together and a
> number of other things, but we can't get away from
> the colonialism that's involved in regulation. It should
> be obvious as far as I'm concerned. (Interview 22)

In this sense, continuous colonization occurs through a multitude of avenues—through reliance on medical systems, legislation and regulation of women's birthing choices. It is a process that causes reliance upon dominant institutions and can result in poor health that many experience because it can disempower people from one another, themselves, the land, health practices and cultural protocols. These outcomes can be traced back to informal and formal regulations on ancient birthing practices.

Regulations on birth are enforced through laws, regulations, fines, nomenclature and licensures. Lee Maracle (1996:93) explains how this affects indigenous people. In her book *I Am Woman: A Native Perspective on Sociology and Feminism,* she writes, "Laws are constructed by the occupying force to facilitate the suppression of any resistance from the dominated people." In the case of the Hawai'i midwifery regulation bill, midwives who are culturally trained and do not have education from a mainland school may not be allowed to call themselves midwives and may be subjected to fines for doing so (Hawai'i State Legislature).

Traditional midwifery and culturally-embedded birth practices are seen as rebellious to the dominant powers. How dare women assert their God-given right to birth the way they want? Furthermore, women making other choices about their bodies, their babies and their care are a threat to financial assets, cultural conditionings and medical dominance in America. The midwifery regulation bill in Hawai'i has certainly enlivened many home-birth mothers and has brought together many women from different walks of life who believe that the government should not interfere with birth and bodily autonomy.

One of the mothers, who home-birthed her first child in the early 1980s, described her feelings about the midwifery regulation bill and how it brought her in the community with other home-birth mamas:

> We've had these things at the legislature over the last few years where we go in and send testimony and all that, and they keep on trying to legalize midwives such that it really would get rid of the traditional midwives, and I'm utterly opposed to that.... But in the talking about it, I have learned that several women that would never have dreamed of it have given home birth to their kids. One is an activist lawyer I knew but had no idea that she was a home-birth mom, and another

was an older woman like me on Maui who is a total activist against all these things, including pesticides, cane burning, and all that stuff, and she is a home-birth mother. I never would have dreamed that because of her background as a scientist, and you know, she's much older, well, she's my age or older. So it has been delightful to see how passionate people are and how many more midwives there are now than there were years ago. I'm actually encouraged, but I'm also worried about them trying again to pass the midwifery licensure bill. (Interview 39)

Unfortunately, the regulations on midwives are not exclusive to Hawai'i. For example, Craven (2010) traces the struggle that midwives and home-birth mums faced in Virginia with restrictive bills and how they relied on "rights-based" and "consumer-based" arguments to argue for midwifery choice. Yet, Hawai'i is quite unique from any mainland state and its various struggles with home-birth choices and access. In Hawai'i, there are traditional, cultural, lay and direct-entry midwives practicing in the Islands, and Hawai'i is culturally and geographically unique as well. The resistance to American occupation and militarism is quite strong in Hawai'i, and its own history with settler-colonialism makes such struggles against various laws and bills quite complex. Part of the resistance to American occupation is reflected in opposition to regulating cultural and birth practices. Some mums also find themselves in complex relationships with settler-colonialism, militarism, occupation, resistance, etc. One mama I interviewed expressed some tensions about this very subject as her husband is in the military, yet she supports decolonization and the Hawaiian sovereignty movement.

I am in a little bit of a sticky position with that because I feel like, as a military wife, I am, in essence, supporting colonization in Hawai'i. But I try my best not to let that seep into other ways of life. My health

insurance and my benefits come from that, so I am,
in essence, a part of that. But growing up in Hawaiʻi,
you can really see how much has changed… the land
here… there's so much land that regular civilians
can't access, and Hawaiians can't access because of
all the bases. We have the US Army, Navy, Air Force,
Marines, all on our little island.

When I used to work in conservation, I really saw
what it was doing to the environment. Not just the
people but the environment as well. They have
so much funding they have to put into conservation because they're essentially ruining parts of
the island. That's been something I've been able to
see and, through my environmental work, been in
contact with. As far as birth practices go, I mean just
what's going on right now with the bill, I think it's
not even just colonization of the Islands, it's also
colonization of women's bodies. Obviously, it has
something to do with colonization of the Islands if
people who live here and grow up here can't practice birthing in their natural ways. It's telling people
you can or cannot do something with your own
body. (Interview 53)

Navigating choices around birth, then, is never just confined to
a singular decision made by a mother; rather, it is situated in various
political arenas, matrices, intersections, influences and constraints.

While many mothers explained that home birth allowed them
to make choices and have experiences that were not available in the
hospital setting, they also explained that their decision to birth at
home was directly the result of a larger worldview that centered on
sovereignty. Sometimes, sovereignty was explained as a project or
resistance to colonization (this was expressed heavily in interviews
with Hawaiian and Black mothers).

Other times, sovereignty was framed in relation to the body where mums framed medical institutions as colonial as these institutions assumed control over bodies via protocols, legislation, medical authority, and the paternalistic culture of hospitals and clinics. These views were nuanced by background, local identity, Hawaiian identity, ethnicity and race. For example, sovereignty was often framed in terms of resistance to colonial institutions (including the hospital) for Hawaiian women, while sovereignty was framed more in terms of rights over one's own body for women from the mainland.

Medical institutions were not only seen as colonial in the context of the American occupation of Hawai'i, but they were also colonial over birth, midwifery and women's bodies (for Hawaiian women and for a majority of the other mothers). Such occupation was often conceptualized as gendered as well in terms of mums expressing that their choices and authority over their own bodies would be relinquished to medical authority during hospital birth.

Doctor Knows Best

Most of us have grown up with the mentality that the doctor knows best. An illness, injury or otherwise unexplainable bodily issue should be addressed by a doctor. At least, that's what we've been programmed to think. And, for the most part, we know if something is a true emergency or if a disease needs pharmaceutical intervention, this is the best case. But, many of us know that there are multiple forms of medicine, many of which do not need to come from a doctor or pharmacy. Medicine also comes from Mother Earth. And healing is often just as mental and emotional as it is physical. The more that people find out about plant medicine, nutritious eating habits, stress reduction, spiritual healing, etc., it seems the less they are to consult doctors for more acute and trivial health matters.

One marker of well-being is the extent to which one feels in control of their own health. And home-birth moms certainly made a point of being in control of their own health and wellness, oftentimes even before they became pregnant. The home-birth moms wanted to make decisions about their healthcare even before they became pregnant. Many mothers also explained that the decision to birth at home (whether in the moment or upon reflection during the postpartum time) was intimately connected to their value of having sovereignty over their own bodies. In many cases, this value-centered decision was backed by the massive amounts of reading and research that mums did about home and hospital births. One mama who self-identifies as Hawaiian, Japanese, German and Filipino, and who is a birth educator, among the many other roles she fulfills, explained how her birth decisions evolved over time:

> Yeah, I have a good friend, and his hashtag is "colonialkills," which is basically a Hawaiian word for colonization kills, and over the years, as I've become aware of what colonization is around the world and then in Hawai'i, it's definitely become a strong feeling and demonstrated actions with regards to childbirth.
>
> My first video was Ricki Lake's video, and I was like WTF! Oh my god. I'm a history person, so that made sense of what happened and how it became overturned, and all the big companies that are investing in third world countries and forcing formula and all of that… it's all about colonizing, and it's genocide… really, it's genocide (breathes in). So, yeah, really strong beliefs about that in terms of demonstrations. We're not out protesting and chaining ourselves to Enfamil or anything like that. I would say a quiet, silent, but very defined set of beliefs and things that we share and things that our family practices, which became very clear at the time we were pregnant and our choice for labor, delivery and postpartum.

Now we really ask our boys to think about some of the things that they're hearing, and about the decisions that they're making, and why they are making those decisions even at eight and eleven, and why and what influenced their decisions and just having those kinds of really basic elementary discussions with them, and then for me and my husband having more of a higher level kind of meta-cognitive conversation about it, and then what does our family do, what does our family represent, how are we going to act, how are we going to demonstrate on that. (Interview 33)

Me: So, can you tell me a little more about how that plays into birth and your decision to have a home birth and kind of the practices that you used and just maybe the feeling and beliefs that you went into birth with, and how is that connected to anti-colonialism?

It was evolving, really, and I don't know if I would have labeled it anti-colonial at the time, but it was definitely more about empowerment for me… that I was going to direct this with all the knowledge and my research, and my body, my birth plan… this is my child. Even legally, this is my child that comes out into the world, and it was more about that, then it was later on when I realized, okay, you have to take this avenue, you have to do this because of your age. You have to do this because of the protocols in the hospitals, and in every visit, there's all these things that have to be done or else your insurance is not going to cover it, so we had to make decisions like vaccinations to decline, and that within the birth plan, we wanted to make sure that in the event we did have to go to the hospital, here's everything we wanted, and here is everything we did not want. So, we wanted to make sure we could work within the system and we could still push through whatever systems were around us.

My husband and I weren't married at the time for our first child, well actually, both my children, so we made sure that there was paternity paperwork for the State of Hawai'i and a notary there so that if anything happened to me and I crashed or something like that, he could make the decisions for the baby based on all of our research.

In our research, I found out how much of birth is controlled by big business. It's controlled by a white, male-dominated medical field who make you feel that you're stupid for making these decisions. I have yet to see any male give birth to a child and know what it's like, and to do that, I will say publicly that no matter what your training is, you are not qualified. You're really not qualified, and with that said, my midwife has never had a child. She gives birth to children as her part of her home birth midwife practice, so how do I defend that decision, you know? If I call some male out on not having a child, but he's birthed one thousand babies and (my midwife) has birthed one thousand babies, what's the difference? She's a female, and her body goes through a cycle that would prepare you for having a baby, so I would say those are kinda some of the things that would be anti-, well, definitely vaccinations, definitely extra tests, definitely understanding the insurance system, the legal system... those kinds of things. (Interview 33)

She begins by explaining how colonialism is harmful and how birth is controlled by males who dominate the medical field and the big business that medicine has become. The business model of medicine seems to disempower women, especially during their childbearing years. This is part of her worldview, and this shapes her understanding of birth, medicine and her perception of how women are treated in such systems. She touches briefly on the stigma that women face for making decisions about their own bodies in a medical birth context. She connects this with Ricki Lake's incredibly popular documentary, *The Business of Being Born,* which, of course, details the for-profit medical-industrial complex as it relates to childbirth. The documentary also details the history of childbirth in America and how uncommon it is for medical professionals to witness undisturbed childbirths (i.e., vaginal, unmedicated childbirths with little to no intervention) in the hospital setting (Lake and Epstein, 2008). The documentary also gives accounts of the harms of unnecessary interventions, including maternal deaths that occurred due to over-medicalization and medical error. This mama expressed that, as a history buff, she was still shocked by all she learned about the medicalization and history of childbirth shown in the documentary. In fact, this documentary was mentioned in eighteen of my interviews as one of the major catalysts for choosing a home birth. (If you haven't seen it yet, perhaps this is your sign to watch it.)

This mama was also able to make connections between the colonization of childbirth by the medical field and various formula campaigns in "third world countries" that actually pushed mothers to stop breastfeeding and to start feeding their children formula. What resulted was an increase in infant and child deaths because of unclean water mixed with formula, as well as nutritional deficiencies. The proliferation of Western sexualization and objectification of breasts as exclusively for sexual pleasure rather than just for feeding babies also occurred. What a disgrace to the millennia of mothers who nourished us with their breasts up until it was marketed as taboo. Arguably, what also resulted was the stigma against breastfeeding and the use of formula as a status symbol. I distinctly remember the moment when I realized this conditioning firsthand.

We went to Uganda to visit family when our daughter was six months old. I was still exclusively breastfeeding her at the time. Many Ugandan women would approach me to tell me how healthy my baby looked and then would ask what I fed her. I would say that she just has my breastmilk. The horror on their faces! They would often demand that I feed her formula right away. She couldn't be healthy just off my breastmilk alone. I would have to say to them that, actually, babies who are growing well only need breastmilk, not formula. But, how dare I, a woman from the US, reject formula?! It is a status symbol, after all. So I was rejecting not only Nestle's conditioning, but also status. This proved to be a mental dilemma for many of the women who were unwitting victims of Nestle's propaganda.

The mama I interviewed about all of this also expressed some reasons for why formula might be considered a status symbol, which tied into her thoughts on traditional practices and home birth. She explained:

> What I see around the world is so many developing countries wanting to be like Western countries, and they see it as an ideal like we'll start using disposable diapers... those must be the greatest thing... or we better switch to formula. In places like Thailand, formula would be seen as much better than breast-feeding. Somewhere like Vietnam, using a disposable diaper is seen as status—I'm rich enough, I can afford disposable diapers. In the parenting realm, it's like they're trying to adopt Western ways, and I do not think it's making things better. I think it's making things worse also in their birthing practices.
>
> I did a lot of research about countries around the world because, with our lifestyle, I could basically choose where to go live and give birth, and so even a lot of countries that had a history of home birth...

for instance, in Eastern Europe or something... I couldn't find a country that I could go to today and have a home birth... an affordable country. There are some northern European countries with wonderful home-birth practices, but they were just more expensive to live in. But so many countries have completely given up their tradition. They've moved birth all into the hospital, and it's really sad. It's like even if the whole world is open to you to choose where to go, there's not a whole lot of places that are still allowing and supporting home birth... so that's why I knew O'ahu was a good place for it. There's a lot of people who are still doing it here. (Interview 49)

Two other mums I interviewed expressed these same sentiments well. One of them even waited to tell her family in Liberia about her decision to have a home birth because they believed that the hospital is safest and perhaps even a luxury that many women do not have:

And it was my mother who comes, this is an African woman, and she said, "That feels to me like living in the city and then going into the bush to have your child." And in my mind, I was like, "Well, what's wrong with that?" (laughs) In my mind, I didn't say that out loud because I didn't want to create an argument, but that's how disconnected colonialism has made the African people to their own culture and to their own knowings. (Interview 35)

Again, a similar thing happened to me. Some of my older Ugandan in-laws could not understand why I would choose home birth over a "safe" hospital. Pain over drugs. Risk over safety. I was rejecting status yet again. And, to be fair, hospitals may be the best place to birth a baby in certain countries/situations where risk factors and location are a life and death situation. But birth is always life or death, no matter where we are. Nevertheless, colonial ideas of birth have proliferated around the globe. Colonization creates a feedback loop when it simultaneously prohibits access to good nutrition, clean water, and medical care, increasing poor outcomes in childbirth and thereby necessitating the hospital setting. When it comes to birthing at home, it seems that we've all been programmed to think of it as an irresponsible choice. And the moms who choose to do it… well, they must be crazy.

Before she had her children, the mama I interviewed from Liberia had a very personal experience the medical system. She was diagnosed with kidney cancer and had surgery to remove one of her kidneys. She was incredibly weak as a result and was told to take the usual route of curing cancer through pharmaceuticals. Instead, she turned to alternative medicine and a shift in mindset. Miraculously, she was able to heal. I don't share this to say that mindset and alternative medicine will cure cancer all of the time, but I share it to show how vital it is to healing.

When this mama became pregnant years later, she was considered high risk because she only had one kidney, but she dived into research and learned different ways to support herself so she could have a home birth. By then, she was determined to birth at home and support her body with alternative medicine. This wasn't the only reason she wanted to birth at home, though. She had also seen a friend's birth in the hospital and was shocked and disappointed by how much her friend had to fight just to have the birth she wanted:

> I told you the story about seeing my friend's wife go
> through that with the doctors and just fighting for
> her right to birth the way that she wanted to… and
> that's when I opted out. I'm not even going to do that
> because there are people who feel I'm going to have
> it the natural way in the hospital just for their own
> security, and for me, I'm just like, once you decide to
> go into the hospital, you give up your rights to have it

the way that you want to have it, or you're just going to be fighting for it, and I don't know if fighting is what you want to be doing at the time of your birth (laughs). (Interview 35)

Me: You're already so exhausted, right?

So, I feel like the whole Westernizing or the colonialization of medicine takes the power out of our hands and into the doctor's, so these people know you more than you know yourself, so you trust the doctor to tell you what to do with your body. Anything else is viewed as being a lunatic (laughs).

This all has to do with money somehow, but so I mean, I don't know how colonization did that, but I just know that's what's going on… whatever happened… and now the power is in the hands of the doctors, and it's taken away from the women who are going through this, and they make us feel or we allow ourselves to feel vulnerable to them so you know we feel like they're doing us this big favor by telling us what to do, and I'm just like you already know what to do, your body is made for this. You're not sick (laughs). (Interview 35)

It's almost insidious the way we are taught to give our power to others, to those labeled wealthier, better educated, smarter, more capable, etc. We are taught to turn away from ourselves and look to others to hold our personal responsibility. It might be easier to do so in the short term, but there are always lasting negative effects. Colonization works much the same. It uses its institutions, medical authority and campaigns to assert power over bodies, over choices, and even over thoughts. It shapes the social imaginary of what is acceptable in terms of body sovereignty and birth. It also shapes societal views of birth and motherhood as well.

These colonial and corporate campaigns and thought processes are still influencing women to this day. The previously mentioned mum (Interview 33) described how she navigated these powerful influences while making birth decisions that were appropriate for herself and her family. She described her reaction not as ultra-political in terms of protesting but in calculated family practices that honor her and her partner's choices in labor, delivery and postpartum. She continued this type of mindful approach in her parenting as she often asks her children about their decisions, why they're making their decisions, what their influences are, etc. These types of awareness practices became part of her lifestyle and shaped how she and her family guide their decisions.

When I asked her about how her birth might be connected to anti-colonialism, she explained that it was evolving. She initially expressed the research she did, the value of having choices over her body and her baby, and how she navigated choices around childbirth and hospital policies. She set up her birth plan so that she could work "within the system" (i.e., the hospital and its protocols and practices) in the event that she needed to go to the hospital. But she also wanted to push back against the system in the sense that she took control over her birth plans and advocated for what she wanted.

She saw hospital birth as situated in big business and a for-profit model dominated by white males who can often have a paternalistic attitude toward women in birth. While she expressed that doctors can make you feel stupid for making these decisions (i.e., making an empowered birth plan and choosing home birth), she also explained that men are not qualified to be making such decisions as they are not the person giving birth. They are not women and will never understand what it feels like to be pregnant and to grow and birth a whole human.

She went through the process of pushing back colonial, male-dominated institutions, including all the judgments and pressures, so she could think clearly about what she wanted and why she was making particular decisions about birth. Seems like such a burden to do while also being pregnant, right? She was able to make informed choices through this process, though, and was arguably empowered despite external colonial and medical forces.

As I heard similar sentiments from other home-birth mothers, I became more and more curious about why they were describing the hospital setting as colonial, patriarchal and paternalistic and what it is about home birth and midwifery that allows for more body sovereignty. While most mothers made this connection, other mothers described the medical model as more patriarchal than anything else.

While I have been focusing primarily on Hawaiian mothers in this chapter, it is clear that colonization and issues of sovereignty also affect mamas of various backgrounds and in various ways. That is, we are all affected by colonization, medical dominance, cultural conditionings, etc. These experiences with colonization shape their experiences, social interactions, lifestyles and worldviews as well—and, they certainly affect birth. In some instances, birth sovereignty, body sovereignty, cultural sovereignty and national sovereignty overlapped to inform the choice of home birth. Women birth at home as a way of reclaiming their power over colonial pressures or medical pressures. In other instances, body sovereignty and being able to have their choices honored were the main catalysts for having a home birth.

One Japanese-American mother I interviewed was a world traveler. She grew up in Kenya, traveled to South America for many years, and finally returned to Hawai'i with her partner. She saw the medical model as more patriarchal and paternalistic. She spoke of the male-dominated industrial, scientific and technocratic views that often seep into and control fundamental human experiences like birth:

> I wouldn't have made the connection myself between colonialism and that type of medical model. I prob-ably would have. I have and do and would make the

connection between a sort of patriarchal worldview and culture and set of values and that system. I know that there are connections between the patriarchal worldview and the colonial one. I just hadn't made those connections on my own.

I think that for me, in addition to it really just being what I believe is best for me, and for my philosophy, and for my body, and for the kind of environment that I feel best in. I also definitely have a lot of criticism of the conventional medical model. I've added to this criticism a lot, actually, since the birth. I've learned more and more about the conventional ways we raise children, and I think that a lot of the thinking and the expertise around that has been defined by men who don't have women's and not necessarily even children's… or human's—I sometimes want to say—although that sounds terrible, so it's probably not true, best interests at heart.

When I think about the time, especially around the beginning of the twentieth century and the first half of the twentieth century, it was an important time for the definition of a lot of these medical models and approaches, and that ended up being really bad for women and babies. I think that has to do with this technical, rationalist, industrial… I would like put INDUSTRIAL in capital letters because I think it affects us so much… scientific approach to studying how a birth should happen, and this is how a baby should be taken care of, and this is how you know, blah blah blah. That's where I feel like my worldview and my politics have kind of created a framework where I'm like, "huh!" Every time I discover a new thing, it all just fits into this male-dominated, technical, industrial, scientific-objective institutional approach to these really

fundamental, human, natural, experiences that have
women at the center of them if we're talking about
birth and child-rearing. (Interview 28)

This critique of this male-dominated institutional approach to
fundamental human experiences, particularly women's experiences
of birth and child-rearing, was expressed by the majority of mums
I interviewed. The institutional approach to birth was described
as "sterile," "cold," "nervous," "scary," "colonial," "impersonal,"
"not informative" and "fear-based." Think of your last medical
appointment, for example. How did the clinic feel? Was it
comfortable, cozy, inviting and safe feeling? Or was it uninspiring,
nerve-wracking, sterile, cold and impersonal? The midwifery model
of care often feels like the complete opposite of the clinical setting
as it is more caring, educational, empowering, personal, holistic and
loving.

There was only one mama who reported that she had a small
issue with her midwife, which had to do with not being fully
informed about a particular medication for thrush that was used
on her baby. All of the other mothers reported that their midwifery
experiences were very positive and so much better than the clinical
hospital setting. Many women found that their midwives became
part of their families as well. That's how close they became! I can
say the same about our home birth midwife with my son. She will
always be etched in our hearts.

Midwifery generally protects women from spaces that diminish
the human experience. On the other hand, clinical settings follow a
protocol of assessment, diagnosis and treatment rather than looking
at the mind, body and spirit holistically. Robbie Davis-Floyd, a
medical and reproductive anthropologist who was featured in *The
Business of Being Born* documentary, has explained that technocratic
and industrial views on birth see women's bodies as defective and,
therefore, in need of interventions (Davis-Floyd, 1992). Women's
bodies are defective bodies, and so anything could go wrong at any

time, thereby necessitating the need for an overseer who is more qualified to manage the female body than the woman herself. This technocratic view on childbirth shapes the experiences that women have during hospital birth and oftentimes traumatizes and dehumanizes them.

Some of these experiences include the use of electrical fetal monitoring, interventions when necessary and unnecessary, and putting a clock on labor (i.e., if a woman's cervix doesn't open up fast enough, it necessitates a need for interventions). Pitocin is often used to open a woman's cervix faster so that the hospital can stick to a timeline that supposedly reduces risk to mom and baby (i.e., prevents lawsuits). Hospitals also routinely prevent mums from eating and drinking during labor, using plant medicine and keeping their placentas. They often use surgical tools, utilize various tests and medicines that may not be necessary, and implement other hospital protocols that are entangled in insurance policies, risk management, litigation, colonial medical treatments and interventions, paternalism, disease management, patriarchy, etc. These measures are also enacted upon mothers in nuanced ways that are shaped by the mother's race, socioeconomic status, gender expression, indigenous identity, educational levels, etc.

For example, a recent article in the *Reproductive Health Journal* found that one out of six women experience some form of obstetric violence during childbirth in the hospital setting (Vedam, 2019). And, out of those surveyed, 33 percent of indigenous women reported mistreatment during childbirth. Even if women attempt to assert themselves in their birth choices, Attanasio and Hardeman's (2019:275) findings "suggest that in the context of childbirth care, women pay a penalty for exhibiting behavior that may be perceived as noncompliant or uncooperative, and this penalty may be greater for Black women..."

Paying a penalty for speaking up and asserting their power is not new to women. This issue permeates society at many levels.

Speaking up can be more dangerous for certain groups, classes, and races of women as well. Several of the Black mothers I interviewed expressed sentiments along these lines; that is, that birth and medical settings intersect in ways that are often harmful to Black mothers.

Black Mothers Birthing at Home

Five of the fifty-nine mothers I interviewed self-identified as Black. Four of the five mums did not grow up in Hawai'i but have lived there for several years. There were various reasons Black mums chose home birth, including distrust of the medical system, being inspired by family members who chose natural births (even in hospital), wanting to connect with their inner power sources, and watching friends birth in the hospital and being turned off by the treatment they received.

Distrust of the medical system stemmed from Black people historically being treated poorly in medical systems, from healing methods being taken away/outlawed in the past, from the high rates of Black maternal mortality, and from seeing family members being mistreated in hospitals/clinical settings. When I asked one mama about what she thought about the intersections of colonialism, medicine and birth from her perspective as a Black mother, she responded:

> We've lost a lot because of it. We've lost a lot of tradi-
> tional birth practices because of it. We've lost a lot of
> belief in the human body to birth the way you're sup-
> posed to because of it. We've even gotten to the point
> where we're almost changing DNA in women who
> have C-sections, and then their child has C-sections,
> and then that child has C-sections. You convince
> people—women—that they can no longer deliver
> this baby vaginally. Colonialism disconnects wom-
> en from who they are meant to be, and a lot of that
> discovery of who you are meant to be happens during

pregnancy, birth and labor. The results of colonialism are devastating in that many women think that there's only one way to do it—in a hospital with doctors. It's medicalized, and we're crazy if you want to do it any other way.

My mom had her children in Nigeria out of hospital and had her three youngest babies in America, and she knows what birth is like. She's had natural birth, but when I told her I was having my babies at home, she was like, "Why? What are you doing that for? Don't do that. That's crazy. Go to the hospital." I'm like, "What are you talking about? You had babies out of the hospital. You've done this. It's normal." It threw me off. It doesn't even sound right, you know? But she's always so proud of me when I do it. I know she wouldn't try to stop me. I mean, she'll verbally try to stop me, but she knows I'm not going to take her advice in terms of that. But I'm so confused that you're giving me this advice when you've done something else well. She's like, "Well, we didn't have that available when I was having these babies." I'm like, "We don't need them. It was never needed."

The hospital has its place, but I bet about 90 to 95 percent of women don't need the hospital to birth, and that's what's terrifying (that anything other) is mental, that you're crazy, or you're old-fashioned for even thinking about it. Like Granny Midwives and how they got pushed out of the ability to deliver babies and help women because of white doctors saying, "Oh no, the baby died because of them. They don't know what they're doing. You have to come here..." Do you guys realize that babies die anywhere, not just in the hospital, not just in the home? It happens in a hospital. These things happen. (Interview 36)

Her response was not unlike the mother from Liberia (Interview 35) in terms of the impacts that colonization has on what their family views as acceptable places to birth. She also mentioned the connection that colonization and medical authority had on the ability of Granny Midwives to practice birth work. The blame that White elite male doctors put on Granny Midwives was interesting to note in that maternal and fetal deaths were blamed on them in an attempt to push them out of birth work. The result, as this mama mentioned, is that people began believing that a woman is crazy, unsafe or old-fashioned for birthing at home. And there was the mindset shift that Black women who had been birth keepers for generations were now suddenly unqualified and unskilled according to White male physicians. Yet, it was the Granny Midwives who had to teach the doctors how to support birth.

Another important note to make is that C-sections, many of which are unnecessary, end up changing the anatomy of women and make it harder to have a vaginal birth. Most impactfully, however, this mum explained that colonization disconnects women from who they are meant to be, and it is through the process of birth and pregnancy that women have the opportunity to reclaim what has been taken from them.

When I asked this mother if her decision to birth at home was in any way tied to the awful statistics that Black women face in the hospital in terms of infant and maternal mortality rates, she responded that this was not a part of her decision to birth at home. However, her decision to be a birth worker was strengthened because she wanted to support better systems of birthing, and she recognized the devasting situations that Black women face in terms of maternal health in the United States. Not only do Black women experience more obstetrical mistreatment in hospital settings compared to their white counterparts (Vedam, 2019), but Black mothers in the US are also two to six times more likely to die from pregnancy complications (Flanders, 2000). Black infant mortality in the US is 2.3 times higher than white infant mortality as well (Ely and Driscoll, 2020).

Another Black mother I interviewed, who birthed her two sons at home on O'ahu, explained that the decision to birth at home was connected to her identity as a Black woman and having a healthy distrust of the medical system.

> My background being a Black woman… I've seen health systems not supporting us. I've seen a lot of mistakes go awry in hospitals. My friend's mother passed in a hospital. It was supposed to be outpatient surgery, just getting knee surgery. But something went wrong with the anesthesia. There are so many other stories, this other woman… anyway, there was a lot growing up and seeing what I saw, especially in hospital care. There was a lot of distrust for the conventional Western approach to health. (Interview 2)

In our interview, she later described how she now takes health into her own hands through eating well, being active, connecting with community, connecting with her cultural values, utilizing preventative care, and even choosing home birth. While this sort of "success story," so to speak, about a Black woman taking her power and health back (and into her own hands), seems to be inspiring, Oparah and Bonaparte (2016) caution us not to read stories of Black women and maternal-health care systems in the US singularly as instances when patriarchal medical establishments control women or as affirming stories about how women take back their power and have natural births, but as more complex. That is, she urges us to see how Black women's experiences of birth and pregnancy "are shaped not simply by violence and coercion by patriarchal institutions but also by the multifaceted ways in which gender interacts with interlocking systems of race, class, age, ability, sexuality and nation (Oparah and Bonaparte, 2016:3). This intersectional thinking can definitely inform how we think about various women's situations when it comes to birth and the obstacles they might be facing.

Another Black mother I interviewed who grew up in Germany and whose parents were both in the medical field (her dad was a developmental pediatrician, and her mother was a NICU nurse), explained that her experience growing up in Germany and then coming to the US shed more light on the American view of birth and women's bodies. She also explained the disconnect American women have with their bodies as well as the complexities around culture, nationality, gender and reproductive health.

> I just never really considered my body or my repro-
> ductive organs to be some sort of shamefully discon-
> nected part of my physical self. So that was helpful,
> and I didn't really realize that any of that was what
> it was until I moved to the US for college and then
> encountered people whose philosophies were just
> so very different from mine. I had been in American
> schools toward the end of my career in Germany
> because I really wanted to go to an American high
> school. German pop culture was very obsessed with
> American prototypes, so I kind of had a taste of the
> fact that people's views were a little bit different
> around these things because we were in Germany.
> Even there, many of my peers were still more liberal
> because they just sort of soaked all that in as well...
> soo, yeah... then we came to the US, and I went to
> an all-women's college... shout out to Spellman! I
> encountered a lot of very different notions about re-
> productive health and Black women's bodies and the
> container that I was now going to be living out my
> adulthood in. That was very interesting, and so when
> it came my time to birth, I really had an opportunity
> to work through all of those different influences to
> some extent or the other. Then, my Hawaiian birth
> experiences began with my third baby. (Interview 41)

One of the other driving forces for this particular mama to choose home birth was her experience at a clinic while getting a check-up on her baby during her first pregnancy. She described the clinic waiting room as being full of women from various backgrounds: Dominican, Venezuelan and many other non-English speaking women. When she talked with them, it seemed like a lot of the care was disconnected from them, and they didn't feel empowered. As an English speaker, she recounts the privilege she had to push back against the medical authority at the clinic:

> I was sitting in the waiting room with all of these women, Dominican women and women from Venezuela, many non-English speaking women, and I was talking with them about when they were due and stuff in the lobby, and there was just a lot of melancholy over the whole experience, and I feel like a lot of the care was disconnected to them. I don't feel like the women felt empowered or positively received there... and I, with my English, had enough to sort of push back against some of the assumptions that were made and create a positive barrier around myself, you know, they would float things, and I would negate their negative connotation with something more positive, and I was conscientious of doing that because I just felt like, you don't know me (laughs) and I'm not here for a long time. I already connected with my midwives. I just needed this because I wanted you close by, and I wanted to stay in touch with my baby. That was interesting, and those women never really left my mind. (Interview 41)

After her first birth experience, which was very positive, she shifted her life's trajectory. She decided to leave law school and become a birth educator. This shift seemed to occur out of a necessity to really follow what resonated with her in her life; that is, she became disheartened by the legal field as she saw the veil pulled back in terms of its allegiance to big business, power and control rather than for social justice. She also found her value in attachment parenting and discovered how societal ideas of acceptable lifestyles were at odds with her own values of home birth, attachment parenting, supporting motherhood, etc. While she expressed that she wanted to give birth on her own terms, she did not express a negative sentiment about hospitals or medical knowledge; rather, she described them as part of a mindset and value system that she did not necessarily recognize as beneficial to her births (but that she would utilize in the event of a rare emergency). She decided later to have freebirths/unassisted births (i.e., unattended by midwives or medical support) with her subsequent children. She also became a doula (and was able to navigate the hospital culture well because of growing up with her father, who was a pediatrician), and she began apprenticing to be a midwife.

In the proceeding chapters, I will discuss this mother's lifestyle and worldviews again because she is not only an interesting person, but her background as a mixed-race woman (Black and White) who grew up in Germany and who now lives an authentic life in alignment to her and her partner's core values is quite dynamic. I do think it is noteworthy to mention, however, that despite her educational and intellectual privileges, she had to navigate very tough decisions like leaving a professional trajectory in order to be the mother she wanted to be, pushing back on societal ideas of "safety" and "freedom" that were at odds with her inner guidance, and witnessing the struggle that other women of color with less privilege have in birth spaces and in the medical realm (in terms of not being able to assert their choices and being subjected to medical authority and control).

Finally, the last Black mother I interviewed was born and raised in Hawai'i. During our interview together, she described herself as Black and local, but also not local in the sense that her parents are from the States (mainland US). She explained that she's both "local and not" because of this and because she's not Hawaiian by blood, but that she was born and raised here in Hawai'i, it is her home, and it is the land she loves. Local is usually used to identify a person born and raised in Hawai'i and one who adopts Hawaiian customs, as well as someone who has a strong affinity for the land, the culture and the people of Hawai'i (Okamura, 1980). It was significant that she mentioned this as it affirms that local identity is often something that cannot be neatly delineated or categorized.

This mama had a midwife for her first birth and subsequently chose to have a freebirth/unassisted birth with her second child (whom she was pregnant with at the time of our interview). She described her experience with her first birth and her midwife as so empowering that she was able to trust in her body and her strength to have her second home birth unassisted. During her pregnancy, she was receiving some care, such as ultrasounds and routine testing, but she was planning to have her birth unassisted (and did so some months after our interview). Because she grew up in Hawai'i, I was all that much more curious about her thoughts on colonization and how they intersect with birth, Black identity and her lived experience. She responded with the following sentiments:

> I think learning more about birth and traditional
> birth practices has really opened my eyes to having
> an anti-colonial mindset. These practices were taken
> from a lot of these communities, from my ancestors
> even. I think that's also the effect of mainstream
> medical practices, that colonial(ization), that coming
> and saying, "Our way is better than your traditional
> way… that's backwards." I think there's been a lot
> of reclaiming lately… I've seen that anyway at least
> with myself and other women of color who choose
> home birth or freebirth. We feel like we're reclaim-
> ing something that was taken away from us and our
> communities. (Interview 19)

This concept of reclamation seems to be widely addressed in birth as it relates to women's bodies and settler-colonialism. In the next section, I address this concept of reclamation in terms of Hawaiian birth traditions and how various organizations are attempting to revive and protect birth practices.

Reclamation and Political Activism

Reclamation of Hawaiian birth traditions continues amongst the backdrop of settler-colonialism, militarization and state authority in the Hawaiian Islands. For example, the Hawaiʻi Home Birth Task Force has mobilized to protect traditional, Hawaiian, and lay midwives despite the restrictive midwifery regulation bill that passed in April 2019. Comprised of midwives and birth workers, the task force is working with the State of Hawaiʻi to prevent the Hawaiʻi midwifery regulation bill (Hawaiʻi State Legislature SB1033 SD2 HD2 2019) from banning traditional midwives and birth practices. Along with task force members, home-birth community leaders have been politically active through community meetings, organized protests at the Hawaiʻi State Capitol, and in writing testimony in opposition to midwifery regulation bills. There are also Facebook groups where the home-birth community has been active in recruiting the home birth community to express opposition to legislation that limits cultural and lay midwifery and birth choice through written testimony as well as speaking at public hearings at the Capitol.

The hearings and community meetings I attended from 2017 to 2019 were comprised of home-birth mums of all economic, racial and ethnic backgrounds. A few midwives, nurses and doctors supported the regulations as they argued that such regulations support the professional development of midwifery, licensure, insurance coverage and improved safety metrics. Yet, the most recent bill in 2019 had testimonies that comprised a 70 percent opposition rate, and the majority of speakers at the hearing in February 2019 were in opposition to the bill as well. Further, the few state legislators who opposed the bill were Republicans, and all the Democrats who voted on the legislation voted in favor of midwifery regulations, perhaps ironically so.

Most mums at the hearings and through their testimonies expressed that they should have the right to choose their midwife and that regulations would restrict midwifery practices. Hawaiian mothers, in particular, expressed that this bill was restrictive on cultural midwives and was a colonial overreach. The midwives and Republican legislators who opposed the regulations argued that it was fiscally irresponsible and would create a financial burden for the state to regulate midwives. The cost of licensure would also be expensive for midwives and would arguably trickle down to home-birth mothers, making home birth less affordable and accessible. This would negatively affect mums who want home births but might not be able to afford the rising costs.

In addition to political activism around the midwifery bill, organizations such as the Hawai'i Home Birth Collective, the Pacific Birth Collective, Kalauokekahuli, and Roots Kalihi's Ka Lahui O Ka Po programs continue to support Hawaiian families and birthing practices and form collectivities in the natural birth community through outreach, training and education. The Hawai'i Home Birth Collective, made up of birthworkers, midwives and home-birth mothers, centers on protecting and preserving the diversity of midwifery in Hawai'i through political and social action related to the midwifery regulation bill, midwifery access, and the diversity of midwifery in the Hawaiian Islands.

Further, the Ka Lahui O Ka Po through Roots Kalihi is a birth prep series that "focuses on the reclaiming of ancestral practices and the cultivation of connection as ways to nurture healthy, happy births" (Roots Kalihi). Such practices include supporting birth partners as well as implementing the key teachings of ho'oponopono (healing relationships), 'ai pono (nutrition), lomilomi (healing, connection with partners, and massage), mo'omeaheu (childbirth and labor), birth plans, hānai waiū (breastfeeding), and lā'au lapa'au (herbs and natural medicines). These key teachings help to prepare mum and baby for birth but are also embedded in protocols that help mothers and their communities reclaim cultural and sacred practices.

In terms of the midwifery model of care, the mothers described midwifery as being supportive of traditional and cultural birth practices that are not always honored in the hospital setting. Yet, even in midwifery there are issues in that regulations on midwifery often favor mainland midwives coming from MEAC-accredited schools, who may practice in a very Westernized fashion. Midwifery care can also be quite clinical and medicalized depending on the particular midwife's training and paradigms on birth as well. The mother I interviewed, who birthed at the Hale O Papa temple (see Interview 22), explained that midwifery is actually different from Hawaiian culture in the sense that unattended birth was the traditional way:

> The default in most cases is an unattended birth,
> right? Traditionally, there wasn't really a perceived
> need for an entire trade of midwifery. It just didn't
> exist quite the same. There was a common practice
> of having people come in and help, but they weren't
> necessarily "trained people." The idea was that
> the mother was just going to tell them what to do
> whether it was a husband or the sister or, you know,
> whatever. Traditionally, that's how it was, and I kind
> of know that because I have known enough people
> who were still in that traditional practice. It's almost
> gone. That's one of the things I really don't want to
> completely disappear, but it's almost gone. It's been
> really squashed out of a lot of fear, but I grew up
> at a time when it was still… there were still a lot of
> people alive who had given birth. They just didn't
> think that much of it. It wasn't the "Oh my god, I'm
> going to die," you know? These were country people,
> and that's what they did. I assume they would go in

if they really had to, but honestly, I never heard of a single transport.

I have heard stories of babies dying, but not at a very high rate. I mean, I don't know of anyone who had a baby—a birth where I heard of a baby dying—but I know it happened. Just like anywhere. I mean, in a hospital. Babies die anywhere, right? So it could happen anywhere. But the idea that the hospital is the safest place to be has just not been proven to be true. I adore midwifery. It's so near to me, but the real truth of the matter is the idea that you actually need a midwife is not proven either. Right now, it's important because people are not conditioned and prepared to give birth totally on their own with no midwife. (Interview 22)

Nevertheless, midwifery was explained as a pathway to reclamation and honoring women's bodies and choices, even if it was not necessary for mums in the past or for some mums nowadays. While some models of midwifery are situated in the industrial, for-profit model of care, many mums described their midwives as part of their family, as someone they can trust, and as someone who offers them time, attention and holistic care, including massage, nutritional advice and emotional and physical support. The midwives filled a gap that needed to be filled in terms of compassionate women-centered care. Midwives are also the sort of gateway to the home birth-experience and, for some mums, the process of reclaiming self, identity and culture. In this sense, midwives can promote healthy lifestyles, compassionate care and informed choice, and empower mums to have choices and experiences not available to them in a hospital setting.

Many Hawaiian moms explained that their home-birth experience allowed them to reclaim their culture and the Hawaiian nation. One mom, in particular, had previously given birth in the hospital with her first son and decided to have a home birth with her second birth. When I asked her about colonization and home birth, she explained how that related intimately to her decision to home birth:

> I'm sure you know of our history here in Hawai'i, especially. I come from a family of sovereignty. I guess you can't say my family, but my partner's family, which is my family now (laughs). Just being around them, I'm learning about their fight for sovereignty and the opposition to the United States occupation here, and that's very political. But I feel like it does relate to my decision to go natural and do home birth (sighs), kind of relating back to going traditional, bringing back Hawaiian tradition in our daily lives, including birth, and just going against the status quo… (Interview 55)

Many Hawaiians and others view the Islands as occupied by the US. This occupation directly influences birth in the sense that it is deeply connected to issues of sovereignty over land, body, choice, mindset, lifestyle, etc. The concept of reclamation, however, is not a romanticization of the past or necessarily of pre-contact/pre-colonization birth, but a way of honoring traditional practices, many of which are deeply spiritual and forge intimate bonds with one another. It is seemingly a way to bring forward values, mindsets and lifestyle choices that resonate with oneself and one's community.

The identities of home-birth mums, their life experiences, and their families and communities also impacted their choices. Black mothers explained their struggles and triumphs with home birth choices and the reclamation of self and of birthing practices that support mothers and babies. While choice and body sovereignty were catalysts for choosing home birth (which will be addressed even further in the following chapters), choices and self-determination are constrained at varying degrees for different individuals. Hawaiian mums, for example, faced various constraints and cultural traumas due to colonization and the American militaristic occupation of the Islands. Their cultural practices, identities and access to ʻāina were disrupted in a myriad of ways, including land dispossession, prohibiting access to birthing sites, losing access to plant medicines and living under US occupation.

It is, therefore, important to understand that indigenous women who have experienced cultural trauma and losses experience them in a multitude of ways that cannot always be understood through mainstream thinking. For example, the experience of intergenerational trauma is more complex than just narrowing it down to women's rights or the fight for reproductive justice. Intergenerational trauma necessitates intersectional thinking (Heberle et al., 2020). Cultural trauma occurs "collectively and intergenerationally among a group of people with a shared social identity or circumstance as a result of state-perpetrated violence or state neglect" (Heberle et al., 2020:816). Reclamation of culture, self and sovereignty, as well as the choice of home birth, has various meanings, and all mothers do not arrive at this decision by taking the same path.

The idea of body sovereignty and multiple interlacing sovereignties (such as sovereignty over choices, national sovereignty and cultural sovereignty) inform the choice of home birth for many mothers. Indigenous mothers, for example, may arrive at particular choices, like home birth, because it is connected to culture, decolonization, body sovereignty and national sovereignty. Such decisions may be based on concepts of interconnectivity between culture, self, connection to land and spirituality. According to Maina-Okori et al. (2018:286), "Indigenous conceptions of interconnectivity view all parts of our identity as inseparable and interconnected, such as our sexuality, sexual orientation, cultural alignment, heritage, lineage, gender, socioeconomic status, spirituality, and connection to the land." In this sense, body sovereignty and national sovereignty interlace and interconnect with identity, culture, gender and connection to land. We are not just connected to our own decisions or to our own families; our decisions are impacted by a myriad of interconnections, and we are connected to everything.

This concept of everything and everyone being interconnected is a common indigenous worldview and one that is increasingly becoming more popular in mainstream thought as well. Even medicine and the medical field are interconnected to a variety of things, such as environmental toxicity, gender roles, food, soil health, colonization, etc. Concepts such as health, birth and biomedicine take on a variety of meanings according to the experiences, identities and worldviews of various mothers. Essentially, it is all connected.

So, when we think about home birth or home birth mums and their decisions, we must understand that it is all connected to our histories, how our society operates, our identities, our cultures, our nations, our education, our health, etc. It is all connected to the womb, which connects us all.

Chapter 4:
What Is Health?

I've always been really passionate about living in a
natural way. I have a background in Hawaiian herbal
medicine and have always just been really interested
in herbals and in natural choice and empowered self-
health. Once my daughter was born, I really went
into the next level, just wanting to make sure that I
did everything as healthy and natural as possible. I try
to buy organic when I can and have a healthy, varied
diet with lots of vegetables and fruits. I try to keep
any sort of chemicals out of our home. I make my
own cleaners and our own laundry detergent, and
just keep a sort of organic lifestyle even in the way
that we live, aside from just having things with chemicals, but just trying to spend a lot of time outside.
We don't really do much screen time, and I am trying
to raise her the way that I was raised, which is pretty
different from how a lot of kids are raised now with a
screen in front of their faces all the time and not play-
ing outside and using their imagination. (Interview 1)

Our collective views on health are always evolving. And how we
manage our own health is incredibly nuanced. Home-birth mamas
tend to value and prioritize their health perhaps more than the general

population; at least, that is what I gathered from my time with them. Unfortunately, not much has been written about how home-birth moms view the concept and practice of health, perhaps apart from stereotypes that they smell like patchouli! ☺ What constitutes good health, how these moms view birth and how they view biomedicine is important to know. We don't know much about how home-birth mums view these things, which seems quite perplexing as having a home birth seems to presuppose that these mums have a deep understanding of their bodies and health. They seem to have an exceptional level of physical, mental and emotional stamina, as home birth does not typically offer the pain medications, epidurals, and other interventions that hospitals offer. Further, home-birth mums' views on birth and their relationship with these views need to be teased out.

How home birth mums perceive and conceptualize the meaning of health, birth and biomedicine is something I ventured to discover. I wanted to understand not only how they conceptualize the meaning of health but how they might practice it in their everyday lives and how their view on birth connects to their decision to have a birth outside of the hospital. How they view health, birth and biomedicine might also tend to inform their views on medical individualism, gender, choice and embodiment, and it may shape the collectivities to which they belong. Health is also connected to economic status in most situations as well. Eating healthy isn't cheap. Good sleep, exercise, health checkups and self-care require time and money that people suffering from poverty generally do not have. This chapter dives into these topics and addresses the complexities of the choice and opportunity to have a home birth.

Concepts of Health

Dominant concepts of health in society have tended to favor the biomedical definition of health, which "focuses solely on the individual's psychological state and the presence or absence of sickness" (Weiss and Lonnquist, 2003:107). In essence, if you are not sick or ill, you are considered healthy. Medical sociologists, like myself, tend to look at various concepts of health, including physical functioning, mental health, social well-being, role functioning, general health perceptions and symptoms (Weiss and Lonnquist, 2003). Medical sociologists also look at health-related behaviors, healthy lifestyles, health protective behaviors, medical authority, gender and medicalization, and utilization of complementary and alternative care (Bird, Conrad, and Fremont, 2010). Yet, even if we define the term, the conceptualization of *health* itself isn't often teased out. We can study certain things about health and health practices, but what does health actually mean?

The idea of health typically tends to favor the biomedical definition, which looks at health as the absence of disease. Yet, this definition does not consider individual and cultural nuances of the term and the practice of health. It also often looks at health as an umbrella term defined by medical authorities from the top down rather than something that erupts and emerges from individual bodies and various cultures. Further, biomedical definitions of health do not connect health with land, while concepts of Hawaiian health embrace reciprocity between people and land, whereby the health of the land and the health of people are interconnected. If the land is healthy, generally, the people connected to the land are healthy. And conversely, if the land is unhealthy or polluted, people's health becomes compromised. Health is not just about land and bodies, though. It is also spiritual and emotional.

Holistic health is important as it can offer a definition beyond just the absence of disease and looks at factors beyond the individual. Complementary and alternative medicine (CAM), which is holistic by design, tends to focus on more holistic and culturally derived definitions of health (rather than Western medicine, which utilizes the biomedical definition of health). CAM includes traditional, alternative and integrative medicine that are arguably quite diverse.

While there are several domains, the following have been recognized as part of CAM: whole medical systems, mind-body medicines, biologically based practices, manipulative and body-based practices, and energy medicines (Torri and Hornosty, 2017).

Midwifery tends to fall under the umbrella of CAM as well, and just as CAM is diverse in its various approaches, so too is midwifery. However, both midwifery and CAM tend to take a holistic approach to the concept and practice of health rather than the absence of a disease approach. All the mamas I talked to favored the holistic definition of health. The mums view health as the wellness of mind, body, spirit and community. This view of health was described as empowering because mothers were able to make collaborative decisions with their midwives, they were able to assert body autonomy, and they were empowered in their health choices.

Empowered choices

While many mamas explained that physical health was an important aspect of health, they saw health as more than just physical. They saw health as based on mental, physical, emotional and spiritual wellness. Of course, we know the holistic view of health sees health as not just the absence of disease but as vitality and balance in mind, body and spirit.

The mums explained that their experiences with midwives were much more holistic and that this approach was much more empowering for them because they could make decisions about their health that resonated with their beliefs. Their midwives took care to recognize the physical, mental, emotional and spiritual aspects of their well-being. Not only did mums feel heard and taken care of, but midwives were also knowledgeable about various health practices that a medical doctor might have dismissed, and as a result, options were expanded for mothers through midwifery care.

This included being able to eat and drink during labor, being able to decline tests and vaccinations they didn't want/need, being able to birth in their position of choice, using birth pools/tubs, using plant medicines, being able to keep and/or consume their placentas without difficulty, and being able to choose who attended their birth. These experiences with midwives and the various forms of "alternative" medicines certainly shaped their understanding of health and empowered mothers in their choices and experiences.

One of the women, a home birth mum of two who studies and utilizes lā'au lapa'au (traditional Hawaiian healing practices), described the connection between holistic health and empowered choices:

> I think that health is an overall wellness in mind, body and spirit. I think that your mental and emotional health has just as much weight in that overall health as your physical. I think that having a healer in every home is a big part of that, too, like having the empowered choices… being able to make empowered choices for your health and your family's health, not having to reach out to a professional who doesn't necessarily have the same values and the same feelings of what your health means. (Interview 1)

Her view of health included not only holistic wellness, but also having empowered choices in terms of individual and family health. Part of this process for her included the importance of having a healer in every home on which to rely. Not only does this seemingly provide empowerment in terms of family health and wellness, but it also reduces reliance on medical professionals who may not share the same values and feelings about one's view of health. Being empowered to navigate health decisions and provide healing to one's family perhaps reduces reliance on biomedicine as well. In this way, it is part of taking one's power back. It is a way to become sovereign in a variety of ways.

Another mum I interviewed, a naturopathic doctor with two children, shared similar sentiments regarding making empowered health choices and utilizing preventative measures to achieve optimal health in mind, body and spirit. When asked what her definition of health was, this mama responded:

> Well, I am a naturopathic doctor, so (laughs) probably a little bit different. I'm always striving for health— we're really big on organic food at our house. I'm very big on education for myself and my patients, making sure that any health decisions we make are well researched and that we're being safe, but also feeling like we have choices in what we're doing with our own bodies, so not being just told to do something and taking that blindly. (Interview 3)

Having empowered choices was a very important aspect of the practice and the definition of health for most of the mothers, and this included not just accepting what doctors say but becoming educated on their choices and decisions as well. Having empowered choices generally meant that there was a level of research and education involved, that informed consent was present, and that women still had choices in terms of their bodies, health and family health. Mothers spoke at length about reading books and articles, talking with friends, watching documentaries, reviewing evidence-based practices, and receiving education from their midwives and other home-birth mothers. Further, mothers often spoke about the concept of choice in terms of their health and as one of the main reasons for choosing home birth. Mothers believed that they should have the right to make choices about their bodies, about their pregnancies, about their births, and about their babies. And they took responsibility for these choices.

While many mamas explained that choices and informed consent are limited in the hospital, I gathered that the concept of choice went beyond just provider-patient interactions and extended to hospital policies and insurance regulations. Such restrictions included having to be induced, be hooked up to an IV, electronic fetal monitoring, compulsory bathing of the baby right after birth, lack of privacy, not knowing the medical providers in the room, having to wear a gown, and not being able to eat during labor.

Indeed, mothers sometimes discussed previous hospital births and their lack of choices as the leading factor for choosing a home birth. Yet, health choices and choices around how women wanted to be treated during their births extended beyond this. It became clear that most women were not taught that they could have choices over their bodies and health. Most women had to go out of their way to learn more, to educate themselves, and to seek out care practitioners who honored their health and bodily choices. This process was described as empowering for many mums as the knowledge they gained seemingly allowed them to practice more power over their bodies and their birth choices. But it was also angering in that mothers recognized that they had not been taught much about birth and pregnancy, that many options were hidden from them, that birth was highly regulated and profits were put before people.

Additionally, mothers recognized that babies deserved to have consent when it comes to what drugs they are exposed to during labor, and what interventions they receive after they are born (including shots, circumcisions, blood draws, etc.). Home birth and empowered choices are not automatically given then. Mothers had to take back the knowledge and the power over their bodies. Such knowledge has been historically taken from women. The decline of home birth in the 1900s and thereafter was not an inevitable decline; rather it was an orchestrated effort by patriarchal biomedical powers and businesses that limited birth options and women's choices.

Many mothers I talked with had previous hospital births and explained that their choices were taken away and were, by and large, disappointed in the hospital setting. Their experiences often led them to choose home birth because of how they were treated in the hospital, because of the hospital feeling unsafe, too loud and too bright, and because certain options were taken from them. One mother of five who is a practicing midwife on the Big Island explained:

> I value my freedom of choice. I value my autonomy and my body autonomy. I feel that what happens to my body and what I do with my body is a really important choice of mine and mine alone, and I don't feel that my hospital birth respected my choices. I said, "No." They did things anyway. I refused things. I was forced into them anyway. Terrible things happened because of the things that they forced me into doing, and I lucked out that it was nothing grave, but it did affect me psychologically.
>
> And so, the thing I valued the most with my home births was nobody pressuring me to take drugs. Nobody pressuring me to speed up my labor. I have five children, and I've been in labor for three days with all five kids, and when I was in the hospital, they were just more Pitocin, more Pitocin, Cytotec, get her to stand up, break her water, oh crap—we broke it too soon, put water back up in there… I just was so trusting of the situation. I am so glad (my daughter) was a girl because I probably would have circumcised (a son) because I hadn't questioned mainstream-ness yet, whatever you want to call it (laughs).
>
> You know, I hadn't really started. I hadn't found myself. I hadn't started thinking for myself, and so when I had a home birth, the cord stays attached until I'm ready to remove it. I think cord burnings are beautiful. It's way better than cutting because it takes long, and it's like a closing ceremony to the whole experience, so we chose to burn our umbilical cord free from the placenta. I believe that although they don't go well in Hawai'i usually, lotus births should be a

choice for women. It's a choice that every woman has the right to make.

I believe that it's my choice to request antibiotic prophylactic eye ointment. I believe that it's my choice to request either oral or vitamin k injection. I believe it's my choice on whether or not I choose to vaccinate my children. I believe that it's my children's choice whether or not they get their ears pierced or they get circumcised because it's their body, and I want to choose what happens to my body. And I want to protect their choice to do whatever they want to do to their body when they have shown that maturity.

For me, home birth was empowering. It was spiritual. It was psychedelic. It was (sighs)… I mean, all of my children watched all of my other children be born, and it bonds your family in ways that you can't ever imagine. Tandem nursing is such a beautiful gift to not just them but to you as the mother because you can't know how amazing that is unless you've actually gotten to see your three-year-old play a little finger game with your six-month-old while they're sharing mom quietly in a gentle moment. If you have a three-year-old or a two-year-old, you know how rambunctious they can be, so you know it's nice to have the soft, loving, quiet times, too. I think by nursing my kids the way I did, allowed them to feel like they were not displaced or had direct competition with the next child. And having a midwife and having a home birth allowed me to have all of the choices to breastfeed my child, to have a water birth, to be in control of the situation, and I knew that if something went wrong in that moment, that it was my decision and not my midwife's fault or not my husband's fault or not anybody's fault because I chose to be in control of the situation.

Sometimes, part of control is knowing that you really have no control. It's surrender, and that's a huge part of birth, and I don't think we really know how powerful we are as women until we really truly give birth on our own terms. And I think that's what they've done to oppress us... they've taken away our ability to birth on our own terms and so we're still just stuck in this preconceived notion because if you let women know how powerful we are, we're dangerous (laughs). (Interview 34)

Her birth experiences allowed her to explore her own identity and power. After experiencing a hospital birth, where she was stripped of her voice, decision-making power, and choices over her body and baby, she was propelled into self-discovery and the ability to really think for herself. This allowed her to question what was necessary for her and what she really wanted versus what the system and medical-cultural messaging had told her.

The other part of home birth for her was this dichotomy of control and surrender. Home birth allowed her to exercise control over her care, body and baby, but it also meant that she had to surrender to birth in all its pain and its unknowns. She described this as a major way for women to come into their own power. To surrender to birth and come out the other end as a mother is incredibly empowering. Yet, this power has been taken away, and women have been stripped of it in the birth room. Most women aren't even allowed to birth on their own terms. Her worldview is that if women know how powerful we really are, we then become dangerous to the system. That is, we can simply stop subscribing to the ways of doing birth, of living a standard life, of being trapped in fear paradigms, etc.

This worldview is perhaps a feminist stance, but I read it as a statement that means something more than just political. That is, women are powerful, and various systems have taken away this power from us. Yet, if we are to know our own power and center that in our lives, we can disrupt systems such as the patriarchy and the male-dominated medical system. We can not only disrupt such systems, but we can also heal ourselves and others along the way. We can bring in more love, compassion, connection, kindness, regulated nervous systems, health, and wellness. This is empowering as we remove ourselves from reliance on the systems and the institutions that keep us from realizing our full power, and we can also transform and heal institutions and power structures through this process.

That is not to say that we have to abolish medicine altogether, nor is it an attack on the many wonderful healthcare workers; rather, we can bring about a new way of reimagining health, wellness, birth, compassion, understanding, empowerment, etc., to transform these systems so we can better serve humanity. We can truly honor the power of the womb.

Many mothers still understand that there is a historically and culturally concerted effort to take away power and health choices from women. Ehrenreich and English (2010) and Worman-Ross and Mix (2013) confirm that there is a directed effort by the male-dominated medical industry to assume power over birthing bodies. Of course, if we trace this back, we find that Rockefeller money and power influenced the set-up of such structures. Their legacies continue to shape medicine to this day and still promote a type of biomedical power in society. If we enter into a patient-doctor conversation or situation, we can often see this play out in terms of power dynamics (especially with pregnant mothers). Regardless of the knowledge one has or ability to articulate oneself, many women are still subjected to situations where their decision-making power and bodily autonomy are at risk. This is often racialized as well.

For example, one of the Black mothers I interviewed explained that her view of health stems from her racialized experience and how she witnessed healthcare systems harming Black people. She cited several stories she has heard over the years where Black people were not being treated well in hospital settings and where choices and bodily autonomy were violated. This led to a distrust of the "conventional Western approach to health" and led her to want to be a doctor to heal people and promote holistic health. While she did not end up becoming a doctor as she became more dissuaded by the medical system's approach to Black health, she did end up in a fitness career centered on health and wellness for several years. Her idea of health continued to evolve into a much more holistic view, eventually including the physical, nutritional, spiritual, emotional, and mental aspects of health. This evolution of lifestyle, clean diet and holistic health led her to have home births with both of her sons.

Other mamas explained that colonization disempowers and discourages holistic health choices in that traditional medicine practices, birth practices and access to plant medicine were taken away or banned altogether by colonizing forces. The continuing effects of colonization, land dispossession, tourism, overcrowding of the Hawaiian Islands, over-development, etc., all impact those health choices today as certain medicinal plants no longer grow or access to them is prohibited. Modern lifestyles and diets increase reliance on Western medicine and hospitals, and access to clean food and water is increasingly difficult to find. When I asked one of the Hawaiian mamas what her definition of health was, she responded by explaining the Hawaiian concept of *ea,* which she intimately connected to health and birth:

> I think one thing that ties into birth with health really
> strongly is the concept of "ea," and I've done a lot of
> work regarding health and *ea. Ea* in 'Ōlelo Hawai'i
> (the Hawaiian language) means the life breath, and
> it also means sovereignty. So, one thing that I have
> looked at a lot as a health person and in my personal
> life has been the connection between sovereignty and

health… *ea* as sovereignty, too. It's not the kind of sovereignty that people learn about in Western culture, where it means government rule and stuff like that.

Ea is internal. It's the breath. It's a life breath, and that's where you get your sovereignty from. Your sovereignty is in the breath of life. It's so important for health because this is the internal breath that every single one of us carries with us, that we have internally, and to manifest in the world health and good relationships to land and food and medicine and everything else we do you know each other.

To manifest that, our *ea* has to be free so that sovereignty has to be exercised. That's where my emphasis has been, largely on returning *ea* to people because they've lost it. We've lost it to the medical system. We've lost our *ea* to the idea that others control us, and that could mean government, that could be the medical system. The idea of delivering a baby… who came up with that word, you know: delivering? Yeah, like pizza somehow. How did the active word in birth become delivery? That's an example of where we have lost our *ea* right. We have lost that spirit inside of us, that life breath and our sovereignty that manifests in the world and is responsible for driving us to do things in our pono manner.

So those are some really important health concepts to me. Pono gets a lot of attention in the health world, but *ea* does not, you know? And I think that the relationship between *ea* and pono (doing the right thing) is very, very important because unless you have your internal sovereignty… and that goes for every single person… you will not have health because nobody else can make you healthy. (Interview 22)

She describes *ea* (the Hawaiian word that means sovereignty and breath) as the basis of sovereignty, of connection, of guidance toward *pono* (the Hawaiian word that means doing the right thing) decisions and relationships with land, medicine, people and ourselves. *Ea* is the basis for sovereignty; it is our breath and our spirits. When it is disrupted, we cannot manifest our health to be optimal. We lose our *ea* to the idea that others control us. Other forces like the government and the medical institutions are then able to control our sovereignty, our health decisions and our life processes. We are reduced to having our babies "delivered" by them and to them. Restoration of *ea*, therefore, means restoration of empowered choices, restoration of sovereignty, restoration of power, restoration of relationship, restoration of spirit and life breath, etc.

She also explains that "nobody else can make you healthy." According to Western medicine, the only path to health is either the absence of disease or their treatment plans to restore health. However, when looking at health from a holistic perspective, doctors cannot make you healthy in this sense, as health goes beyond the physical elements and available pharmaceutical treatments.

Furthermore, this mother explains that *ea* is the internal power to manifest in the world, whether that be our health, our relationships, our births, etc. In McMullin's article, "The Call to Life: Revitalizing a Healthy Hawaiian Identity," she describes that this concept of health is more holistic than the biomedical understanding and that for Hawaiians, health has a more nuanced meaning:

> What it means to be a healthy Hawaiian contributes to our understanding of the taken-for-granted state of "health." By examining concepts of health for meaning and social order, we see that health entails more than individualism and self-control, but rather is embedded in family relationships and the land that you and your ancestors occupy.

In other words, the body and thus health cannot be
"detached from living situations." In recognizing that
health is embedded in a social and historical context,
the study of concepts of health moves us away from
"naturalized" notions of the unhealthy other.
(McMullin, 2005:818)

McMullin (2005) describes health as more social and historical
rather than a fixed understanding of what is healthy versus unhealthy.
She sees health as embedded in the relationship with family and land
rather than just individualism. Health is influenced and shaped not
only by broader social structures but also by social relationships and
collectivities. McMullin (2005) argues that this concept of health is
always socially and historically situated for Hawaiians. For instance,
home birth mothers explained how important eating locally is to
health. That is, connecting to 'āina, growing one's own food and
eating non-genetically modified foods treated without pesticides are
all part of this relationship to health.

Certainly, the Hawaiian sovereignty movement has also
addressed issues with pesticides and genetically modified foods,
particularly genetically modified taro/kalo, considered a food staple
and literally an ancestor in Hawaiian culture. In terms of empowered
choices, then, health is not just an individualistic choice, but it is also
informed by various social and historical processes and collectivities.
It is also informed by our *ea*.

Balance

Balance was another key theme described by mums when asked about
their definition of health. Many reported that being healthy is not
possible without some sort of balance. This balance was described as
physical, mental, spiritual and emotional. Many mothers suggested
that while one's physical health could be optimal, they might not
actually be healthy if their lives are unbalanced, and they are enduring
mental and emotional stress. A home birth mama of multiple

children, who is a student midwife, described her understanding of health and balance:

> What's my definition of health? That's a good question. Well, health is a balance in the body for me. It's a balance mentally, physically, spiritually, emotionally, and feeling balanced and recognizing when you're not. Lack of health is when you recognize that you're not (healthy). I think somebody who's healthy understands the limits of their bodies. The biggest thing is just understanding your body and your mind and your physical self needs.
>
> So, I recognize that I am a breastfeeding postpartum mom, and exercise isn't always number one on my list, but eating healthy and eating a variety and eating enough calories is, and meditation and things like that… things that help me keep myself sane and balanced, you know? And if that means I'm overweight according to the world standard, that, to me, doesn't determine whether I am healthy or unhealthy. I can get up and walk with my kids and do whatever. As long as I can do those things and find joy and peace with myself, then that's health. (Interview 36)

Her understanding of health and the way she keeps herself healthy is through awareness of her and her family's needs. She knows that balance includes the awareness of her body as a breastfeeding, postpartum mother. The physical, emotional and mental effort one needs to have to recover from childbirth and breastfeeding is incredible. Many mothers need to balance this with taking care of newborns, other children and away-from-home jobs. Balance can be difficult, especially for mothers. For this mom, balance meant that she could take care of her family and be at peace. She understands her needs and has the awareness and resources to cater to those needs. While her definition of what is healthy for her may be questioned by standards of health in the Western medical model, she accepts that her idea of health is very individualized as well. It is not a one-size-fits-all approach.

Another home-birth mama of multiple children who lives on Maui described her understanding of health and balance:

> To me, health would be really tied to physical health. It would be really tied to mental health as well. For me, I always try to find a balance of not just doing what's good for your (physical) body but what's good for your mind and in your mental health as well. A lot of that could translate to being outdoors, activity (like) that. Just the full body picture as much as possible. (Interview 21)

When mothers talk about balance, as this mama did, they always relate it to a holistic view of health. In a medical context, balance might be measured by biomarkers being in a good range, eating a balanced diet, and having a body relatively free of injury. Yet, mothers described balance as holistic—mind, body and spirit. Balance was also often described in a choice-based framework in terms of being able to choose activities that are optimal for balance, such as meditation, walks, being outside, being with children, not working too much, etc.

Mothers recognized the constant demands of motherhood and how important sleep, time to self, praying, meditating and exercise were to maintaining health. A single mama of three who home-birthed her youngest daughter, described health as the following:

> Health... mentally, physically... just making sure you're balanced. Everybody has work, and kids, and life stresses, but to take time to do something that you know will help you mentally, physically... like praying, meditating, exercising...

Despite the demands of work, family, life stresses and being a single parent, this mother still tried to make time for those practices that helped her achieve balance and, therefore, strive toward her idea of health.

Spirituality

Spirituality is, of course, connected to concepts of holistic health, culture, religion, etc. Many mums told me that spirituality was a pillar of health for them and their families, whether through personal, cultural, and/or religious practices. Spirituality was described by a Polish home-birth mother living on O'ahu as foundational to connection, health, and self-actualization. When I asked for her definition of health, she replied:

> Oh, you asked me that on the beach… I remember you told me about it. The first thing that comes to me is really embracing your spirituality… really embracing the aspect of you being connected to Mother Earth, being connected to the heavens and beyond, and being connected to your higher self… to all the senses, which are you… and be willing to explore all the aspects of connection to Mother Earth and to the spirits and everything that lies with it. I feel it's so important.
>
> Through my study as a holistic health practitioner and as a healer… massage therapy and all that… (it) confirmed what I always knew: that you can have the healthiest diet, you can be exercising every day and taking the best supplements, but if your soul and your spirit are not healthy, you can forget all of that (other) stuff. You will not be up to being healed or fully healthy. For me, I feel like first is this spirituality which comes as the top priority, what I need to concentrate on, and then after is everything else as far as diet, of course, 100 percent, and then being active, using your body, and all that stuff. (Interview 29)

For her, embracing spirituality meant having a connection to Mother Earth, to the heavens and to oneself. Spirituality is a necessary component of good health for her. Exploring her connection to spiritual life solidified her conceptualization of health in that she was able to see health as holistic. Her identity was also wrapped up in this concept of health, as her career and lifestyle aligned with her spiritual practices and her health choices. She reiterated that physical health and diet were not the singular marker of good health, however. Instead, without spiritual health, optimal physical health might not ever be possible.

She also spoke about intuition and spiritual connection when navigating her pregnancy, her birth choices and even during labor. She explained that her spiritual connection and intuition gave her the insight to choose the right foods, lifestyle, birth practices, midwife, etc., during her pregnancy. She spoke about how intuition and spiritual connection also saved her from the fear-based rhetoric one doctor bombarded her with, as well as how she utilized her spiritual connection to her ancestors to navigate hard parts during labor. She wanted to use her own inner voice and inner knowing to make decisions for herself rather than succumb to decisions based on fear or coercion by medical professionals.

The Business of Being Born documentary details at length how the medical-industrial complex oftentimes uses fear-based arguments to coerce pregnant women into tests and interventions, many of which are unnecessary (Lake and Epstein, 2008). Many of these interventions and tests are not necessarily evidence-based and are often utilized to avoid litigious outcomes should something go awry during pregnancy or childbirth (Lake and Epstein, 2008). These interventions are routinely pushed upon birthing women, often without regard to whether they are necessary or wanted (Block, 2007; Craven, 2010; Ehrenreich and English, 2010; Oakley, 1986; Oakley, 2016; Oparah and Bonaparte, 2016; Worman-Ross and Mix, 2013). By design, the atmosphere of fear and risk avoidance in hospital settings disrupt a woman from following her own intuition and having faith in the design of her body. Perhaps what is worse is that this design teaches women not to rely on faith but to engulf themselves in fear.

Having faith can sometimes lead us to understanding that we have the power within. We, as women, were designed to birth babies, pending any injury, disease or defects. While some women choose not to have babies, we are all born with biology that promotes reproduction. Having faith in this design was very important for many moms. Their faith in their bodies and their strength allowed them to do one of the hardest things a body can do: give birth. Unfortunately, home-birth mothers have been called irresponsible for making their own birth decisions and for following research that contradicts biomedical authority.

Perhaps even more disruptive to medical authority are the mothers who choose to follow their internal and spiritual compasses when it comes to decisions over their bodies and their babies. Having faith disrupts the doctor-patient power dynamic as well. Nevertheless, following their inner guidance provided them a level of balance and access to empowered choices (within particular social and economic constraints), making it possible to practice some control over their own healthcare choices and ability to follow their own intuition, even when people called them crazy or when doctors scared them into doubting their bodies.

Birth

Birth reveals social and cultural norms and reflects and shapes how women view their bodies, social identities, relationships, abilities and natural instincts. Birth shapes and reflects how we view the world and how we view women. When birth is conceived of as a natural, normal life process, women are generally treated as capable, strong and able to birth their babies. When birth is viewed, on the other hand, as an emergency, women are to undergo a variety of technocratic medical measures to manage their bodies and their babies. They must be saved from themselves. Of course, depending on the situation, such viewpoints are on a spectrum and may change depending on the unique situation.

The women I interviewed saw birth as a natural life process and viewed their own experiences as part of their lived identities as well. They also connected their decision to birth at home with their lifestyles, which tended to focus on living authentically, healthy, active and family-centered lifestyles. One home-birth mama, who was a trained chiropractor and healthy lifestyles advocate, explained that her decision to home birth was connected to her priority to be as healthy as possible:

> I chose to do a home birth because I feel I was able to have more preferences honored than if I had been in the hospital. But again, it's a huge priority to be healthy and knowing the health benefits of having a natural, vaginal delivery for the baby... they need the pressure to squeeze extra fluid out, and the vernix, and how they get inoculated with the good bacteria, and there are a lot of health benefits for both mom and baby. When you do it naturally, healing time is quicker for the mom. So, doing a natural or home birth is connected to my priority of being healthy, and there are less risks for infections and other things versus if you were going to have a C-section or give birth in a hospital.
>
> (In the) research I was doing I learned that women would die if they were to have their baby in the hospital because the obstetricians wouldn't wash their hands in between, (for example). I know you can in certain hospitals and other hospitals (are) attached (to) birth centers now. But I wanted to have worship music in the background and essential oils. I wanted

those things. I wanted to feel like I could. I wanted a more peaceful, holy spirit-filled environment, and I felt like I could foster that more in my home versus in a hospital. (Interview 32)

It was clear that not only did she want the most natural birth possible because it was healthiest for her, but that doing so was a way to honor her spiritual devotion as well. She explained the many benefits for both mum and baby to birth at home (all of which are backed by evidence). These benefits include being able to have skin-to-skin contact with baby right after birth, reducing exposure to pathogens, centering family health, and having cultural and personal wishes honored. While she did not say it's impossible to have the preferred choices, the health benefits, and the spiritual practices honored in a hospital setting, she did allude to the various risks and constraints that come with hospital birth.

Other mothers explained that home birth allowed them to have control of their own experience and their bodies. Women have been taught to disconnect from their bodies. We live in such a mind/intellectually focused world now, and the pressures of work often make us disconnect from our bodies. We are taught to fight through exhaustion and to subscribe to a higher authority rather than listen to our bodily wisdom. Many women throughout the world do not have much control over what happens to their bodies, and home birth can be a unique experience in that women get a say in what happens to their bodies. While this is not always the case, of course, most women explained that their midwives were keen on informed consent and education throughout the birth process. This type of care was empowering to women and allowed them to really have control over their choices. Women weren't just forced into a prescribed set of rules on their bodies. Women wanted to have control over their birth setting, their care and the choices made before, during and after childbirth.

While they expressed that birth is about letting go of control, it seemed that mums wanted control over their birth choices, providers, and settings so that they could *actually* surrender into the birth process. Perhaps this is like how we want to make enough money to have control over our lives as well. That is, we want power over how we use our bodies and our time. We are in a world where most of us do not have the money, power, control or energy to assert that power because of so many pressures. The ability for mums to trust in the "natural" birth process at home allowed them to feel in control and yet surrender and let go. This is an incredible feat that can translate to other areas of life and inspire us to regain sovereignty over our lives in many ways.

Think about all the decisions you make because you are forced to or because you are afraid. Now, imagine if we, as a collective, began to operate out of faith, family-centeredness, spirituality, health, and love of community. The faith and strength a mama has to have to give birth at home might inspire us to let go of fear-based thinking and prescribed ways of being in the world. No wonder home birth is so routinely shunned!

Many of the mothers had experience being birth workers themselves, including practicing midwifery and doing doula work in and out of the hospital setting. The mums who were doulas often explained that their catalyst for birthing at home was inspired by their past experiences with clients in hospital birth. They explained that women did not have choices in the hospital, that the hospital staff did not always treat them with compassion and kindness, and that their individual needs weren't honored. One mama connected her lifestyle to her decision to birth at home. When asked about why she chose home birth, she explained:

> It's just kind of a certain type of lifestyle, and I think it probably has something to do with wanting to be in control of our experiences and in control of these raw and important moments. I worked as a doula for a few years, and I only attended hospital births. And

I just saw what was taken away from the experience for some of the moms that I worked with, and I just knew that I didn't want that… it just wasn't gonna be for me. (Interview 1)

Me: What kind of things did you see that were taken away?

I saw decisions being made for them in moments where they maybe couldn't answer in the way that was expected. For example, there was a mom that I worked with that had told nurses that she didn't want an epidural, and a nurse came in while she was in the middle of a contraction before anyone could stop her, and she said, "You look like you need more," and she pushed the button and gave her more epidural and it made it so she couldn't push. It was just so sad to me because she had voiced what she wanted, and that was not respected. And even for me, in my place as being an advocate for her, I didn't even have time to stop her (the nurse). I couldn't. I was just so thrown off that she would do that after she was told that (the birthing mother) didn't want any more epidural.

Women (were) not being given the chance to find an empowered space for themselves and not being able to tap into their primal birthing power. It's sad to me that gets stripped away. It's a medicalized view of birth: you're pregnant and you're sick. It's an ailment that needs to be cared for, and to me, that's not how I feel, and that's not what I wanted. (Interview 1)

Perhaps the most important thing to note here is that women's choices are often taken away from them and that pregnancy and labor is not a sickness. It is a healthy, normal process according to this mama. She witnessed disempowerment inside the hospital, where the other birthing mum was given medicine against her will, and this impacted her birth. In this sense, medicine was part of an unhealthy, dominating system. While it's not uncommon for women's choices to be routinely taken from them in patriarchal societies, it struck a particular nerve with this mother that her client's wishes weren't honored during such a "raw and important" moment. Such disempowerment from the primal birthing power seems to disconnect birthing women from their innate power and capacity to bring about life into their world. It seems to me that this is perhaps the most perverse attack on humanity in both the spiritual and the physical realms.

Others explained that home birth is an extension of a healthy lifestyle and part of their holistic lifestyles as well. A naturopathic doctor from the Big Island who birthed outside the hospital explained that her decision was evidence-based and that it was the healthier option for her. She explained that the C-section rate at Hilo Hospital was over 30 percent, and they have an extremely high infection rate for things like MRSA. She did not believe that giving birth was a pathological event nor that she needed hospital care for her birth. She did end up needing some postpartum care in the hospital, which she was grateful for; however, she still was frustrated with the medical view of birth, placing fear around everything having to do with pregnancy and birth.

> I definitely have issues with birth being viewed as a pathology, and I mean even with insurance coding and stuff right now. That is exactly how it is looked at: a pathology. And that's a bit frustrating. I think the medical system these days has put a lot of fear in everyone. I mean around everything, but I feel like especially birth, and it takes a lot of power away from the mother. I definitely have some frustration with that. I've heard way too many women saying they didn't feel like they had a choice and things, and they just wanted to walk around, and they weren't allowed

to walk around, and that's a simple right you should be granted during something as difficult as childbirth. You should be able to be in a comfortable position. Somebody should not be telling you that you can't move. The whole Cesarean rate goes up significantly right before long weekends, you know? I just feel like there are a lot of unnecessary interventions that put the mother and the baby at risk, and financial strain on the family as well, that do not need to be there. That definitely played into why we made our choice because I do feel there's over-care and over-fear in the medical system these days around birth. (Interview 3)

When I asked her if she had anything else to add about her view of home birth, she explained that there was still a lot of stigma about home birth, such as women being viewed as crazy, irrational, misinformed or risky. She felt that people view home-birth mums as hippies who are into natural medicine and that home birth is non-evidence-based. She explained that people still think it is "natural" and therefore not safe as well.

However, the women she sees choosing home birth are her most educated patients as far as higher education goes. She thinks it's important that people know that many home birth mums do massive amounts of research from scientific sources to arrive at their decisions. They were also well-educated and did a lot of research on home birth as well. This urge and ability to research seemed to be derived from the mothers' educational levels, however, rather than their social classes.

Further, this mama attempted to destigmatize home birth by professing that it isn't just some "hippie-dippie" person making this "unsafe" decision but, rather, that home birth is actually safe for low-risk women, as evidenced by facts and science. This is interesting in that many mothers also expressed that natural lifestyles and home birth go hand-in-hand and that natural ways of living are not only important but are also backed by scientific evidence. For example, spending time in nature is linked to lower stress levels (Hofmann, et al., 2018), natural plant medicine is thought to be easier on the body than pharmaceuticals, and eating organic foods reduces exposure to cancer-causing pesticides (and organic foods are arguably better for the environment as well, although this is somewhat contested depending on the proximity of the food supply chain and the energy/environmental costs of shipping food).

Nevertheless, mums gravitated toward natural lifestyles and birthing and found evidence (scientific or otherwise) to support such practices. Their practices not only expressed their shared values and ideals, but certainly such practices reflected the perspectives of the home birth collectivity. Many of the women, for example, submitted testimony in opposition to the midwifery regulation bill that referenced scientific studies confirming home birth as a healthy option for low-risk women. From my experience with this community, I also found that many of the women I interviewed are connected to local farmers and organic food producers in the Islands as well. These perspectives of the collective, which values home birth, non-toxic lifestyles, medical freedom, questioning of routine medical treatments including vaccinations, and local non-genetically modified foods, entered the individual mothers' value systems to shape their lifestyles and worldviews.

Trust

Trusting in birth and labor, with all its pain and moments of doubt, is not an easy feat. Most women come to a place of self-doubt right around transition (about eight to ten centimeters dilated), and they have to dig deep to transcend this self-doubt so they can get through birth.

Trust was explained in many other ways including trust in their midwives and partners, in their babies and their bodies, and trust in the natural process of life. This concept of trust was certainly embodied as well, with many women explaining that they chose a home birth because they trusted their bodies, they trusted that their body was made to birth, they trusted natural life processes, they trusted God, they trusted God's design, they trusted their ancestral wisdom in terms of birth and life, and they trusted their choices. They trusted their decisions and beliefs in the natural way of birth at home over the hospital. This level of trust requires great strength when the messaging and conditioning in our culture is that the hospital is the safest place to birth.

These mothers practiced discernment between their conditionings and their intuitive nudges; that is, they had the trust in themselves and their intuition to choose what was best for their births. They viewed the hospital as a place that cannot always be trusted in terms of birth. While the hospital *can* be trusted in terms of emergencies, certainly, and all mothers expressed their gratefulness for hospitals in emergency situations, they did not trust the hospital for their births. They did not want random people in their room, they did not want tubes and medications, and they did not want someone else to manage their birth. They trusted birth.

I am always fascinated by people who trust so deeply. Indeed, I have given birth at home myself and have taken this journey of trust. Yet, I am still in awe of the amazing power of women to trust birth and creation. I suppose it's what we have been taught to do in various religious and spiritual circles. That is, to trust in God's design, timing and plan. We are supposed to trust in birth because it is our place of human creation. We are supposed to trust in life and death as well. These are natural. However, they are not easy. At the same time, we have been conditioned by the biomedical field to distrust our bodies and nature.

I don't wish to paint the picture that medical science ultimately disrupts God's design, but there is something to be said about the tropes that have come from the biomedical field, including that

145

doctors have a "God complex," that "doctor knows best," that birth and creation should be managed, that there is risk in birth, that death should be managed, etc. The idea that science is the ultimate truth begs the question of who's science, what constitutes science, what method produces the right truths, who funds the science, etc. It does make me wonder if medical science was designed to oversee and manipulate God's design. I am not speaking about healing itself as many healing knowledges, plant medicines, etc., include prayer practices and honor of God's power and the ability of our bodies to heal themselves. But I mean the proliferation of biomedical power. The massive reliance on Tylenol, for example, to cure a headache rather than the intuitive knowledge that perhaps a headache is caused by overworking, overthinking and underhydrating.

Science gives us an out when it comes to taking care of ourselves and living life at a pace where we can listen to our intuition and to God's plan. That is, we can just pop a pill and move right along. We can give up responsibility in this way. We don't have to face our power or our fears. We can drink caffeine instead of rest because the alternative, as many might suspect, would be to not have the energy to work and keep up, and if we don't keep up in this economy, we might not survive. Home birth mothers showed me that there are different possibilities. We can survive beyond what is prescribed to us. And it all starts with birth. And it all starts with trust. And it all starts with the womb.

Trust also extended to partners and midwives. One mama who birthed her children on Kauai and who essentially lived her life outdoors (she chose not to live in a home and instead chose to live in a tent near the ocean) for many years explained that it was her partner who really helped her to trust herself for her first birth:

> My first partner was a big part of me being able to really trust myself because he was just so at ease with it as well, and he was like, you know, women have been birthing for millennia, and I'm sure your body knows

how to do it. His 100 percent trust in me was such a relief, and I knew that if I said I wanted to birth in a hospital, he would trust me in that. But he really just trusted me, and that was such a good feeling, and so for that birth, it was just us in the room, and he pretty much just watched, I mean he gave me the coconut water, that was his big job (laughs). (Interview 4)

Apart from three mums who had to convince their partners/ husbands that birthing at home would be a good decision, the rest shared similar sentiments in that their partners or husbands trusted their ability to birth at home. Of course, the home birth midwives also trusted that they could birth at home. Beyond this trust in the birth process itself, many mothers explained that the trust they built with their midwives was so important to them. That is, they built deep, unwavering relationships with their midwives.

Many home birth mothers had tandem care, which essentially meant they chose to birth at home and see a midwife throughout their pregnancy, and they also saw an OB or nurse midwife in the clinical setting for things like routine check-ups, ultrasounds and labs. Most explained that the sterile medicalized setting was more "fear-based," "appointments were short," "wait times were long." Sometimes, they would be seen by whichever nurse midwife or doctor was on duty at the time, whether they knew them or not, and the clinical environment was generally uncomfortable and inconvenient. The mistrust of the hospital setting seemed to come from the very valid fear that they would be mistreated, that their choices wouldn't be honored, that they would feel uncomfortable, that their babies might receive unwanted vaccinations, that they wouldn't know their care provider, or that something would be done to their bodies that they wouldn't approve. This made it more difficult for the mothers to establish trust with their medical care providers.

Distrust of the hospital setting and the patriarchal and paternalistic culture of medicine led mothers to practice choice over their medical experiences and birth setting. Sometimes, mothers feared giving birth in the hospital because they had witnessed hospital births where their friends or doula clients were disempowered. They saw that the doctors and nurses did not listen to the birthing mothers, or they did things to them without consent. They often broke trust with mothers. Things that were promised to be honored were taken away, like not doing delayed cord cutting, vaccinating children against their mothers' wishes, bathing the babies instead of letting the skin-protective vernix seep into their skin, performing episiotomies on women without consent, giving medications after refusal, doing membrane sweeps without approval or knowledge from the mother, checking cervical dilation against consent, letting people come into the birthing room without consent... the list goes on and on. That is not to say that all nurses and doctors fail to listen to mothers; it is more of a critique of those who do not listen and a critique of the way hospitals and the health care field manages birth. Certainly, it was expressed that the for-profit medical care system incentivized doctors to push unnecessary treatments and interventions that disrupt birth and disempower women as well. The medical paradigm that sees birth as a process that should be medically managed also turned mothers off as they did not trust the medical professionals to honor their choices during pregnancy and birth. As a result, they decided to take birth choices into their own hands.

While there was mistrust of the clinical/hospital setting for birth, the mothers expressed that midwifery care was completely different. Midwifery appointments were described as longer, more comfortable and much more informative. Midwifery appointments usually occurred at the mother's home, so there was no commute or wait time (making it easier for mothers of young children). The appointments lasted at least an hour or longer. Midwives took the time to get to know the mothers and asked them about their emotional and mental health, their diet, their connection to their babies and their families, etc., rather than exclusively focusing on the physical aspects of the mother's body and her baby. Midwives asked about what mothers wanted to do before, during and after their births, placing the power back in the mothers' hands. Midwives became close friends, almost like family, for many mums as well. One O'ahu mama of multiple young children explained that very sentiment:

> Yes, so it's definitely different from my OB appointments. Basically, our midwife really felt like a part of our family, and she did become a part of our family. She came over, and she interacted with my children. She included my kids in our appointments. I guess I didn't even… it feels weird even calling them an appointment. It just was weird to even call it that. She would come to our house, which was amazing for me. I interviewed her at first. I think that was one of the selling points to me. My son can be kind of reserved, and he takes a while to get comfortable around people, and that was not the case with my midwife. She really put in an effort to make a relationship with my kids and my husband also, which is really important to me.
>
> Everything was just natural. And she would include the kids in listening to the baby's heartbeat or taking my blood pressure, and nothing felt forced. It was just a totally different experience than anything I had ever… in a good way… experienced with my previous two kids. It was amazing. It was amazing. She is amazing. I seriously love her. (Interview 17)

Women-centered and family-centered care was so important for women and allowed them to build that trust with their midwives. It is often said in the home birth community that being comfortable and feeling safe around the people who are in your birth space is so important as disruption, force, and feeling unsafe disrupt the progression of birth and the flood of hormones that allow birth to occur naturally and spontaneously. While not every woman ends up with a midwife they trust or becomes part of their family, most of the mothers expressed that their midwives became like family. They trusted them, and they were comfortable. This relationship and the trust they built with their midwives contributed to their positive home birth experiences. And, it wasn't just because midwives honored mothers' choices. It was about their warm demeanors, their knowledge, their voices, their presence, their humanity—something that is often lacking in the medical realm.

Being surrounded by the right people whom they could trust was vitally important to mothers in trusting themselves and their own bodies during childbirth. One of the Black mothers I interviewed, who lives on O'ahu, explained that she expected her midwife to check her cervix often because that is what occurred in the hospital during previous births. When the midwife told her that she trusted her body to open and for her baby to move down, this mother was able to really settle into trusting herself, her body and her baby. She explained that her midwife helped her to trust herself again during her home birth:

> It just brought me where I needed to be in that mental space and trusting that whoever was with me had my best interest in mind and at heart. And that helped me to trust myself. To be able to feel your power—and it's powerful—and know you've created a life, and now you're... every part of you is using every single muscle or all your entire energy is now committed to bring this life earth side, and no one else can stop you from this, because this is your purpose at this time.

> The transformation was knowing that I am a powerful being, and I've always known it, but feeling it, and internalizing it, that I can do this... it's feeling on top

of the world. I can do anything… if I can do natural birth. And you don't even have to be the one having a natural birth, you could just be in the room with the woman who is doing that. You feel that power is unstoppable. That, for me, was the biggest transformation: understanding my power has no bounds. It has no bounds. (Interview 36)

Feeling one's own power is an incredible experience, particularly for women. Perhaps this power is enhanced particularly during experiences that women have been taught are to be managed by others (such as birth). This level of empowerment might not have been possible without women trusting themselves and their bodies and resisting social norms that pressure them into medical settings where they risk loss of power over their bodies and choices.

Worman-Ross and Mix (2013) had similar findings when they found that mothers resisted reliance on technology and hospital interventions and opted instead to follow natural and intuitive ways of knowing. They also found that midwives' trust in the birth process and in birthing women is a women-centered approach that honors women's needs, intuitions, bodies and babies (Worman-Ross and Mix, 2013). The next section details the importance of trusting oneself, particularly during pregnancy and childbirth.

Trusting Oneself

In continuing with the theme of trust, most mothers explained in one way or another that the process of birth required some level of trust in oneself. Trust was cultivated and experienced in many ways. Following "one's own intuitive knowledge," "educating oneself," "trusting in the female body's ability to birth," "trusting in God's design" that women are biologically shaped women to give birth, and trusting in one's "own strength" (mentally, physically and spiritually) were all discussed throughout the conversations I had. When I asked a home-birth mama on Oʻahu, who grew up on the mainland, why she valued home birth and how that connected to other parts of her life, she explained:

> It is connected to my value of trusting myself in all areas. Trusting that I can make decisions for myself and that I'm capable of researching, and finding, and understanding information. It's related to my value of independence and my value of respect for my physical self, as well as mental and spiritual self. Independence pretty much is at the base of it for me, and that kind of trickles over into independence and how I raise my kids.
>
> You mentioned that you co-sleep with your kids. We co-sleep with our kids. We chose to vaccinate them on a different schedule. We want to choose. Being able to be independent about that, and trusting that I can find good information, and make a decision based on that, and not necessarily have it spoon-fed to me from a medical professional. That's all pretty related to me being able to trust my body and being able to trust in the natural rhythms and the natural processes that it goes through, and it's also taught me a lot about how to endure different kinds of pain (laughs). Not just physical, but that I am able and capable to live through and endure a lot (laughs) and that it's going to be okay at the end, you know. (Interview 18)

The level of trust and faith that this mother cultivated and practiced gave her the freedom and responsibility over her own choices and her family choices. Rather than take a recommendation or piece of information at face value, she researched home birth and did her own due diligence, as well as tuned in to see if it worked for her. This sort of deviation from external authority seemingly gave way to trust in her body and to trust in the natural processes of life.

Trust also extended beyond birth into other areas of her life, such as in decision-making, mothering, working, etc., which was empowering for her and allowed her to really shape her decisions, choices and lifestyles in the way she wanted.

While almost all mothers explained that they chose a home birth due to evidence-based practices and research that confirmed the safety and benefits of home birth for low-risk women, they also explained that part of that process involved following and trusting their intuition—or internal knowledge—to steer their decisions and experiences. Trusting one's intuition or knowledge from within shows that knowledge can be embodied. Our bodies hold so much wisdom and intuition. They are our guides. And, of course, knowledge can come from within as well as from outside of us.

Our systems and society today generally steer us to consume and follow knowledge outside of us rather than follow our own intuition and our own embodied wisdom. When it comes to trusting oneself, particularly during something as intense and mysterious as childbirth, this requires great trust in one's own voice over the loud messages of society. The home-birth mamas were natural divergents because they tended to listen to their own voices rather than biomedical authority and dominant birth norms, such that they were willing to face the stigma and pain of home birth head-on. They saw intuition as a naturally occurring ability that guides them towards the right decisions and experiences for them. This paradigm certainly challenges the idea that knowledge comes exclusively from some objective apparatus or scientific method.

While there are processes and social norms that aim to take away our intuitive abilities and make us doubt ourselves, these home-birth mothers took their power back and made choices that were most in line with their intuition. They did not let cultural, medical or social messages overtake their own power.

The Liberian mother mentioned in the preceding chapter explained that power during birth typically is taken away from women in the medical realm and that trusting yourself is one way to shift that dynamic. These power shifts were also embedded in colonial and Westernizing practices over women (particularly Black and indigenous women). Making people feel vulnerable or crazy for trusting themselves and/or resisting the colonizing medical authorities is part of the process of taking power away from women. It makes women feel like they are crazy for making a decision that goes against the grain. Of course, this is part of the stigmatization of home birth, and the for-profit medical system certainly plays into this. This mama believes that our bodies are made to birth and that pregnancy and birth are not sicknesses, yet these forces make women feel vulnerable and incapable of trusting their bodies by pathologizing their bodies and assuming authority over them.

There are critiques of the alternative/home birth movement as being a choice-based, individualistic paradigm on birth and that it doesn't address women who lack the autonomy to make such decisions (like disabled and incarcerated mothers, those who don't have access to midwifery care, or even high-risk mothers who cannot birth at home). There must, therefore, be a level of choice and power that goes into home birth as home birth is not an accessible option for all women. The women who chose home birth had some level of power to do so.

There is also a level of knowledge that mothers had cultivated and engaged with that helped them to trust themselves as well. Yet, to say that this type of birthing and these birth communities are individualistic is a stretch. Many home-birth mothers explained that family, community and culture were central factors in having a home birth. Yes, they had the ability to birth at home, but it was not due to selfish reasons. They wanted the best for their babies, their bodies and their families. Many women did so as an homage to their cultural practices as well.

Women chose to birth at home because, ultimately, they trusted their choices, their bodies and the ancient birth energy more than they subscribed to the idea that birth only belongs in the hospital. In the hospital, women are often given the message that their bodies are not to be trusted. Davis-Floyd (1992) writes about how hospital birth becomes ritualized through various practices like gown wearing, stirrups, cervical checks, electronic fetal monitoring, etc., which signal to the birthing woman that she is not capable of trusting her body or birthing her baby without technocratic measures and "professional" assistance (despite evidence that such measures are often unnecessary). This becomes the acceptable standard, and these rituals have meanings.

Think about movie scenes when a mother goes into labor, and as soon as she enters the hospital, they put her in a wheelchair. She is given the message that she is unable to walk, is unable to manage pain and needs assistance. Women in labor can and should walk and stand (as needed) as such positions help with opening the cervix and managing contractions. Such rituals, like the wheelchair, are enacted upon mothers for "safety" and "concern" for their bodies and their babies. These rituals signal to women that they can't trust their bodies, that the doctor's instructions override their intuition and that they are in need of being rescued. These rituals create meanings that place female bodies in a hierarchical system; that is, Western medicine and white male knowledge become superior to female bodies and their intuition. Trust in oneself and one's body to birth on its own without such rituals and interventions seemingly poses a threat to the dominant powers. Tension is created when women challenge such rituals, and they disrupt medical power when they assert alternative possibilities.

If you have not noticed, there are few circles in society that encourage women to speak up and claim their own power. But once women start speaking up and questioning things, it has a snowball effect. This is why many home-birth mothers question things like medical intervention, colonization, patriarchy, childhood vaccinations, conventional diets, etc. All of a sudden, they realize they have a choice, can trust their intuition and don't have to go with the status quo. They tend to start making choices for themselves, not based on their conditioning. This tension shapes their worldviews in that women tend to question dominant ways of birthing, living and parenting such that they begin to make decisions for themselves and what ways of birthing, living, and parenting resonate with them rather than uphold conventional ways of doing/being and uphold dominant power systems.

Embodiment

We all live in a body. But, as we know from lots of psychologists, books, trauma experiences, etc., not all of us really live in our bodies. Most of Western society is very heady; that is, we spend so much time building our intellectual skills and put most of our awareness in our brains (rather than in our bodies). I alluded to this earlier as well. The concept of embodiment means that we consider our lived experiences in our bodies. It means defining our experiences through our bodies. Some feminists caution against this as they believe that embodiment reduces women to our biology and doesn't take into account nuances.

However, living in a female body that experiences birth and the process of becoming a mother is an incredible experience that is shared by mothers around the world. Feminists and feminist theory should not be so quick to dismiss those experiences. They are often quick to assert that biology does not impact our experiences, identities, roles and expectations. But I know it does because I have experienced the massive transformation of birth and the incredible flood of hormones that allowed me to bond and nurture my own children. This is written into our DNA as mothers, and to assert otherwise is an attack on mothers. That is not to say that all women bond well with their babies, but we have to consider why that is the case. What was disrupted to make that so? Did she have to return back to work while she was still bleeding during her post-partum time? Did she experience abuse?

Ultimately, we cannot dismiss the importance of being in a female body, having female hormones, and having female experiences, however nuanced they may be. And, yes, the experience of birth is nuanced according to each body, background, identity, baby, labor and birth. Yet, there is something to be said about a shared experience that all mothers go through when they give birth, particularly when that birth is at home. Some call this a rite of passage. It's what bonds us as mothers and as people responsible for perpetuating human existence and consciousness. It is essential to our existence.

I was talking with a good friend and home-birth mama several months ago about the rite of passage that is pregnancy and birth and how that connects us as mothers. The whole experience is designed in such a way that we drastically change—from our brains to our bodies. We go through the experience of bringing a soul into this world—in physical form. We also talked about how in Western society, we do not have rites of passage that help women feel embodied and to honor being in a female body. The way we collectively dismiss menstruation and menopause are great examples. Rather than preparing females for their first blood and celebrating their cycle, we have tended to keep it hush-hush. We push women to follow a schedule that is energetically male rather than based on the female menstrual cycle. We don't prepare our women physically for their blood and for the labor that is birth. We dissociate from the body consequently. We dismiss its signals, its needs, its intuitive nudges.

Plato once argued, "the 'follies' of the body 'contaminate' the pure search for truth and knowledge." This quote always makes me laugh as I think about these "follies" and how they are the reason for human life. Plato's flawed thinking about our bodies and the infinite wisdom that emerges from them has resulted in dualistic and binary thinking today about the wisdom of our bodies and even about women's health. The "follies of the body" are always tied to women, as they are constructed in terms of being natural, animalistic, leaky and excessive. Our hormones, blood, milk, natural instincts, birth power, fat, etc., are all just follies that contaminate the pure search for knowledge—according to Plato. How absurd. These follies are the building blocks of life, intellect, connection and love. How could they contaminate when they are us, and we are them?

I have a hard time separating the body from knowledge, as so much knowledge comes from the body. In fact, there is no human knowledge without our bodies. And, our birthing bodies carry the knowledge of human perpetuation—the greatest knowledge of all. Still, so many schools of thought have tried to dismantle our connection with ourselves and our bodies. We have arguably become a disembodied society as a result. We have failed to listen to the wisdom of the body. We have tried to overcome nature. But we are nature. We have traveled too far from the womb, and as a result, we have collectively lost its deep wisdom. Thank goodness for midwives and mamas who always come back to the womb with all its infinite expansiveness.

Yet, we are taught to ignore our bodies and not trust their signals. At the same time, in a weird twist of events, women are also defined by their bodies and treated in certain ways by the medical field for having a female body. Women are sexed, raced, classed and otherwise categorized according to binary schemes situated in the body. These categories are used by biomedicine to make assessments and judgments on diagnoses, treatments, interventions, cures, etc. For example, being in a female body means that the medical gaze will prescribe a certain set of protocols based on the reproductive life of a woman.

Being in a female body also means that most females experience reproductive cycles, changing hormones, childbirth, menstruation, menopause, motherhood and sexual activity. These experiences impact health, the lived-bodily experiences of women and certainly the health care that women receive (which is often paternalistic). Embodiment is also an opportunity to become more in touch with their bodies, to learn about childbirth, to leverage options in terms of health care, and to resist the mind/body and nature/culture dualisms in Western thinking.

The home-birth mamas recognize embodiment as the place from which they gained their power. Certain bodily processes and changes during pregnancy and birth call attention to or rather demand attention from women so they may become more embodied and connect with the infinite wisdom that pregnancy and birth offer. After all, pregnancy and birth are probably the most intense embodied experiences in a woman's life. Perhaps mothers have this opportunity more so than others because of these drastic changes (people with disease or athletes also experience being more present in their bodies even more so than the average person). Oftentimes, mums expressed this sense of embodiment through sentiments such as, "I was made for this," "God designed our bodies to give birth," "I trusted my body," "I trusted my body to know what to do," "Women have been giving birth since the beginning of time." One O'ahu mother with four children, two of whom were birthed at home, explained:

> I feel like the way in this moment that feels most
> organic to describe is a place of deep trust and know-
> ingness. The way that I experience it is just this deep
> knowing, in a sense (that) no matter what happens
> in the birth, everything is going to unfold in the way
> that nature has intended it to, in a sense. So not in
> a disempowered way of like oh, whatever happens,
> happens, but a real settling into the surrender, into
> the mystery, and the way that transferred over in my
> body is feeling the kind of energy that I sense would
> be how we would be.
>
> How I would describe the ancestors helping to open
> the channel of me to be able to birth a human into
> creation, and the way that I experience that in my
> body is this very deep surrender of being able to

relax and allow my body to truly be in the flow of creation. It's funny, because you know, I think that for some people that looks a certain way. But even in the pain and discomfort of that, birth for me was an actual knowingness… to go toward that and to face all that as something that our ancestors have always done, and that's part of the process of self-initiation, in a sense… going through this initiatory process, of going into that which I fear the most, which would be death like dying from childbirth. (Interview 52)

Her statement reminded me of a metal placard I once saw on a rock at Barton Springs in Texas. I was walking just above the springs when I saw this curious quote etched in the placard that was embedded in a large boulder. The quote by Walter Prescott Webb reads, "Civilization shouts, gives orders, writes rules, puts man in institutions, and intimidates him with a thousand irritating directives. In return it offers him protections, soul salvation, and a living if he can find it." The "civilization" he described reminds me of the system we live in, the medical institution, the colonizing forces that promise safety and comfort, but also promise disembodiment and perhaps even relinquishment of sovereignty over oneself. Home birth seems to pollute this entire sentiment in that it is primal, embodied, female and untamed. But it is also loving, protective and civilized in its own beautiful way.

Mothers described having to surrender to their bodies, to nature and to the design of humanity to birth their babies. This surrendering to the body, with all the pain and discomfort in birth, allowed women to enter places of fear and doubt (perhaps even potential death, as it is with all birth) and emerge empowered. That is, they did not have to rely on any other institution to help them. They could thrive and face their fears themselves (of course, with loved ones surrounding them).

But of course, such initiations and rites of passage like home birth are nuanced, and each woman goes through her own initiation during birth. A Maui mama, who is white but also was formally adopted by a member of the Anishinaabe tribe in Minnesota, explained that embodiment is also connected to sovereignty in various ways. When I asked her how home birth connects to her value system, she explained:

> I would say just trusting in what is and being accept-
> ing of what is in front of you are really big values in
> my life that I hold pretty high and trying to remain
> present and honest. I think all of that plays into a
> home birth, and I don't think you can separate the
> two. I think that every value of just love and honor-
> ing and gratitude and all of that is fully encompassed
> in the birthing process at home or the hospital. But
> home birth is to trust the process, and I trust the pro-
> cess. I know what my body was made for, and birth
> is not an emergency. It's not abnormal or dangerous.
> It's normal.
>
> Births are beautiful and amazing, and I'm incredibly
> grateful for Western medicine and the hospitals for
> when we need them 100 percent, and I also never
> judge anyone else's choice. I think that birth sover-
> eignty is as important as national sovereignty to any
> indigenous people. You know it starts with birth,
> and I believe that the woman's right to choose how
> and where and with whom she wants to give birth
> is of the utmost importance and can set lots and lots
> and lots of people free if we all had birth sovereignty.
> (Interview 40)

She was confident in the process of birth, and she also locates birth as the beginning place for national sovereignty. While we see various laws and declarations regarding indigenous and bodily sovereignty, such documents and practices in the dominant context do not necessarily locate sovereignty in the body or during/at the time of birth. But this mama offers home birth as an opportunity for freedom, seemingly in all ways. What a miraculous truth that freedom can be found through the body.

Lee Maracle (1996) utilizes the concept of embodiment as she situates and locates health in the body of the native. She writes that embodied spirituality is the life force for the people. Spirit and body are at once separate and one, and the body can heal itself from *dis-ease* and *disease* in the medical sense (Maracle, 1996). This is, of course, counter to the medical model, which does not include "spirit" in the healing process, nor does it recognize that the body can heal itself without treatment (i.e., a doctor's diagnosis and prescription for treatment are necessary). Maracle (1996:115) writes:

> "Indian doctoring" is the harnessing of spiritual energy. Our healing process is based on the assumption that illness, dis-ease, is inside the body. The whole of the body is ill. Healing will be done primarily through the spirit. Spirit and body join together against the illness. What Native medicine does is harness the reserve of spiritual strength to assist the body in purifying itself of the disease. All the methods of healing that Native doctors use are directed at purification. This makes sense if one considers that the major cause of disease is the presence of toxins and foreign bodies in the body.

"Dis-ease," as opposed to disease, is important in understanding what embodiment means for indigenous medicine. Dis-ease presupposes that there is something wrong that has disrupted ease, something situated in the body causing uneasiness or disruption, something is split in the body or spirit when it should be whole; but disease isn't necessarily there, though dis-ease could present itself as such in the form of a medically diagnosable illness. The illness may be a disconnect from community, a lack of identity, a grappling with personal trauma or a presence of foreign bodies in the body (which I read as both a sign of illness in the biological sense but also of embodied foreign concepts that are harmful to the spirit such as certain ideas and lifestyles).

In this sense, Native embodiment is both a site for identity, resistance to ongoing colonizing processes (which are a source of dis-ease), and an opportunity to heal. Home birth may represent a cure to the dis-ease of many ailments in our society today, ranging from occupation to militarism to doubt to fear to powerlessness.

Home birth offered several Hawaiian mothers the opportunity to experience embodiment, resist colonial practices and reclaim/ reconnect to themselves, their culture, 'āina and birth practices. Part of birthing at home also allowed for connection to ancestors and connection to 'āina. One Hawaiian mother who home-birthed her son, explained:

> I think it was a primal thing. My ancestors were
> there to support me, like, you got this, there's no way
> you need to go to a hospital, you are a primal being.
> Actually, now that I think about it, when I was preg-
> nant and deciding to do a home birth, I was like, our
> ancestors did not have hospitals, they just went and
> did it. And think about animals. They don't go to the
> hospital, they just do it. It's remembering that primal
> nature all of us have. We are primal beings, and I feel
> that living in the country, not in the city, I am able
> to connect with that more, being more connected to
> nature, hiking, surfing a lot. I remember that I am a
> part of this rhythm, this fickle life that is hard to feel
> when you're in a city. (Interview 11)

Reconnection to 'āina, to ancestors, and to cultural traditions and practices arguably helps heal the dis-ease caused by colonial traumas as well. To birth at home is a form of embodied, cultural and national sovereignty for many Hawaiian women and for many women of various backgrounds (Hawaiian women tended to rely on the discourse of cultural and national sovereignty more than others).

While discourses of embodiment do not often take into consideration spiritual aspects of the body, concepts of holistic health and, indeed, indigenous health and existence account for the spiritual side of health and embodiment. In the mama's statement above, it becomes clear that a return to our primal selves via home birth—or even living outside of city life—offers the opportunity to live a more embodied, healthy life that is connected to all things.

You Don't Get a Trophy for Having a Natural Birth

There is an expression that "you don't get a trophy for having a natural birth," meaning that there isn't some reward for going through the pain and presumed risk of home birth. This is usually a saying told to mothers who are about to give birth or for those who talk about birthing unmedicated. Perhaps well-intentioned, it is facetious in the sense that mums know they don't get a trophy. They know that birth is not about getting a trophy or about boasting. They know that having a natural birth isn't something women do because they want to be rewarded with accolades and prizes. We birth unmedicated because it can be safer that way, it can allow for the full experience, it can allow for us to be embodied and connected, and it is intuitively the right choice for many mothers.

For those I interviewed, there was a sense of pride, strength and empowerment for going through pain and doubt and coming out the other side stronger, more trusting in one's body, and more in awe of the feminine power. Mums explained that their experiences were incredibly rewarding. Home birth was empowering, and their births prepared them for motherhood. The pain taught them something valuable about being a woman and being a mother, and their midwives offered them care they hadn't received elsewhere. The pain had a purpose. The pain was not just agonizing; it was empowering, strengthened them, taught them patience, gave them a sense of trust in oneself and prepared them for motherhood. So, I suppose they did get their trophies after all, didn't they?

I remember some years ago watching a video on how a Native American nation, I forget the specific one, prepares its girls for their first blood (menses). The video showcased a young woman about twelve to thirteen years old. They decorated her and then made her dance to the beat of a drum for a whole night. She was not allowed to sit or even to wince, even when she was tired or her feet ached. Many people might view this experience as painful or abusive, but if they look deeper, it had a purpose far beyond pain. This rite of passage prepared the young woman for childbirth. It prepared her mentally for labor, for enduring pain, for staying up late with her newborn baby, for the mental stamina required, etc. It taught her the responsibility that comes with the first blood, which is that pregnancy can now biologically happen. And with that, motherhood. It was a beautiful celebration of this young woman's strength, endurance and grit. I often think about whether we would need so many pain medications for birth in the United States if we had such rites of passage before birth and pregnancy.

Concepts of Natural

The concept of "natural" in relation to birth is also widely debated as there are so many various understandings of what "natural" means. For example, one may view hospital birth as natural if there aren't any interventions during the birth. Natural birth generally means, however, that a spontaneous, vaginal birth occurs. In the home birth community, the location of that birth would be at a freestanding birth center, at home or in nature. Outside of birth, the term *natural* was often used by mothers to describe lifestyles that are free of toxins, free of too many industrial products, robust in outdoor time, and full of nutritious organic, unprocessed foods. I found that the mothers tended to define a natural lifestyle as non-toxic and as one that was a form of health risk management as well.

Birth is a natural, biological process. Birth is primal. Birth is essential. It is the mechanism through which physical human existence continues. It is an embodied experience in which a cascade of hormones activates various sensations, feelings and physical changes that open the cervix and ultimately result in the birth of a baby (if all goes well).

But birth is also social and embedded in social relations and meanings. Likewise, the preparation for childbirth is both social and natural, as Rothman (2014) asserts. While the concept of natural is generally perceived as untamed, wild, etc., Rothman (2014:5–6) offers a different perception of natural as she writes what that means in terms of knowledge and dominant forms of knowing as well:

> We learn, manage and prepare that which is natural all the time. Women are preparing themselves and using expert assistance, as Mitchell and McClean (2014) show, to avoid medical interventions, which themselves have become the perceived dangers. What medical dominance has done is not only take over from midwifery and woman's own embodied knowledge of birth but denied that such knowledge ever existed or could exist. Scientific or "medical" knowledge is real and authoritative; other knowledge is reduced to "intuition" or "spiritual knowing," made all but laughable. But when a baker adds a bit more flour because the dough is sticky, is that "intuition"? Or is that knowledge based on craft, skill and deep knowledge of the hands? When a violin maker rejects a piece of wood in favor of one lying next to it that looks just the same to me or to you, is that "intuition"? Or experience, skill and craft? And when a leading neurosurgeon examines a dozen stroke patients who all present pretty much the same way on all of their tests and feels hopeful about some and concerned for others, is that "intuition"? Or knowl-

edge based on experience, using a range of senses and information that may not be captured in the tests?

Perhaps what is most notable here is that there is expertise and knowledge inside the natural, embodied experience (and that knowledge is not just found through the standard scientific method). Embodied knowledge of birth is natural and is full of wisdom (as many mothers reiterated). But "natural" is also meticulous, trained, experienced and wise. I do disagree with Rothman's approach that tries to decenter birth knowledge from intuition and spiritual knowledge. In fact, intuition, spiritual, scientific and embodied knowledge do not have to be separate. Birthing knowledge can be both intuitive and experienced. It can be spiritual and can carry the wisdom in our DNA. We do not have to use either/or arguments. Intuition can lead us in the right direction, too. Intuition doesn't have to be separate from scientific knowledge.

Oftentimes, intuitive knowledge ends up preceding scientific knowledge. Remember when bone broth was only consumed by indigenous cultures until "scientific knowledge" decided it was healthy and all the rave? Another important thing to note here is that more and more knowledge continues to erupt from the connection between body and knowledge. That is, our bodies hold infinite intuitive wisdom. They can tell us so much information, they work so hard to keep us and our babies safe, and they carry the wisdom, the memories, the traumas, the triumphs, etc. throughout the generations.

Going "Natural" to Reduce Risks

Intuitive female knowledge encompasses calculations, observations and tools just like "real" science does. However, scientific tools fall short in that they still cannot capture the knowledge that erupts from female bodies and their ability to give birth to new life. Female energy and bodies have been labeled as synonymous with nature, the wild, the untamed, etc., and the female body has been framed as risky. They are deduced to being managed, like an overgrown yard, by tools. It seems women are labeled as part of the mysterious yet conquerable wild, the natural, the risky, the untamed. Perhaps this has biblical implications with the Adam and Eve story. Indeed, even intuition and natural design (i.e., God's design) are often perceived as risky. Birth is also risky (especially without technology), as the medical authority has told us. Yet, the mothers did not view birth as risky, and they certainly did not view being "natural" as risky either. In fact, they draw upon this concept of natural living as a form of risk mitigation and management.

Natural living is a way of life for these mothers. When asked about their lifestyles, most explained that they lived a very natural lifestyle; they were very aware of the dangers of genetically modified foods, toxic household cleaners and chemicals, the overuse of technology (particularly the overuse of screen time), etc. They view natural living as a risk management strategy whereby they prevent disease in themselves, their families and their environments by consuming only organic fruits, vegetables and meats whenever possible; they reduce screen time for their children, they spend time outdoors (on hikes or at the beach was most cited), and they make their own non-toxic household cleaners (or purchase the least toxic items). All these lifestyle choices were made to reduce the risk of disease, optimize health, show their love for their family, be environmentally sensitive, and connect culturally and spiritually.

No matter their socioeconomic status, the mothers engaged in these practices at various levels and lived this sort of non-toxic lifestyle to the extent possible. They did so as a risk-management strategy on several levels: first, to reduce disease, but also to return to a way of life more aligned with their cultural and spiritual values. Because they viewed health as holistic, they wanted to make a chemical-free and toxic-free household for their families. They also chose to eat a variety of diets (including vegan, paleo, vegetarian, etc.), all of which included non-GMO foods whenever possible. They connected to local growers to support sustainability. When possible, they also engaged in outdoor activities to destress, connect as a family and reduce their exposure to EMFs (electromagnetic frequencies). They connected to the land to develop a relationship with it.

One of the major issues concerning mothers was toxins in their environment and finding ways to avoid exposure to toxins. This often meant avoiding conventional household cleaners, fast food, and synthetic ingredients and clothing, wearing menstrual cups rather than fragrance-laden tampons or pads, eating genetically modified foods, eliminating petroleum-based products, etc. It also meant spending more time in nature and, when possible, designing their lives to be less stressful. This also meant staying out of toxic workplaces and not listening to people who denied their intuition, spiritual and cultural knowledge. One mama explained that this extended to her place of work as it was having negative effects on her health. When I asked her about health and non-toxic lifestyles, she responded:

> Being happy is number one. That's the whole reason
> I quit my job. I realized I was so unhappy because
> it was such a toxic environment, and I had serious
> health problems from it. I think you have to have
> good, positive, healthy, happy energy around you. I
> think that's number one because my health has never
> declined so quickly otherwise. And then definitely
> working out every day... I try to surf every day, or I
> also try to walk. That's my other thing. Then eating
> healthy, so all that pretty much in that order. (Interview 31)

Avoiding toxic environments extends to the people they are around as well. Their vibration and frequencies can affect you positively or negatively, as this mama experienced. Natural living was presumed to be better for them in many holistic ways—from people, food, sleep, cleaning products, stress levels, etc. Several mums surfed or swam to destress and unwind. Several mums did yoga regularly. Many made a daily effort to be outside in the sunshine. And, while they didn't necessarily reject modern conveniences and technology, many saw these as things to be managed and reduced for their family's health. This is perhaps opposite to the modern paradigm that natural things should be managed and that technological advancements are entirely positive for the advancement of individual and societal civilization and happiness.

When it comes to birth, mums see birth as natural and normal. Many explained that undisturbed births are important as they allow for the undisturbed progression of hormones that allow for baby to be born naturally. Hospital birth was viewed, generally, as a place where natural birth is usually disturbed by fluorescent lights, paperwork, interruptions, interventions, and the lack of body autonomy to move around and eat/drink during labor. Midwifery care also felt more natural in terms of human connection and safety, rather than the sterile, cold and clinical environment with an unfamiliar physician. Hospital interventions like Pitocin, Cytotec, epidurals, electronic fetal monitoring, etc., were viewed as unnatural (although sometimes necessary in emergency circumstances) by many mums. Additionally, most mothers practiced some form of attachment or gentle parenting whereby they breastfeed, babywear, co-sleep, and, even in some instances, homeschool their children. This was seen as the most natural and positive way to parent and take care of young ones for many mothers. It also calls for a level of responsibility and sovereignty over one's life, choices and family.

In general, the concept of natural is seen as positive and viewed as a lifestyle paradigm that reduces the risk of disease and poor health outcomes. Plant medicine, like essential oils and herbs, for example, was utilized during their pregnancies, labors and postpartum periods. The next section explains how some mothers view the concept of natural, including natural birth and natural lifestyles, as a path to the reclamation of culture and, at times, as colonial resistance as well.

The concept of natural is utilized as a deviation from the dominant society and perceived US lifestyle, which includes long hours of hard work, fast food, little connection to nature, high-stress environments, lots of electronics and television time, little movement, reliance on biomedicine, etc.

Reclamation of Natural

"Natural" was sometimes utilized as a concept to support the reclamation of cultural and birthing practices. I recognize that utilizing the concept of "natural" in relation to indigenous peoples can essentialize and romanticize their ways of life (and perhaps even add to the idea that indigenous people live in ways that are not "modern"); at the same time, I recognize that colonial forces thrust ways of living that can feel quite unnatural upon people of all backgrounds. There is a lack of spiritual and natural alignment in much of "modern" life. I am sure you can feel that statement in your bones. Does modern life feel rushed at times? Scary? Frenzied? Unregulated? Exhausting? Can you feel yourself crumbling with the weight of all the things we have to do to survive in our society today? Do you feel sad that you cannot live according to your body's need for rest, good nutrition, low stress, etc.?

Natural living is a way of life more aligned with our intuition, nature, cycles, nervous systems, and bodily needs. It is not necessarily meant to identify indigenous ways of life exclusively. It extends to ways of life that can happen now and in any family. The mothers view "natural" as a place and a practice of reclamation of culture, birth, 'āina, sovereignty, responsibility, alignment, balance, wellness and health. This does not mean, of course, that home birth mothers reject modern advancements, modern medicine, technology, or even Western values entirely. Rather, it means that dominant ways of living are often put aside for more aligned ways of living—that birth can be natural without instruments, that food doesn't have to come in a box or from a grocery store, that productivity doesn't have to mean lack of sleep and excessive stress, and that we can design lives according to our female cycles.

"Natural" was also a concept connected to reclamation—reclamation of our power as women, reclamation of land, reclamation of Hawaiian birthing practices, and reclamation of sovereignty. Part of this reclamation process meant that women decided to birth in the ways that their grandmothers/ancestors birthed, that they meticulously rid their homes of toxic chemicals, that they studied, grew and used plant medicine (when possible), that they opted for forest bathing, grounding (walking barefoot on the land), and swimming in the healing ocean salt water, etc. One Maui mama explained:

> That whole turning point into going into the nat-
> ural birthing route was when I started looking at
> my great-grandmother who home-birthed sixteen
> children. She was knowledgeable in Hawaiian Lā'au
> Lapa'au, you know, like using plants and herbs for
> healing, and so that's when I started getting into es-
> sential oils and looking at essential oils for supporting
> our overall wellness, more preventative. That's when
> I really buckled down on what I was buying as far as
> the ingredients. I call it perimeter shopping. I try to
> stay on the outside of the grocery stores, like the pro-
> duce. Sometimes I'll get meats and stuff, but as far as
> the snacks and all the packaged stuff, I usually won't
> even, because it's like half of the stuff that's in there.
>
> After watching a few documentaries, you're like, oh,
> what the hell are we eating (laughs). In the begin-
> ning, I was (really strict), but it just drove me crazy.
> Pick and choose your battles on it, and just know that
> when you're at home and when the kids are at home,
> you know, that's where I can control most of it, and
> that's where I empower our kids and our family to

make the choice. It is a choice. You know what's good for you, you know what's not good for you, so you pick and choose. I think that's empowering for my children because one day they'll be teaching their family as far as eating, birthing, you know, all of that. And that's huge, especially with the world that we live in, where everything is packaged or made in labs. And it's like, oh my gosh, that's why everybody's sick. (Interview 10)

Another Hawaiian mother (mentioned in Interview 57) explained that she felt called to birth more in nature rather than in Kahului because the city was like a "concrete jungle," and the energy there was ungrounded. Her lifestyle was already quite natural as she grew a lot of her own foods, lived somewhat off the grid, and utilized and taught plant medicine in her midwifery practice. The space she birthed in was surrounded by trees and was much more natural than the city. This made her feel grounded and more prepared for birth. This was a space far away from the sights, sounds and smells of colonial artifacts and "developments." This natural place was a safer, more spiritually aligned place for her. It is like that feeling you get when surrounded by forest—your heart beats slower, your mind feels less foggy, your body stops aching, you notice the air on your skin, you hear the birds, and you feel connected and free. This is the place that feels safer for many people. In fact, there are so many studies proving all this to be true, not that we needed studies to know this.

Another Hawaiian mama from Oʻahu explained that natural living is part of connecting to life, to others, to ancestors, to culture, etc. This was part of a strong philosophy and value system she held. She explains:

Well, now that we've had a home birth, I think it's become for me a mind and heart philosophy... a life philosophy which is basically that the people

we, the kūpuna, the ancestors, hold the key and
the answers. When we rely on those things, we can
have our babies at home without fear because this
is ancestral knowledge that can guide us into doing
this. It's an expression of our belief that our culture
and our history connect to everything that we do. So,
choosing to have a baby at home is just a piece of the
puzzle. It's like choosing to grow your own food at
home, choosing to eat at home, knowing where your
food comes from. So, I think it's like a strong pillar
in our philosophy. I'm telling our girls where babies
are born, and they're like, "at home?" Yes, at home!
(Interview 45)

She explains that birthing at home is a piece of the puzzle in a
natural lifestyle and one that shapes her worldview and philosophy,
which she passes down to her keiki (children). This mother was
particularly fond of growing her own food and really being mindful
of sustainable island living as not only a natural lifestyle that reduces
toxic load but as a way of connecting to her ancestors, to her cultural
way of life, and to her future visions for her family and community
as well. Arguably, Hawai'i—in terms of location, geography, and
culture—is more natural than other places, given the ocean, the trade
winds, and the mountains, oceans and rivers. It is hard not to notice
the beauty of Hawai'i nature. Hawai'i's favorable climate for year-
round food growth, as well as the various plant medicines that grow
there, also contribute to its natural environment. However, it is also a
place paved with concrete, packed with tourists, occupied by the US
military and reliant on most of its food imports.

This "natural" way of life and one that seeks reclamation of
natural ways of living, being and knowing is constantly constrained
by colonization, land dispossession, cultural trauma, ways of living
that make us work excessively hard just for money and food, and
ecological and environmental pollution, among others. Living

a healthy, natural lifestyle is, therefore, always situated in and constrained by social processes and larger forces. Likewise, how birth is conceptualized and the ability to have a birth at home are constrained. These constraints are nuanced and vary from woman to woman. The next chapter addresses more of the connections between home birth and healthy lifestyles, as well as how the other issues we face today affect the lifestyles of home-birth mums in Hawai'i.

Chapter 5:
Healthy Lifestyles

> Health is wealth, you know. I think our bodies are the vessels for our spirit. So being healthy... staying hydrated, being active, staying fit, eating real foods, live foods, not packaged, not processed whenever possible is really important. I don't drink soda or anything like that. Health... it's like loving life too, just being grateful for all that is, knowing that we're a part of this process of nature. (Interview 11)

Mums tended to view their lifestyles as healthy and natural, and they understood their home birth as part of this lifestyle choice. Their lifestyle choices, like eating organic foods, being balanced, exercising, spending time outside, avoiding toxic chemicals and processed foods, connecting to family and connection and love for 'āina are part of what keeps them healthy. In medical sociology, health lifestyle theory is defined "as collective patterns of health-related behavior based on choices from options available to people according to their life chances" (Cockerham, et al., 1993; Cockerham, 2005; 2011; 2013). Health as a category with a variety of consumption options (like gym memberships, organic foods, non-toxic cleaners, etc.) is certainly an indicator of status in our society today (Korp, 2008). And it is sometimes presumed that home birthers are upper class or are "crunchy" with lots of resources to be healthier. Yet, the conversations with home birth mums showed that living a healthy lifestyle was not motivated by wanting to gain status, nor was a healthy lifestyle out of reach even for mothers who lacked comfortable financial resources. Rather, they engaged in lifestyle choices to promote family health, connect with ʻāina, reduce reliance on the medical industry, and avoid toxins that are harmful to their bodies and the environment.

The healthy lifestyles were shaped by the mothers' connection to place through their identities, cultures, families, connection to land, and their spirituality. Many felt called to revive birthing traditions and chose more traditional ways of living by connecting to the land, growing their own food, being outdoors, connecting with nature, fostering spiritual connections, fostering a sense of community, seeking natural healing methods, and perhaps resisting or limiting their use of modern advances like vaccines, fast food, pharmaceuticals, etc. One mama expressed the following:

> We go on hikes on average once a month, and another part of our lifestyle is that we aim to be, what's the phrase, politically conscious. I wouldn't call myself highly politically active. If anything, a lot of my lifestyle choices are also wrapped up in my spirituality and my spiritual practice. And so, for me, the political awareness part is also being aware of how spirit is playing in the different realms of the world and just taking note. And I am. A big part of my lifestyle is doing my best to choose, to make better choices, to consciously add to a situation rather than take away, and that's part of even the mechanics of the day-to-day.
>
> We aim to not be so consumeristic because, in my opinion, we live in a consumerist culture. And so we try to tone that down. For example, I started making

my own laundry detergent. I started making my own
pads for (laughs), you know, that time of month, and
I wish I had known how simple it could be. Our lifestyle is minimalist while at the same time, we're aiming to be green while aiming to be futurists because
we still want to be progressive, but it's almost like our
progressive view and lifestyle also aim to bring back
what was lost from traditional culture. (Interview 2)

A wide variety of mothers expressed that they wanted to
distance themselves from consumerism and wanted to "bring back
what was lost," whether that was traditional cultures, traditional
medicines, ways of eating and preparing foods, growing one's own
food, healing methods, and even birthing methods. However, this
return to tradition was viewed as progress and progression. Quite
ironic, isn't it? Especially when we've been taught that tradition is
backward at best and barbaric at worst. Yet, progressiveness should
be about improving and offering choices for better living all around.
The dominant culture is clearly failing at doing so in a myriad of
ways, from our mental health crisis and our unclean food and water
to the massive amounts of chronic illnesses. While there is a level of
social progressiveness that is offered here, most mamas did not view
their lifestyles as a political project as much as it was a commitment
to wellness and culture:

Yeah, it's definitely not political. It has to do more
with a wellness mindset. Like, how can you be well if
you don't have the choices and then empowerment
to make those choices? It has nothing to do with
(the) political. It's about kind of living your best life,
like an Oprah-ism (laughs), you know... like just
living your best life, really. (Interview 24)

This wellness mindset was key to many of the values and lifestyles
that home-birth mums lived out in their daily lives as well as in their

birth choices. There were, however, some political mindsets that do overlap with such a way of life. Rather than centering on political activism, social movements or political parties, many mums viewed their political resistance as embedded in their lifestyle choices.

> I don't trust that institution of the hospital, while at the same time really wanting to reclaim my body… reclaim what is natural versus a system that is telling me you must do it this way. Really wanting to reclaim my innate power and ability to birth, and that decision was radical. I may not be a politician. I'm not out there marching the streets. While at the same time, I do feel like a lot of my lifestyle choices, the day-to-day, is choosing to alter… that alternative lifestyle. That is part of my political resistance. Birthing at home was a big part of that. For both of them, I had home births. (Interview 2)

Rather than identify their choices in relation to consumption patterns, mums tended to identify their choices through a health-centered worldview whereby they distanced themselves from dominant consumer systems and lived "alternative lifestyles" focused on health, wellness and body sovereignty. That in and of itself is a sort of silent political resistance. Rather than rage against the machine, these mums often just ignored the machine and led their lives in an authentic, natural way.

Chris Bobel's (2002) book on natural mothering expresses similar findings in that "natural mothers" distanced themselves from mainstream ideals and opted instead for home birth, extended breastfeeding, plant medicines, alternative health care and homeschooling. Bobel (2002) found that mothers understood their decisions and parenting methods as part of a social movement and collective that chooses to follow nature over social obligations. Most interestingly, Bobel (2002) also found that they resisted the rat race (i.e., the drive to acquire and increase economic and social status), so to speak, and instead opted to rely on natural ways of living and rearing their children.

The findings certainly confirm Bobel's findings as the mothers see themselves as part of a collective of shared interests having to do with living a healthy lifestyle, taking care of their minds and bodies, practicing attachment parenting, breastfeeding, and living in ways they consider to be more natural, and perhaps even more spiritual, than the standard American lifestyle (which is riddled with imbalances, poor health, stress and unnatural paces of life).

How are Healthy Lifestyles Defined by Home-Birth Mothers?

A healthy lifestyle meant that mums had good holistic health, felt balanced in mind and body, felt vital, could spend time outside, made their own health choices, and reduced their time on screens. Of course, we all do this imperfectly, and health is a spectrum for many people, and our bodies and lives are constantly changing. Things around us are always changing as well. However, mothers navigated the ebbs and flows of health and were able to connect with family. They were able to exercise and eat clean foods to the extent possible, they utilized preventative and complementary medicine, and they reduced their reliance on the biomedical field.

> Our main medical doctor that we use is a naturopath. We do acupuncture, see a chiropractor… different Ayurveda are the main modalities that we use. My kids never, ever, ever, ever get sick or have any issues that come up, and we always attribute that to our natural lifestyle. I just feel that you know those kinds of things are enabling us to not ever get sick, to not need medical intervention because we're not putting anything unnatural into our bodies, to begin with. We try to stay pretty positive and mentally and emotionally balanced. I always feel that helps with the disease

in our bodies as well. We definitely do more Asian and Indian medicines and nature—and naturopaths. (Interview 16)

Healthy lifestyles also included an awareness of healing methods and experiences outside of the dominant medical paradigm of health. This mama explained that, at times, there were conflicting paradigms in her family in terms of what it means to have a healthy lifestyle and what health means. Her health practices included things like being outside, deriving health from the 'āina, using naturopathic doctors, and birthing at home, but this also meant that she resisted dominant medical paradigms about health and birth.

> We've always been very interested in spending a lot of time outside. We've definitely gotten a lot more intentional about our health and working with our naturopath doctor (has) also helped to congeal some of that for me. I was always interested in herbs, and I've always been pretty esoteric as far as crystals and things, but my understanding of how to wield those things has definitely grown much more… I was much more like a supplement kind of person.

> Here in Hawai'i, it's a much more normalized life-style to rely on the 'āina for your health care and health, and also having the opportunity to work with naturopathic doctors has just given me another shortcut into the resources that I need to deepen my understanding. And then I've been able to practice on my family. I see that whole idea of upsetting the set-up… having the birth the way that we did causes us to question the entire medical paradigm and my parents are deeply entrenched in it, so there was some… I don't want to say conflict, but contradictions there. There's no animosity behind it, so there was an

opportunity to juxtapose the two paradigms and then
just choose what resonated. (Interview 41)

For Hawaiian mothers (as well as others), healthy lifestyles
also meant connecting to 'āina, to ancestral wisdom, and to family.
Connection with 'āina is a cultural, spiritual, and health-building
experience. Using alternative medicine was also a huge way of
bringing in that natural lifestyle value while continuing to bolster
family health.

Navigating Constraints to Healthy Lifestyles

These healthy lifestyles and connections to 'āina were, at times,
constrained by various factors, such as financial constraints to afford
organic food, access to land and other environmental constraints caused
by colonization. While it is argued that one's ability to participate
in certain consumption patterns or behaviors is made possible by
economic means, constraints and life chances, I would argue that life
chances and constraints are not as impactful on the lifestyles of home-
birth mums in Hawai'i. That is, they were resilient and resourceful,
finding ways to support their healthy lifestyles. From the interviews,
it appears that they assert a high degree of agency over their lifestyle
choices despite their economic backgrounds.

For instance, while all mums have some level of higher education,
fifty-six percent of mums also defined themselves as being working/
lower class. Certainly, they made sacrifices to afford organic foods;
however, most mothers were able to have a healthy lifestyle despite
their economic status or relation to the means of consumption. Some
mothers just made their own soaps and household cleaners and grew
their own food. Many breastfed and used cloth diapers to save on
costs because it was healthier for them and their babies and because
it honored their value system.

Many mothers used plant medicine rather than spending
money on allopathic doctor visits as well. While this isn't possible
for everyone, particularly populations who aren't well-educated or

who have chronic illnesses due to environmental and economic factors, all mums were able to assert agency within various structural constraints such that they were still able to live a healthy lifestyle within their various constraints. While I don't believe that all home-birth mums have agency to afford an entirely organic diet regardless of their social class, their value systems seem to support the desire to choose foods that are non-toxic and nutrient-dense.

Within various constraints, mothers still strived to honor the values and the lifestyles they believed most aligned with their value systems. For example, while many mothers expressed that they couldn't always afford organic food, they would strive to purchase local produce instead or grow their own food. Or, if they did not have time to go to the gym due to childcare responsibilities, they would go on a walk or jog outside with the stroller. Yet, constraints weren't always attributed to economic means but were also impacted by colonization. For example, many Hawaiian mothers expressed that access to certain plant medicines and healers/healing mechanisms are difficult to obtain now due to colonization. That is, the banning of traditional healing over time eventually erased and silenced the healers. Several non-Hawaiian mums also blamed colonization for why people are reliant on health care/biomedical systems.

The US lifestyle that indigenous populations, and truly all of us, have been forced into isn't conducive to health. Environmental toxins and pollutants were also discussed by a handful of mums and were framed in a critique of colonization of the Islands and the poor health outcomes that have resulted from colonization, militarism and tourism. Accordingly, in their interview study with twelve Hawaiian adults in Waimānalo, Keli'iholokai, et al. (2020) found that 'āina is intimately connected to health and resilience, and that three major findings included that 'āina is everything, 'āina is health, and 'āina provides community healing through collective initiatives. Keli'iholokai, et al. (2020) also found that the connection to 'āina is not only part of addressing health but that this connection may help address historical trauma and environmental issues resulting from colonization as well. Therefore, constraints to health are also shaped by negative colonial impacts on land and access to land. The US military, for example, has bombed several areas of land and sea in and around Hawaiʻi. The lasting effects of the bombings and the chemical and fuel leaks have poisoned land and water—and, eventually, people, too.

Home-birth mums have a shared resistance to dominant, colonial powers that often harm women, the earth and families. Most mums expressed this resistance to dominant biomedical powers over birth and healing specifically, even if they did see the value in hospitals in emergency situations. The collectivity of home-birth mothers generally viewed their decision as part of their worldview that supports family and women-centered care and resists medical authority as well as colonial violence. Relying on these worldviews and lifestyles over the institutions that cause harm and disrupt natural ways of being was also a shared value expressed by the mums. A home-birth mama who had her children on Kauai explained that her lifestyle and her choices and paradigms about her body are connected to her larger worldviews:

> I've become really passionate and outspoken about the Hawaiian sovereignty movement and just sovereignty in general, like personal sovereignty and the sovereignty of all people on the earth, regardless of what color they are. Watching people in the Midwest have pipelines put through their backyards… doesn't matter what color skin they have… they're objecting to it. And yet the overlords are saying, too bad, we're going to do what we're going to do to make money and to extract the wealth and it doesn't matter who we step on. That's just colonialism of the entire planet over all of the non-elite people.

Hawai'i is like this glaring case study of colonialism still in a very obvious way... I never really knew, when I was growing up, how deeply that wound is and I'm learning about birth and also natural medicine versus allopathic medicine. It's remarkable how much the white man has tried to dominate every aspect of life and every bit of power or magic that they don't understand. They've needed to dominate and every time I'm watching a show with my daughters, and they are portraying birth, and the women are just in agony screaming and they're on their backs, and I'm, well, maybe you should get up and work with gravity a little bit. But, oh, it's very convenient for the doctor to be sitting on a stool with legs open in front of him compared to following the mother walking around and trying to get her to cooperate with their monitoring and their poking and prodding. Their self-importance, you know, they need to feel important, they need to feel in charge, and that's what has so many women afraid and not trusting themselves. In one way, women have given their power, but in another way, it's certainly not their fault that their power has been taken and they don't even know that their power has been taken. (Interview 4)

Most mothers shared similar sentiments and expressed strong feelings about these topics. These feelings were shaped through historical trauma, colonization, embodied living as a birthing mama, biomedical dominance, media and power. Such feelings motivated mums to embrace lifestyle choices that are reflective of the family-centered, indigenous, anti-patriarchy, women-centered and anti-colonial worldviews they hold. Accordingly, indigenous status also mattered, as many Hawaiian women explain their health choices and lifestyles as being family-centered and more centered on traditional, cultural and communal practices and living.

Health has individual and communal importance as well in the home-birth collectivity. Not only were practices like eating organic foods better for the body but they were also described as better for the environment. Similar to the holistic concept of health and the Hawaiian concept of health, McMullin (2005) describes it as community-centered and connected to 'āina, one home-birth mama explained that health is not exclusively individual-based.

> Health has a lot to do with community connection. I see health as communal a connection and being in a healthy relationship to the land and nature, and also nourishing, treating our bodies again with utmost respect... having that kind of relationship with the body and all levels. I could say my body, mind and spirit, but essentially bringing in all those levels and layers to combine into a place of health, not tugging on all those threads or thinking that they're separate, rather (that) communal health is like individual health. (Interview 52)

This communal idea of health is part of an indigenous and family-centered worldview that informs the choice of home birth through lifestyle practices like reducing exposure to toxins, eating clean, using plant medicine, growing food or participating in CSAs, etc. These practices are considered healthy for the body, family, community, and 'āina/environment. But they are also mainly centered on love and aloha for self, others, nature, community, water and land.

Health Lifestyle: Shaping Identity and Worldviews

Most people in American society do not view home birth as a healthy decision, despite evidence suggesting otherwise for low-risk women. This choice most certainly would not be viewed by most of society as part of a healthy lifestyle choice due to the stigmatization of home birth and the idea that it is a risky, selfish decision. How dare a mum choose for herself? How dare she put herself or the baby at risk? Yet, the mums describe it as the healthiest, safest decision (from a mental, physical, emotional and spiritual lens) as it was described as best for their bodies, safety, family and babies.

Home birth was often described as just another part of their lifestyle as well. It was also a way to protect their babies. It was described as part of the holistic approach to their lifestyles, which included eating clean, stress reduction, mindfulness, exercise, outdoor time, family time, avoiding toxins, choosing natural methods for healing and the use of complementary and alternative medicine (i.e., acupuncture, lā'au lapa'au, lomi, chiropractic care, essential oils, naturopathic doctors and midwives). Home birth was often described as part of a value system and lifestyle approach that seeks to reclaim female empowerment, indigenous sovereignty and body sovereignty as well. It was also described as incredibly natural. Some mums even said birth is as natural as going to the bathroom.

Collectively, the mothers practiced shared ideals, worldviews, choices and lifestyles. Living a healthy lifestyle is important, and they expressed that this came down to valuing land, community, family and one's own body. While home birth, for example, has been critiqued as expensive and only available to upper, middle-class white mothers, the mums I interviewed (of various backgrounds and races) found ways to pay for their midwifery services such as paying in full, bartering, negotiating costs and establishing payment plans. Race did not impact the decision to birth at home. Of course, not all mothers everywhere can have home births and issues of birthing justice extend to women who are economically disadvantaged, incarcerated, those who have experienced obstetric trauma and even those who are houseless (Oparah and Bonaparte, 2016).

I found that mums actively make conscious health choices and decisions, which includes home birth. Twenty-three percent of the mums work as birth workers themselves and advocate for birth choices and cultural reclamation of birth practices for women in Hawai'i. Most of the mothers have also actively resisted midwifery regulations through political action, including writing testimonies, attending and speaking at hearings, and through community meetings. These women are not only choosing to home birth, but they also do so in connection to their collectivities, social networks and value systems.

Additionally, while all mums had critiqued medicalized birth and described home birth as natural, they also believed firmly in the benefits of hospitals in case of emergencies and even modern medicine at times. They also found, however, that modern science and medicine still often rejected the benefits of natural plant medicine, healers, midwives, home birth and more natural ways of healing. They were sometimes worried that doctors would treat them unfavorably because of this. Certainly, instances were brought up when a mum might need to make a home birth transfer to the hospital and that those mums were treated horribly by medical staff (and sometimes even CPS was called!).

Ironically, while indigenous and female healers know of the benefits of many natural health practices, science often lags behind. For example, things like consuming bone broth and turmeric, extended breastfeeding, delayed cord cutting, birthing at home for low-risk mothers, and skin-to-skin contact in birth (all mentioned by mums) that have been previously dismissed have now been "proven" by science to have a positive effect on health. Many explained that science supports home birth. For example, one mama explained the following:

> I was in school for biology. The whole point of science for me is trying to get to some kind of truth, you're trying to get to some point—at least basis of fact—like the fact that most women can just give birth without a whole lot of intervention, and that's not the way the medical system was set up. So, I did feel that I wanted to take my power back. Especially after feeling so helpless at the hands of a doctor, I'm glad I got that

experience so early on and that it didn't happen later in a birthing suite or whatever. I wanted that power.

Watching when my friend gave birth, like I was telling you, seeing that she had full control over her environment, I feel like if I'm giving birth, I want control over my environment. My sister gave birth about two months before I did, and her story was full of people coming in the room and just poking her and prodding her, and then the shift changes and there's like a whole new set of people and they're not communicating, and I was like, that sounds like a nightmare, that sounds horrible. I don't want any part of that. I don't want random people I've never met sticking their hands in my vagina. (Interview 7)

So, while mothers tended to resist medical and scientific impositions on home birth, many also confirmed that scientific evidence supported their decisions and their health practices, and they trusted themselves to make the right decisions for their births. Mums felt empowered to make their own health decisions based on both science and their cultural, natural and intuitive ways of knowing.

Medical Individualism, Biomedicine, and Neoliberalism

Medical individualism means that individuals can make health decisions for themselves. This is relevant as it presumes that individuals can manage their lifestyle choices and that they have the freedom to do so. Mums, unsurprisingly, tend to favor a medical individualist approach to their health care, pregnancies and births, and lifestyle choices. They told me often that they "wanted control" over their births, and they wanted to "make decisions" about their health and their bodies. Much of this was rooted in distrust of the biomedical field to oversee their births in such a way that honored their choices and intuition. A few mums expressed that they were fearful of what would happen to them in a hospital birth, that their choices wouldn't be honored, that they would be cut open, or that they would be subject to unwanted medical interventions.

One O'ahu mama, for instance, explained that when people called her brave for having a home birth, she called *them* brave for having a hospital birth. Only a handful of mothers expressed that they were comfortable in hospitals, and many said that "the hospital is for sick people," and they wanted the choices in birth that only a home birth setting would allow. Many mums fell somewhere in the middle; that is, they felt the hospital was okay for emergencies, but that birth was not an emergency that necessitated hospital care. All expressed that that they wanted control, choice and informed consent over their medical decisions and felt that that wasn't possible for them in a medical setting.

Having agency over one's health has a positive effect on physical and mental wellbeing. Mums expressed their positive experiences with having control over their birth decisions in the home birth setting. Such positive effects included feeling loved, being safe and comfortable, willing to choose what they wanted during birth, connecting with the older kids, connecting with their family, learning more about their own health and healing modalities, avoiding unnecessary toxins and medications, reclaiming cultural and spiritual birth practices, etc.

To start off or continue the journey of motherhood in such a loving, empowered way is essential to the health of the mother and the family. Being able to have control over one's birth or at least have a sense of agency over what happens to them during childbirth is vitally important for mothers. Rather than having things done to them, mamas get to feel like they are part of the process, are centered, and their needs are honored. They are welcomed into motherhood in a peaceful way, which shapes everything from bonding with the baby to reduced rates of postpartum depression and mood disorders.

Mums were able to make lifestyle choices and medical

decisions that aligned with their view of holistic health and their value of birthing babies in a peaceful, loving environment. Asserting authority over one's own healthcare decisions can be incredibly empowering as well. Christian home birth mum of three, who is also from the Netherlands, a home birther, and a business owner on O'ahu, described some reasons why medical individualism might be considered important amid biomedical practices and authority:

> I think the worst part is what I said earlier… obstetricians, in general, seem to think that they know best and there's no communication with their patients. There's no respect, and there is a lot of abuse. I am also an active doula, and I own a doula group, so we do a lot of births. And it happens: verbal, emotional abuse is common practice, and it is a problem. That plus the overuse of a drug called Pitocin creates moms who come out of their births confused and not empowered, but disempowered, insecure in their ability to mother. And we know that Pitocin increases the chances of moms having post-partum mood disorders, especially post-partum depression.
>
> So now we have moms that are struggling to care for their children. In addition, we have a lot of separation. People don't live near their families anymore, and their support system is lacking, and so you're gonna have these babies who aren't cared for and aren't loved in the way that they're supposed to, and that is going to have long-term effects on our society. You can already see it. We have mass shootings. We have a lack of empathy. We have children with disabilities. All my kids are in elementary school. Each one of them has a child with severe autism or something else—a behavioral issue that they need a full-time aide in every single class. I think it's that sticker: "Peace on earth begins at a birth." (Interview 5)

Her first-hand experience with doula clients in the hospital and seeing them mistreated and, at times, abused shaped her worldview regarding medical individualism and the rights of birthing women and their babies. She connects this with wider societal issues as well, explaining that disempowering women through obstetric abuse and toxic medicines disconnects us from our babies. It is a trauma that is difficult to heal. She explains that in society today, there is also a lack of support, and babies and mothers aren't cared for or loved in the ways that they need to be. This results in all sorts of disabilities and violence in society, according to this mama. Several other mums reiterated these exact sentiments as well.

Imagine, for a moment, that you are being born in a hospital. You are about to become separate from the one person who you've connected to for the past nine months. You are making the transition into this world, and instead of being greeted by your parents' loving hands, you are born into a bright, cold and sterile room. There is an unfamiliar person with gloves on who pulls you out and whisks you away from your mother—your whole world, your peace and comfort. All these unfamiliar sights and sounds and people scare you. You feel funny from the drugs they gave your mum. They bathe you, taking away your vernix and your baby smell, which inhibits the bonding with your mother. They poke and prod you, and if you are a boy, they also cut one of the most delicate, tender parts of your body (i.e., foreskin). Finally, after all this trauma and nervous system dysregulation, they return you to your mother. You remember her smell, you taste her milk and you feel safe again, for now. But that initial imprint is left on you for life.

Why have we accepted this as the routine way in which to welcome souls into this world? What violence! And we now find that people are feeling increasingly disconnected, lonely, depressed and anxious. Is it any wonder when this is often what people experience the first few moments of their lives? The way that mothers and babies are treated has a significant impact on our society, and to be frank, I don't think we are doing so great right now as a society.

Medical individualism is one possible way to circumvent these issues. If mothers can make autonomous choices over their bodies and have loving support, this positively affects society and the individual. Imagine how we could heal and make our world such a magical, safe place to be if we changed the way we do birth in this county and all around the world.

Ironically, even though American culture tends to value individualism and freedom, individual agency is often restricted and stigmatized, particularly if these choices don't support dominant power systems. Despite these quite reasonable and loving choices, home-birth mums are stigmatized for making an "individualistic" choice and for having freedom of choice over our bodies. It is quite reasonable to conclude, then, that the dominant culture only appreciates "freedom" and "individuality" when it fits a certain agenda (oftentimes, the agenda/propaganda is entangled in large financial benefits for certain companies and families in the United States, i.e., the Rockefellers, the Rothschilds, Blackrock, Vangaard, Big Pharma, and other unnamable aristocrats). Anything that doesn't fit the profit and control agenda—like having a home birth or declining certain medical treatments—gets immediately ostracized. It's okay to be an individual as long as you go along with what they want. It's okay to have freedom as long as you do what they say.

Often, such restrictions on freedom and medical individualism get enacted into law. In Hawai'i, these restrictions function at the legislative level where they enacted rules around who can call themselves a midwife, even if their families and their whole lives have been dedicated to birth work. Several mothers explained their frustration that the midwifery regulation bill in Hawai'i restricts particular midwives from practicing and is restrictive in terms of when women "risk out" of home birth (i.e., if they go over forty-two weeks, if they have a breach baby, if they have gestational diabetes, etc.). These restrictions are colonial by nature; they remove sovereignty from the individual, family, and culture and place that power into the hands of the state.

One Hawaiian mama who lives on O'ahu, for example, explained that restrictions on birth have included preventing women from taking their placentas home and following cultural protocols on the afterbirth. More generally, she explained that birth has been impacted by colonial mindsets in hospital settings and that her choice to have a home birth was impacted by restrictive medical policies.

> I'm a Native Hawaiian, and I think that the colonial mindset definitely has impacted birth and the way that birth is practiced. The whole medical model is not Hawaiian at all. I think a large part of why I did not want to go to the hospital is because I did not want to subscribe to a lot of the medical procedures and policies, which are very patriarchal and Western. That made a huge impact on why we choose to birth at home. (Interview 45)

The point at which individual choice supports communal and cultural reclamation, rejection of unchecked consumerism, and indigenous sovereignty, the powers that be then enact political, cultural and social policies that remove autonomy. That is, the dominant culture promises autonomy and self-governance only so far as it doesn't challenge dominant power systems. Such big systems are also able to place blame, at the same time, on indigenous communities by asserting that individual and communal choices have led to certain failures rather than placing blame on colonial structures and intuitions. Medical individualism, therefore, is only accepted insofar as individuals embody biomedical and neoliberal values that do not challenge systems of power. This is why home birth, perhaps the most blatant form of medical individualism, still isn't accepted in dominant society.

Of course, various groups face differing levels of stigmatization and social control, as neoliberal paradoxes and pressures do not stop with indigenous peoples. The unacceptability of home birth and various forms of medical individualism is not limited to race, gender, class or indigenous status. Further, challenging the medical system also poses a threat to dominant powers, but not doing so also poses a threat to individual choice, the sacredness of birth and honoring the entrance of a new life. A midwife on Oʻahu who home-birthed her two children explains the following:

> I am very much in the decolonization movement of bodies in our medical system. There are way too many people who don't realize that even if you're going in for a root canal, you're allowed to say no. Or if you're sick and you're at the hospital and they want to run 700 tests on you. You can say, "Well let's do one at a time." And I really feel like the medical system has taken a hold of a lot that is sacred to people, and of course, when it comes to birth, I feel like the spiritual side of bringing a baby in is completely lost in the medical model.

> I've found, as a midwife, that in an unlicensed state, it's my duty to uphold that deregulation because it isn't. Women are choosing out-of-hospital deliveries so they have more choice and more control, and they have more respect and autonomy, and so I am not super into mandatory licensure because it serves the whole population. Even if it's only two percent of the population that doesn't want it, they are humans, and they have a voice, and they should also have a space. And especially when it comes to something as spiritual as bringing babies or choosing not to bring babies. It's your body, your choice.

> I feel the same way with vaccinations. I'm not for or against. It's up to you what you want to do, look at

195

what works for you and your lifestyle and your exposure. Same with circumcision. I have a personal belief
system about it, but I also know that it is not my duty
to make choices for others. I work as a doula as well,
and if a heavily medicated birth is what you truly feel
suits you and it's the only way that you'll actually enjoy bringing your baby in if you have the information
and the education, then there's no reason why you
shouldn't be able to do what you want to do. (Interview 30)

Empowered choice is certainly both part of a healthy lifestyle
as well as part of medical individualism. Craven (2010) argues that
neoliberalist values support choice-based and rights-based rhetorics
only so far as they support "consumer choices" in the neoliberal era.
Human rights and birthing justice are not as paramount as they are
not packaged neatly into consumer choices that reflect neoliberal
values of free markets and consumer choice. In terms of gender,
women have historically struggled with asserting consumer choices
and neoliberal values such as individual autonomy when it comes
to the medical field and birth (English and Ehrenreich, 2010).

With the proliferation of neoliberalism, however, women have
leaned on rights-based rhetoric when it comes to supporting their
health and birth choices (Craven, 2007). The women have certainly
ascribed to a rights-based rhetoric when it comes to their births,
lifestyles and consumer choices. For example, many women assert
that they engage in green/wellness consumerism, participate in health-
building practices and support individual choices over their bodies.
This is reflected in the conceptual model (Figure 1) as neoliberalism
is placed within the category of health lifestyle because neoliberalism
connects to medical individualism and particular health choices.
Yet, women also see home birth not as a neoliberal, individualistic
occurrence but as one that is intimately tied to sisterhood, family,
community, spirituality and culture.

Neoliberalism tells us that the full human is the one who engages in a certain level of consumerism (Brown, 2016) and in acceptable ways that reify dominant systems of power, of course. Instead of being a beacon of freedom, neoliberalism ranks and files us according to our ability to consume and according to our ability to assert our choices in society. This, of course, has a disadvantageous effect on marginalized communities and on women who don't fit the bill of being the best consumer (i.e., the fullest, most moral human). People have argued that home birth is only for upper-class women or that it's part of a bougee lifestyle. The Hawaiian mother in Interview 22 alluded to the fact that birth shouldn't be framed in neoliberal frameworks and that we should be critiquing the foundations of patriarchy and industrialization as they relate to birth instead:

> We really need to remember that every single one of us got here from thousands, thousands of home births. There was no such thing as a hospital… that's like only in the last three generations or something, right? Before that, that's how we got here. That's how our ancestors got here. All of our ancestors. Our great-great-great-grandparents and their great-grandparents and their great-grandparents and their great-grandparents all got here from traditional birthing practices, pretty much with maybe some exceptions, you know. If you happen to be royalty or something, but with very few exceptions. Pretty much that's how we've been doing it for many, many, many, many, many, many, many, many, many years, and I think that it's part of the essential practice of being human.
>
> We can't forget the birth wisdom that is in each culture is wisdom about a certain power of women within whatever context might have been happening. There might have been total patriarchy. There

197

might have been many other things going. There could be poverty. There could be patriarchal oppression. It could be a lot of different things. But in the process of birth, by the fact that we're here, something worked, you know. The whole practice of out-of-hospital birthing for many, many, many generations has been an essential human practice of female power, and it is important for us to reclaim that power as part of our return to being fully human. Industrialization has taken (that) away from us. To be fully human, it's crucial to understand the basic power that is in our body. It's not just a mental understanding, but on the physical level, we need to understand wellness, the power that comes from wellness and wholeness. And that is where traditional practices come from.

Ancient traditions are essentially about taking that which is natural and making it a little better, you know (laughs), not changing it, but making it a better experience. That's what traditional practices are, right? You're taking something that already naturally exists, and you're adding a way of doing things that makes it just that much better. The thing is, we're at a time where people may be afraid of going "backwards," but really, what we're doing is, we're drawing up from the past and putting it forward. (Interview 22)

She explained that to be fully human is to recognize our power, to recognize the power of birth, and health and wellness, and to recognize that traditional practices help us to be more whole and to be more fully human. This kind of power does not erupt from neoliberal policies and processes, and it does not trickle down from power holders. This type of power is not consumeristic nor competitive—staples of neoliberalist values. It is internalized, and it is embodied, and it is part of her Hawaiian identity. It is how she sees the world. Home birth for her is about honoring that internalized and embodied female power. This is expressed in the conceptual model (Figure 1), showing that identity, women-centered worldviews, anti-colonial worldviews and spirituality can all influence the choice of home birth. One home-birth mama from O'ahu, who is an acupuncturist and doula, explained that home birth is women-centered, and institutions have disempowered women around childbirth throughout history:

> I just started thinking about it more. I was doing doula work, so I was doing home births, and I was doing hospital births, so I was really seeing the contradiction, but I want—I always want—to tell every woman. Because so many people are like, you're so brave, and I'm like, what are you talking about?! You're brave to go into a setting with a stranger with a huge spotlight between your legs, in stirrups, and hope that it works out. I don't know. It's not even that. It's also just, I feel in the core of it that somewhere along the line in the history of birth, they took this sacred ritual, this sacred transformation, and disempowered women. You know, basically illegalized midwives… all the men back in that period, all the doctors in that period were men.
>
> There were so few women, so it was men down there, which is just the most bizarre thing. You go to any country in the world, third world country, they don't even let men near births, and yet all these women today just give their power over to these—even if it's a woman, it's the way they've been trained—and it's just they've lost the sacredness of it. We've been somehow programmed not to believe our bodies can do it. I know I'm preaching to the choir, you know all

this, but it makes me sad, and I'm so glad that women
are starting to demand these changes of baby-friendly
hospitals and breastfeeding, and I mean, it's so sad,
but I think it was part of a whole disempowerment of
women. I don't know how women let that be taken
away from them. (Interview 8)

It saddens me and so many other women to know this truth—
that our most sacred rite of passage, our most spiritual experience,
our most amazing ceremony has strategically and purposefully been
taken away from us. And, we unknowingly have come to the place
where we no longer understand the sacredness of birth. It's like we
have had our precious jewels stolen, but we are unaware that they
even belong to us and that they have been taken away.

Home birth is an opportunity to realize the spirituality of birth
and allow us to claim our birthright. Of course, not every home
birth goes according to plan, and there are bad outcomes (just as
there are in the hospital). Regardless of whether birth is at home
or the hospital, it is necessary to preserve women's power and the
sacredness of bringing a soul through. We have been reduced to
objects that undergo policies, procedures and instruments rather
than people with spiritual journeys who need love and compassion.
In my opinion, part of healthcare and birth experiences must include
this spiritual aspect. Yet, the concepts of health we have today don't
account for such nuanced, individual and spiritual aspects.

In her book, *The Healthy Ancestor*, McMullin (2016) describes
the various concepts of health and healthy lifestyles as well as how
Western medicine abstracts bodies; Western medicine detaches us
from our lived experiences and situations and instead uses instruments
and a guidebook to treat ailments (rather than individualized,
compassionate, person-centered care). Health is then described as a
normal, abstract state of being that does not consider individual, lived
experiences and perhaps even gendered embodiment or indigenous
identity (McMullin, 2016). Health is the abstract description and

ideal type for bodies that function and includes things like exercise and eating well to maintain a long-lasting body (McMullin, 2016). But health is also a spiritual and cultural experience and identity. Health is about feeling whole just as much as it is having good cholesterol levels.

The mamas talked about how health, like birth, must honor the individual, and a healthy lifestyle is part of a nuanced identity. We all have individual things that help us to feel healthy and whole. Engaging in a healthy lifestyle does have its constraints, of course. Mums aimed to have the healthiest lifestyles and make the best, most informed decisions over their bodies and for their families, yet they also resisted dominant power structures and consumerist identities. They engaged in wellness consumerism but resisted identifying themselves as part of toxic consumer cultures. I noticed this when mums would talk about the challenges they faced with food purchases. Many would explain that they shopped for natural, local foods whenever possible but sometimes had to go to Costco. Or that they wished they could afford a one-hundred percent organic diet but had to cut corners because of the high expense of organic food. Their eating habits weren't done so in a pretentious way; rather, they wanted to be healthy, they wanted healthy families, and they wanted healthy environments.

Like their decision to birth at home, individual choice was often situated in a broader need to distance themselves from the harms caused by dominant power systems. Staying away from the hospital setting was one way of avoiding colonial structures that reify colonial and cultural traumas. Neoliberal pressures constrained individual choice, yet choices were made that were not centered on neoliberalism.

Mums did not practice non-toxic lifestyles, organic food consumption, exercise, babywearing, breastfeeding, attachment parenting, etc., to show that they were superior to others, or they somehow mastered the professionalization of motherhood. Rather, these practices were part of their family, indigenous and women-centered worldviews and reflected the values and beliefs of the collectivities to which they belonged. They engaged in these practices because they centered on family, respect for self, freedom, culture, tradition, safety, sovereignty, love of 'āina, respect for ancestors and holistic health. The next chapter addresses personal themes that mums brought up regarding the meaning of home birth and how it shapes their identities, lifestyles and worldviews. These deeper themes center on spirituality, "gut" wisdom, ancestral strength and deep human bonds.

Chapter 6:
Back to the Womb

For me, I feel that no matter what your ethnicity, your religion, or your racial background, we've all been slightly colonized. And you know we've been stripped from our roots, and I think we've been stripped from our roots about food, about our way of life, about jobs, about living, and health care, and having babies. Birth is at the core, the most natural thing that anyone could ever do as a human being. I feel that would be the foundation of where that fight needs to begin, you know. I feel society has stripped us from connection to growing our food, and connection to healing ourselves, and living the lives we want to freely, in a day-to-day basis (and) education of our children. You know people have been birthing since the beginning of time, or there would be no humans (laughs) or there would be no life at all really. (Interview 54)

We have all had our roots stripped away from us, and we've all experienced this to some extent, no matter our background. People have struggled for so long to return to their roots, to live life in a way that is authentic to them and their communities. The proliferation of our economic system and the way we are taught to live our lives often removes us from this authentic way of living. Birth, however, offers a return to those roots as well as a catalyst for building freedom and connection with one another. The womb is the starting place, the root, of understanding who we are as human beings. It is, after all, the point at which we all enter this world and into conscious existence. The womb is the place where we begin our social relationships.

This chapter describes the importance of the womb, the process of microbiome transfer during childbirth and what this means for our relationships. This chapter also describes deeper meanings and worldviews the mums held, which include ancestral strength, relationships with midwives and how these relationships often empower women and restore humanity, pain as an experience that is meaningful, gut wisdom and spirituality. This is reflected in the spirituality category's conceptual model (see Figure 1). Mums know the importance of centering and returning to the womb. The womb is the root from which all things grow. This collective of women value the process of returning to their roots in various ways, some of which have strong cultural connotations, some of which relate to them as women, some of which relate to them on a health level, and some of which are family-centered and anti-colonial.

Decolonizing Our Babies – The Microbiome as Our Warrior

Colonization over lands, practices, cultures, indigenous peoples, healing methods, birth, women's bodies, etc., was repeatedly brought up in the conversations I had with home-birth mums. The pain of such things tends to linger in our DNA year after year, generation after generation. I always feel that we have this tension in humanity between sovereignty and violence. It always seems some system or group of people try to take others' freedom, and this results in so much trauma and violence. Yet, that fight for freedom lives in our

DNA just as much as the pain. We are meant to be free and to help one another. We are meant to heal. We are meant to protect that which is sacred. That is the mother energy, or divine feminine, as many call it. It's that inkling within us to question things, to follow our guts and to resist any disruption to our sovereignty.

Many mothers explained that one way to heal these generational traumas, honor our ancestral connections and disrupt the sterilizing mechanisms in hospital birth is through the microbiome. By now, you've likely heard about the microbiome and how important it is for our physical, mental and emotional health. You can easily find thousands of articles on the importance of gut health, the latest probiotics, how poor gut health affects our physical and mental health, etc. In essence, the importance of the microbiome cannot be overstated.

During vaginal birth, the microbiome gets passed from mother to baby, where the mother's flora and fauna colonize her baby's skin and mouth. This process contributes to the gut health of babies, as well as to their immune systems. Confirming these sentiments, a recent article in *Science Daily* (Wellcome Trust Sanger Institute, 2019) reported that during birth, the baby comes in contact with bacteria from the mother's gut. The study discovered it was the mother's gut bacteria that made up much of the microbiome in the vaginally delivered babies. It is important to realize here that our guts are connected to our mothers' wombs. We know that even those who we live closest to will share similar gut microbiomes.

Dill-McFarland, et al. (2019) sampled the stools of over 500 individuals (who had to be part of a sibling pair) from the Wisconsin Longitudinal study to examine the intersection between the microbiome and social relationships. It was determined that human interactions, especially sustained ones, influence the microbiome in the gut such that we share similar microbiomes with those we spend the most time. This biological mechanism for linking human relationships and health (via the microbiome) informs our social relationships, our connections with one another, our biology, and our health (2019). Our guts literally forge our deep connections to those around us. Certainly, this reaffirms the importance and connection between mother and baby at the gut level. And what's more, the gut microbiome is like a second umbilical cord carrying the nutrients of ancestral wisdom, immune health, intuition, healing energy and womb connection.

Mums who talked about the microbiome did so in a way that informed their relationships and deep, lasting connections with their babies as well. The importance of the microbiome to the familial connections and to the health of babies and mothers was also highly stressed. When I asked about medical births and doctors and how they impact birth, familial connections and the microbiome, one Hawaiian mother who is a holistic health practitioner and has several home-birthed children, said the following:

> I've come to realize, and this is with any profession, nobody knows everything, and it's impossible to know everything. They do know a lot, but with re- gard to birth, I think a lot of their education is within the framework of keeping people safe and alive and not so much looking at the long-term impacts of how we are born. It's more like that immediate, is every- body safe and alive? That's the objective. I think that might be one of the approaches: safety, being alive, which are obviously important, but not so much when we're getting into things. We're like, okay, yes, we want safety, we want alive, but we also want a healthy microbiome, we want a strong connection between mom and baby and partner and siblings, we want a healthy breastfeeding relationship. I think that contrast has informed a lot of my decisions, too. Yes, I want safe and alive, we all agree safe and alive is good. That's the primary thing. But can we get more than just safe and alive? (Interview 58)

Many mamas, including this one, explained that medical interventions during birth disrupt the connection with the baby as well as with oneself. Although mothers generally pass down their vaginal and breast milk microbiome to the baby during and after birth, this process can be disrupted through a variety of mechanisms in the medical setting. If medical practitioners bath the baby right away, they remove the protective vernix and vaginal microbiome from the baby's skin, which can leave babies exposed to germs and compromise their immune systems. They also take away the smell of the vernix, which is intoxicating to the mother, making her want to connect, smell, hold, feed and nurture the baby through a cascade of hormones designed to support connection.

The microbiome connection is also negatively affected by C-sections, sterilized environments and medications that disrupt the microbiome. While home-birth settings were described to be the most ideal place to foster healthy social relationships and bonds with their babies, this was not impossible in the hospital. One mama explained that babies born by C-section can still receive their mother's vaginal microbiome by smearing vaginal fluid on the baby's skin upon birth. This process essentially gives the baby the mother's microbiome without having to go through the vaginal canal. Passing down the vaginal microbiome promotes better health outcomes, a stronger immune system, and a stronger connection between mum and baby. It might be difficult to find a doctor willing to support this practice, however. But that doesn't mean you cannot do it.

A home-birth mama of two on the Big Island explained that she experienced the benefits of passing down the microbiome to her own children, and she saw how important gut health and the process of passing the microbiome down to the baby was in terms of building a healthy immune system and shaping long-term health. As mentioned, medical testing, sterilization processes and medicines in the hospital often disrupt this gut flora/microbiome, so it was very important for this mama to keep her microbiome healthy and free of these sorts of colonizing measures. She explains:

> Before I had babies, I was a breastfeeding peer counselor up at the hospital. I'd work with new moms to establish breastfeeding, the benefits of breastfeeding, and help them get hooked up to resources in the community. And what I would do is call and text and follow up with them for the first six months of the baby's life to help them meet their breastfeeding and pumping goals, returning to work, whatever they have to do.
>
> One of the things I really learned about was the gut microbiome, and our gut health and protecting that. One of them really sets the tone in terms of protecting baby's gut and what it means for their health in the future. That was a huge thing for me in terms—I don't know why I got so into it. I think it's because I was working in breastfeeding, but colonizing them with all of our good flora, it can really be diminished in the hospital.
>
> For both pregnancies, I was GBS (group B strep) positive and declined antibiotics and chose to treat it holistically. For my first time around, I was fighting tooth and nail with my midwife. I'm like, this is not evidenced-based care. This is ridiculous. I don't meet any of the guidelines or markers for being predisposed to gestational diabetes. Let me give you my food history, let me give you this, my diet. I told them I don't drink high fructose corn syrup, and if you let me put this shit in my body, my blood sugar's gonna spike, and I'm gonna go psycho. So, the first time around, they let me like do the fasting and do the eating. I'm like, you're telling a pregnant woman

to fast, this is so fucked up. So, the second time around, I really want evidence-based care. I want an evidence-based model, and I'm seeing that the hospitals are really tied. Waimea Hospital now has been bought by Queens Medical Center, and they're tied to all these regulations, so now, unless you fight for it, they give every single woman Pitocin after having a baby... yeah, they're like, that's just the guidelines now. It was a huge reason (for) choosing a home birth.

The second time around was having evidence-based care... that was probably number one, now that I'm thinking about it all. In making informed decisions with me being GBS positive, my midwife laid out the options. She was like, okay, here's the research on it. Here's what other countries do. I can get you antibiotics if you want. We can do it during labor, or we can do the garlic protocol, or we can do yogurt, or whatever it is. But me being able to take my health into my OWN hands... whether it's healthcare, having a home birth with me being in charge and making informed decisions. I see people sitting back, and they're like, I don't know, I'm not the doctor, and I'm like, well, the doctor doesn't know a lot of stuff too, or the doctor there's an OB here in Kona, and he's been practicing for forty years, he went to medical school forty years ago and hasn't had any continuing education. Things have changed. We've learned a lot in those forty years. (Interview 51)

This mama was particularly concerned with her options and decisions as she was GBS or group-B strep positive. GBS is a bacteria that pregnant women are tested for late in the third trimester and is commonly found in the vaginal canal and rectum. If babies come into contact with group-B strep during birth, it can be harmful only on very rare occasions. Doctors and hospitals would prescribe IV antibiotics for the mum during labor as a preventative measure in such situations, despite the low risk. Debates continue over whether GBS poses enough of a risk to prescribe antibiotics, as antibiotics come with their own risks, such as wiping out good gut bacteria and leaving people more susceptible to a variety of imbalances. Protecting the microbiome is difficult when protocols, routine testing (like the gestational diabetes glucose test), and disruptions occur so routinely in hospital birth.

In my own experience, I should have protected my daughter and my gut microbiome more carefully. I was GBS positive during her pregnancy and did not have all the options presented to me for treatment, so I listened to my midwives, who gave me IV antibiotics during labor with her. I likely didn't need them at all, and unfortunately, I believe they added to her extreme colic during the first few months of her life.

Do you ever have that gut feeling? Maybe it's that feeling you get when someone in an authoritative position tells you to do something that doesn't resonate with your inner knowingness. Or maybe you know what's going on in your body, and someone keeps telling you it's all in your head? Resisting messaging that doesn't resonate with your own intuition is difficult. But when our guts tell us to do something, we should listen. And, when there are forces trying to disrupt your gut microbiome (i.e., the pharmaceutical industry, the processed food industry, the pesticide industry, the fashion industry, etc.), it is important to engage in practices that protect your gut health and microbiome.

That Gut Feeling

According to various studies, our microbiome (gut) impacts our decisions, health, moods and social relationships (Clemente, et al., 2012; Dill-McFarland, et al., 2019; Tritten, 2014; Wilson, 2015). Of course, our microbiomes are also impacted by our social relationships, what we eat, our stress levels, and where we live. But our microbiome goes beyond just present-day biological and social relationships. The microbiome is also part of our past, our generational strength, our "gut wisdom," and our humanity. The mums also described the microbiome as the root place from which we derive our wisdom and our intuition—and how we connect to our past. The conversation I had with the Hawaiian mama below addressed this in more detail, and she offered thoughtful words from her indigenous worldview.

> I think (colonization) definitely had an impact on how women choose to have their babies, and it's sad because what I think we are learning is important for the microbiome and how all of these things get passed down from the woman to the children right through natural birth. I never really understood the saying, follow your na'au… follow your gut. I never understood how much the organisms in your gut are actually biologically tied to your mother, and to her mother, and to her grandmother. That's been a really big piece for us to realize… the microbiome and where the seeding of the microbiome happens, and the recognition that a lot of the ancestral knowledge that occurs in the gut is actually passed down from the mother to the child.
>
> And then, to put yourself in a sterile hospital environment where you might be at risk because of C-section, its really scary. Then, also to realize how much your baby is colonized—to use that word—colonized right after birth. So we were going to choose to have them on our farm, in the place where they will be raised, and we're going to colonize them with all of those bacteria from birth. The realization of the microbiome and the importance of it has added that layer of appreciation to our choosing to have the kids at home. Our kids can say they were born in

the place that they were raised in, and I never really, really, really, really understood how important that was until I started learning about all of the microorganisms that are present around us. (Interview 45)

Me: That makes so much sense now… the way you're saying it. I just read something this week that said that the synapses in your brain are… or like the neuron transmitters are… created in your gut first and then, so even the way we think… not just our, you know, spirit… they're not separate things… that even the way we think and make decisions are all connected.

Yeah, like, you don't, I mean, there's a reason that so many people say, "follow your gut." It's because it knows, you know, and it knows, I think, not only because of yourself, but it knows because of that ancestral link that goes all the way back to the first grandmother, right? And I didn't really understand that either. You know people say they're "hangry," you know all of that… right? It's true because it's what's in your gut that's driving so much of what you're doing, and we just are only now beginning to particularly understand that, but our ancestors knew and even on a scientific level too, you know, when you look at their language. I think that knowledge is there. We just don't have the tools to access it. (Interview 45)

This natural process of passing the microbiome from mum to baby during vaginal birth provided not only a protective benefit but also a sort of spiritual guidance and connection. When we think of going back to the womb and honoring its wisdom, we cannot leave out the microbiome, which functions in the preservation of ancestral wisdom and the health of humanity. The gut was also understood to be an inner guidance, a spiritual advisor, and an ancestral connection that directs us to make decisions that are best for us. Trusting one's gut and intuition was highly respected by the collective of women I interviewed. They lived much of their lives by following their guts. While this is looked down upon in our very heady and intellectualized society, our guts provide wisdom and intuition that is ancient and refined. Why not follow it?! Our microbiome is something to be protected and listened to, not something to ignore, sterilize or wipe away. The honoring of the gut microbiome, packed with its intuition, ancestral wisdom and spirituality, serves as a protective effect on the health of babies, and it transfers immunological protection, wisdom and ancestry from mum to baby.

Ancestral *strength*

The gut/microbiome and the womb serve as the place from which several mums honor the past, present and future. They also connect us to our ancestral strength and help us draw upon that strength during birth. Many mothers understand the microbiome as something that has been passed down from mother to baby for millennia and as something that carries wisdom and spirituality. In the conceptual model (Figure 1), these connections are demonstrated and showcase that women draw upon both collectivities and spirituality in their choice of home birth. One mama from the Kona area of the Big Island, who primarily identifies as white but also has Native American ancestry, talked about her reason for choosing home birth and how that experience connects hers to spirituality, to herself, and her intuition:

> I think in my root of choosing a home birth, I did
> focus on what are the traditional ways in this land
> that a woman would give birth. That's why I had my
> girlfriend Leialoha come for that grounding of Ha-
> waiian spiritual support… do an oli (chant) during
> the time of my birth… I was chanting and singing
> Hawaiian songs during my labor and to really tap into

that mana (power), that extra spiritual, supernatural energy to raise myself out of my physical being to give my best healthy birth.

I get growing up in Hawai'i and growing up with a Hawaiian family that did things like navigation on the makali'i and hoko - hokulea… really lived Hawaiian style, Hawaiian life, that when you make that decision, when you put that pau'a in the ground and you value your sovereignty… when I read letters from the queen or, any type of antiquities, texts, I never think that when they're asking for you to take on your sovereignty, that they're telling you to ask from someone else to give you your sovereignty.

We're born sovereign. We are born free, and as soon as you stop thinking that someone else can give that to you, you empower yourself. To name yourself sovereign and all actions that you do forward, whether it has to be legal or just choices that you make to remain sovereign… that's how you become sovereign. If that continues within each household, then soon enough, you have a nation of sovereign people that can collectively push that colonizing energy out of your town. (Interview 47)

Looking back to texts, letters, values and practices, this mama is informed by ancestral strength and sovereignty in her choices. More deeply, she connects to this ancestral strength through prayer, chanting and cultivating a birthing space that honors spirituality and intuition. Later in the interview, she described herself as the most living body of her lineage. This was such a beautiful sentiment to me; that we are the most living body of all our ancestors, all their blood passed down through all the births of each mother in our lineage. She draws upon this concept and her ancestral strength and wisdom to make particular choices, which included living her life most mindfully, most naturally and most in line with how her ancestors lived (to the extent possible). While most of the world is influenced by external factors and what society tells us to value, many home-birth mums center their lives around honoring their intuition, their ancestral wisdom and their na'au's.

For another home-birth mama (Interview 52), the connections between colonization, ancestral strength and birth shaped her worldview in that she utilized the concept of remembrance to reclaim her power and to uncover the ways in which she had knowingly and unknowingly given away her sovereignty and her power:

> As far as being an embodied woman, it's (child-birth). It's the most powerful so far in my experience (laughs), a place of wisdom. I see the colonization of birth and the control that has come through in trying to manage birth per se, and manage a woman's choices, and limit those things... it's just a root-core place of colonization. It crosses all the boundaries and barriers of separation based upon our skin color and the land that we came from, and knowing that like the body as being the vessel connected to all the things that we've been discussing... this is such a root place.

> The cervix is literally the root of our being. So if we're opening there in terms of "natural birth"... birthing the way that we feel whatever that is like, however we feel, wherever we're at... that is 100 percent up to us. Like that's what we are destined to reclaim, that needs to happen NOW. I sense from a colonized standpoint, this is the declaration, you know, for us to say like no, NO! Our bodies and, therefore, our land and everything else that's also interconnected from that root are to be sovereign... giving ourselves the opportunity to know and re-member that we have that. To know and remember

that we have the ability to see now more and more as we're able to digest the reality of living so long in a colonized state and also how we participate in that.

Making choices from that place for me is how am I participating to saying yes to being colonized. On any and all levels. How am I just unconsciously being a part of that colonization of my body and my life, you know? For me, that was something I didn't understand cognitively while making the choice to swap from from the hospital to home. As it settled in and landed in my body, it's, oh yeah, that's exactly what I was doing. I was declaring that, kind of like, wow! I didn't even know how much had been chosen for me and how much I had given my power away because I just didn't know. I didn't even know. I didn't even know there was another way. I think it's just an incredible and important conversation to speak about it in the way of colonization because it has everything to do with ownership, and it has everything to do with reclaiming the ownership of our body. (Interview 52)

Reclaiming our bodies and our sovereignty is a spiritual process. Our embodiment as mothers and makers of humans is spiritual. Our cervix is spiritual. It all is connected. By utilizing the cervix as a concept and as a literal root of our existence as humans is so powerful here in that it expresses an opportunity for reclamation of choices and a portal of wisdom that may help us to peel back layers of colonization and colonial mindsets so that we can reconnect to the root of what it means to be interconnected and what it means to be human again. The cervix is the route to the womb and an opportunity to return to ourselves. This return to and opening of the cervix is a metaphor for the return to home birth, to return to spiritual humanness, for opening spaces that have been subdued and silenced. It is reclamation. It is remembrance. It is ceremony. It is intuition. It is a return back to the womb.

These interconnections offer a pathway for liberation. While it is not to say that we are not human or somehow less human as we live in a colonizing power apparatus or if we choose to have hospital births, there is something about our way of life and our medical system that dehumanizes and something about decolonization that restores humanity. And home birth is an opportunity to decolonize even that which touches the deepest places inside of us, such as the womb. The root place is also quite metaphorical here in the sense that mothers tend to utilize complementary and alternative medicine and take a holistic health approach. Such approaches are often described as getting to the *root* cause of illness or disease rather than just treating the symptoms.

Getting to the root, whether that is the womb or the place upon which we recognize our ancestral strength, was central for the mums. Drawing upon ancestral strength was nuanced, however. At times, ancestral strength was connected to Black identity, spirituality, empowerment and even anti-patriarchy/anti-colonization. For example, one of the Black mothers I interviewed (described in Interview 41), who had several freebirth babies and who is a birth worker and educator, talked about drawing upon ancestral strength to not only get through her pregnancy but also through her birth. While she and I talked about drawing upon our sisterhood as birthing women, referencing that as we were laboring, over 4,000 other women were also laboring at the same time, she also talked about how being Black was situated in various historical and contemporary violences and traumas. She described how Black resilience and strength inspired her and how she drew upon ancestral strength to get through the last weeks of her pregnancy and get through various challenges she faced:

> I just felt like I had really connected during my labor
> with this concept of laboring simultaneously with all

these women around the world. That's a visualization tool that I have since given to a lot of my clients. (Interview 41)

Me: Is it like 4,200 women are laboring at exactly the same time? I remember thinking about that, too, during labor. I can do this because I'm with other women who are doing this.

Yeah! So, for me, that became a really metaphysical concept. I had confided in one of my law school colleagues. He was a Black man. I was just tired one week, and it was late in my pregnancy. He and I had been studying together, but he had just had a death in the family due to some sort of police violence. He was feeling exhausted. And he said we just have to persevere. Imagine if you were one of our ancestors and you were working in the field. You wouldn't get the day off. You'd have to give birth to your baby right there and strap it on your back, and continue working, and so lean into some of your ancestral support. And it just stuck with me. I had this vision, this concept, of not only am I birthing with women simultaneously across the planet with widely varying circumstances, but also in my masculinial lineage. I can draw on people who had to deal, who just had to fucking deal, you know what I mean? That really resonated with me. I wanted to repay that. I felt like I had leaned into women, and I wanted to be able to reinvest that. That sparked my desire to do childbirth education.

My dad is a doctor, but also a teaching doctor. It's important to him, which is interesting because as we continued with our early attachment parenting phase, we were making all these choices that were different than what my parents had put out there.

He's a pediatrician and just thought we would follow his trajectory. But having such an empowering birth experience allowed me to question all the fundamentals. I'm like, well damn, you told me just to have an epidural as an easy button and didn't tell me how empowered I would feel not doing it that way, and how much I saved my baby from having to take all these toxins, and all this stuff. And so, what else should I question? Then, we chose not to vaccinate. This decision I don't think is really relevant to what you're doing, but it's interesting. My dad's solution to that was telling us to go to lecture… I think I might have shared this with you before. He wanted to lecture his residents on why we were choosing not to vaccinate.

Education's just always been a very important component. I started there, so then we got to our second baby, and it's time to have a home birth. But we were living in Georgia now, having left Jersey and law school, and I started looking for a midwife, but I was back with this obstetrician. Meanwhile, the one who I had seen early in my first pregnancy before I moved, and I was thinking, this is great… she should be so excited. She was curious about our first birth, and I told her how wonderful it was, and she was so happy for us. But then I was dealing with some depression with my second pregnancy (I think I just really hadn't been as on top of my nutrition as I should have been). I was dealing with depression, and she was just very nonchalant. She's like, well, you know, second baby's not nearly as exciting as the first. Now you're dealing with reality. I told her what I wanted for my hospital birth. I don't want monitors, can we be negotiable? I didn't actually get any monitoring or anything my first birth. I had tested group beta strep

positive, and I had anticipated needing antibiotics,
but then, because I was complete when I arrived to
the hospital, they didn't have any time to give me any
IVs, and I was like, I didn't fucking need any of that.
(Interview 41)

It is certain that this mother drew upon her ancestral strength
and Black resilience to navigate her choices, her fatigue during
pregnancy, her births, and her decisions about the care she wanted
to receive (and not receive). Oparah and Bonaparte (2016) write
about Black women navigating maternal healthcare systems and
the complexities around it all, such as obstetric violence toward
Black women, sterilization of Black women and the hospital as a
white, male-dominated culture. While this mother might have been
a shining example of a Black woman taking her power back, and
indeed she is, her choices were also situated in historical, ancestral,
gendered, racialized and familial constraints. She at once drew upon
her Black paternal lineage and ancestral strength but also navigated
the medical paradigm with her father's training and his vocation.
Birthing Black babies while also witnessing the pain of her friend's
loss due to police violence added another layer of trauma to her as
well. Her birthing decisions are as inspiring as they are multifaceted
and constrained.

Ancestral strength and wisdom are as inspiring, liberating and
empowering as they are constrained and situated in various power
structures and mechanisms. A Hawaiian mama I interviewed, who
is a home birth mama to two young children, talked about how she
drew upon her ancestors for strength during the birth process and
how this process was cultural for her as a Hawaiian woman.

Well, I feel like it was a cultural thing for me, a cultural practice for me, to feel that my ancestors had
done this before. I feel like I'm kind of an old soul.
So I can kind of relate to that, and I wanted to do it

as an inspiration for my children, for the future to know that they can do it, too, and that they can know that their mom was able to birth them naturally and at home comfortably, and not in a medical facility or sterile medical facility. That kind of just goes along with how we practice at home, too. (Interview 26)

Her home birth was as much a cultural practice as it was a way to honor who she is as a mother. She also drew upon her inner strength to inspire her own children so that they would know that they were strong and didn't have to necessarily rely on medical facilities for birth. This extended beyond birth, though. It was a mechanism to teach children not to rely on outside voices to shape their decisions unless those decisions resonated with their intuition and inner knowingness. It's about not giving up one's voice or relinquishing responsibility to systems. It's about not abandoning oneself. This was all connected to her lifestyle as well, which aimed to live authentically, to be more naturally focused, to engage in functional movement practices, to center life around her family, and to design her life to be as peaceful and as natural (i.e., not as reliant on outside institutions and structures) as possible.

In her fieldwork with fifty-two home birth mums in Australia, Emily Burns (2015) also found that spirituality, ancestral connection and childbirth interlinked and correlated to positive health and birth experiences. She also discovered that the collective imaginary of ancestry and undisturbed birth informed her participants as they drew upon ancestral strength and spiritual birth preparation (called blessingway) through collective memory (Burns, 2015). She writes:

> By naming other generations, the blessingway partic-
> ipants simultaneously call upon and co-create a child-
> birth mythology, a fictional time "in the past" where
> "all" women supported each other, did not have to
> be taught about birth, birthed naturally, at home—
> and importantly, without mention of complications

or infant and maternal morbidity rates. Birth was instinctive, communal and birth knowledge was "inherent." Most importantly, birth during this time was, by default, natural and normal, rather than technocratic and risky. (Burns, 2015:792)

Burns (2015) also found that her participants experienced strong connections with one another by way of the spiritual experience of birth, their relationship with nature, and the collective imaginary of female ancestral strength (i.e., what she calls the "nostalgic imagination of women through time and space"). Similar findings came up with the mothers in Hawai'i, who expressed similar collective experiences, relationship with nature and connection with female ancestral strength. These experiences and connections translated into political action against midwifery regulations as such regulations were seen as disruptive to ancestral connections by way of removing cultural midwives and birth choices.

Mums fiercely protect their right to birth as they choose and with whom they choose. Many also questioned vaccines (as, at times, they were viewed as unnatural and unsafe, and mums preferred to rely on natural immunity). Many also participated in non-GMO groups that engaged in political action and community education on the harms of pesticides and engaged in political action against state overreach (i.e., fighting against the building of the Thirty Meter Telescope on Mauna Kea as cultural, spiritual and political action).

Pain

Drawing upon the female birth energy and ancestral strength also gave many mothers the strength to navigate the physiological changes in pregnancy and birth. This included enduring pain. Regardless of whether the actual process is pain-free or excruciating, moving through the growth and changes that come with being pregnant and becoming a mother are difficult and oftentimes painful. I do not mean this in a negative sense, however. Our conceptualization of pain in the dominant culture and dominant biomedical paradigm is that pain is negative and something to be avoided at all costs. It is indicative that something is going wrong in the body. It is a reason to pathologize. Yet, pain can be viewed as a motivator, a spiritual test and an opportunity to become stronger.

Likewise, childbirth is described in the dominant culture as being the most painful experience a human can go through. There are a variety of medications and routine interventions to lessen the pain of childbirth, which is a welcomed relief for so many laboring women. But pain is not always necessary to avoid. Many respondents in a mixed methods study on cultural conceptions of pain during labor expressed that there was value for the pain felt in childbirth in that it prepares a woman for motherhood and helps the bonding after birth as well (Mathur, 2020). The perception of pain was also often judged along the lines of cultural and even racial assumptions and expectations (Mathur, 2020). And, arguably, having a home birth presupposes that the mother understands she is going into an experience that will be extremely painful.

I have gone through childbirth twice, and although it wasn't anywhere near pain-free, pain was just a small part of the overall experience. This is contrary to the idea that the entirety of childbirth and labor is painful. There is little knowledge in the dominant culture and media on childbirth that there are breaks in the pain; that is, there is relief between contractions, and there are spaces that are not full of pain and doubt. Even in the pain, there is the opportunity for relief and elation as well. Pain is productive. Pain communicates that something is happening in the body. It is the body's way of talking to us and giving us important information. The contractions of the uterus and the opening of the cervix generally cause pain in most cases, but it also opens the pathway for new life to emerge. And this contracting is not always painful for all women.

Yet, pain is part of the opening for many women, and they describe it as an experience that allowed them to trust themselves, prepare for motherhood, feel empowered, witness their own strength and capacity, and appreciate the joy on the other side of it. Pain is meaningful and is part of the identity development of these mothers in that pain was described as necessary preparation for becoming a mother. Pain was not described as debilitative but described as capacity building and transformative.

The mama I mentioned in the last section (Interview 41) described the concept of pain in her own births and how she navigated ideas about childbirth with her actual lived experience (which had the absence of intense pain). When I asked her about this, she responded:

> We definitely are actively questioning people's pre-conceived notions and prescriptions and trying to just live life authentically and trying to make space for our children to do the same. That's what's import-ant to us. After our first birth, we were very happy and content, and we had already pushed back against some norms in getting to that place. We felt pretty positive, and then having an unassisted birth really solidified with us that we just really needed to upset the set-up and that we should question everything because this was one of the pinnacles of things that people impress upon you as fear-worthy, and like the most intense, painful, dangerous thing you may ever experience, and to take it all in our own hands and have an incredibly peaceful experience… it just made us feel like we wanted to question everything and be intentional about the decisions that we made rather than just bumping along the stream. I think that's our lifestyle. But what does that look like: unassisted free birthing, cloth diapering, organic as much as possi-ble, unschooling, bedsharing, breastfeeding, all those things? (Interview 41)

Her freebirth experience was very peaceful and made her realize that ideas that were impressed upon her, and indeed all of us, are not always true when it comes to lived experiences. That is, we don't have to accept the conditionings that have been thrust upon us. This gave her and her partner the guidance and confidence to question other things that have been impressed upon them and other social norms that might not actually be best or necessary. This empowered them to design their lifestyle more according to intentional decisions they make rather than going along with social norms and expectations. Their authentic lifestyle and birthing choice congeal in this way.

One home-birth mama from O'ahu described the fear-pain connection and how potent it is in US culture to shaping birth paradigms and to the embodied childbirth experience:

> I think in our culture, in the United States, there's so much fear associated with birth, and people are always told these negative stories. That's why birth is painful for women in the United States. Whereas in some countries, it isn't even a painful thing. It's looked at very different. In the Hypnobabies course idea, instead of managing the pain, you could avoid the pain. I wouldn't say that... I definitely didn't have a sensation-free birth, there were some sensations there, but so much of it is mental, based on what our expectations are. If women are always told, you're going to fail, you're going to ask for the drugs, you're going to try a natural birth but it's not going to work out, don't even bother to try just ask for the drugs... and they're just not exposed to birth anymore.

> For most women, these days, the first time they give birth is the first time they've seen a birth happen. I think I was really lucky in the sense that I had been present for two births before I had babies. I was there for my sister's vaginal birth, but with an epidural,

and then I was there for my sister-in-law's scheduled Cesarean section due to transverse breech presentation. I got to see firsthand how people can be treated in their birthing time and what it's like for baby to be born. In the US, (most) people have never seen a baby be born, whereas in (the) old days, maybe you were there when your sibling, or your cousins, or somebody else... there was more of a communal tribe where people were around birth, and they saw it could be okay instead of it being this scary unknown thing that causes fear because the fear causes the pain, and the pain makes it more scary. I really, really think if we could all support each other more in telling people that birth can be a positive thing. It can be a good experience. (Interview 49)

Because of the shift from home to hospital and because of the daily lives we live now in modern times, we are often removed from birth and even birth preparation and ceremony. We then hear stories about what it is like from popular culture, media, movies, horror stories some mums tell other mums, etc. This process makes birth seem mysterious and scary and, therefore, increases pain, according to this mother. It is psychological, in other words. We have a preconceived notion that we place upon an experience rather than letting the experience just be what it is. If we let every birth be its own experience, without the fear of pain, perhaps birth would be much more celebrated, revered, and honored. Maybe it would still be painful, but how we process and experience that pain would be different.

Other mothers described their birth experiences as painful but that the pain was productive in building internal trust and empowering them in early motherhood. A Chinese American mama who had her first birth in the hospital and then decided to have a home birth with her second child explained the process of pain, trust, connection and overcoming the fear that she experienced during her home birth:

I kept saying… kept coming through me: I trust, I trust, I allow, I allow. And I just kept trusting and then allowing my body to do the work, and then I kept saying… I connect to all the women who come before me, and for some reason, that brought me so much comfort… just by connecting to the collective of all the women who have given birth before me. There was a power in it, and I kept listening to that. I kept saying I connect to the women who've come before me. I call on the women who've come before me. I trust, and I allow.

There were two points where I felt like I had slight hold-ups in the process of her coming because the contractions were intense. They started two minutes apart and then just continued to increase to almost nothing in between. There wasn't clearly like a break. It just kept going, and there I had a fear of the burning, like the ring of fire, and I had fear of the actual coming out, and Medra (her midwife) stopped me for a second. I was yelling and holding onto Jaymie (her other midwife) at the edge of the tub, and she said, your energy, your energy, you're sending your energy out to Jaymie… you need to focus it within. It was true. It was helping. Jaymie was supporting me and looking me in the eyes. I was yelling, and she was taking some of my pain, but Medra was telling me to use that pain and work it inward and pull it in, and then once I did that, I was able to push her down and almost out, and then her head was in the birth canal, and we could even feel it, but it felt like a little stuck, and at that point, it was a fear that I was still holding. Medra said there's no room for fear anymore, and for some reason, those words made me come to this point. It was this pivotal thing in my life, really this realization that you'll always fear something scary.

You never actually get rid of it, the fear, you don't become unafraid, you just decide that you're strong enough to meet it. So, in that quick moment, I understood I'm going to just step toward this door. I'm not going to be unafraid of the pain, but I'm choosing to come toward it, and in that power, I was able to completely push her through and allow.

It was this thing that I've carried with me since after the birth. It taught me something about myself and about life that I had all the power in me and that you're never not afraid of something you're afraid of. You just are choosing to meet it, and I tend to be a fearful person when things arise. So it was something that I carried with me, and that connection to the essentialness through and empowering birth where I did all of it… I found the strength in myself and in my ancestors and in the women who all come before me… that all came through me with such power of the divine. That's nothing that could have ever happened to me in the hospital. Just by being in my home and being supported by birth workers, women and my partner it was… I was in full control of my birth. Then she just came straight out, and then they said, you can pick her up. I looked down and she was looking up at me in the water. It was the most amazing thing. I just scooped her up, and I lifted her to her first breath. (Interview 54)

This home birth experience allowed her to shift how she related to fear, to herself, to her ancestors, and to the women around her in deeply profound ways. She describes this experience as empowering and as one that she would never have experienced in the hospital setting. The pain was a catalyst for her to overcome her fears and to be in a relationship with her fears rather than avoid them. The pain was an opportunity for deep connection rather than disconnection. When we take away that opportunity to feel—to really feel—birth, imagine what we are taking away from women. Of course, not every woman wants to experience that pain, but to take away that choice through fear-based rhetoric and hospital interventions is unfair. Pain can empower women in certain circumstances. Pain can open up possibilities within that we never imagined. It can activate our strength. It can prepare us for motherhood in ways we never thought possible.

Another mum also explained that the pain was productive to tapping into her intuition and her own voice. She also explained that this process has broader implications for how we relate to one another in society:

> Home birth can teach you so much. It was exhausting, and it was painful as hell, I'm not going to lie (laughs). There's nothing joyful about pushing a child out. There were a lot of ups and downs, especially toward the end, but looking back at the whole thing… it was just magical. Like, oh my gosh, this is amazing. Also, the value of listening to yourself and your intuition and giving that more credit… people need to get back on that. Trust yourself, and when you think it's right, it will be right. If not, it will be different. (Interview 44)

> Me: How do you think the world would change if we were more trusting, patient and simple with our lives?

> It would be a better place (laughs). I think there will be a lot more contentment and happiness, which then leads to different interactions… the way humans interact with each other and treat each other. Only positive things, yeah, absolutely. (Interview 44)

Pain also helped to shape these mamas' identities and expand their capacities, as they described labor pain as an initiation/preparation for the challenge and reward of motherhood. Home birth offers the opportunity to explore the transition from maiden to mother. Further, there is a shared understanding amongst mums that the pain of childbirth that is not known until felt and experienced. I remember asking my midwife when I was pregnant with my daughter what a contraction feels like. She laughed and said, "Oh, you'll know it when you feel it!" And moms everywhere who have experienced contractions know that they are a unique sensation and perhaps one of the most intense physical sensations one could ever feel.

Spiritual Home Births

Many mums described getting to a place in birth that was incredibly spiritual. It seems the pain is a portal to this spiritual realm. It is the sort of linkage between the womb and the spirit world. Part of this journey through pain and birth included "trusting" oneself, relying on one's "intuition," and the "love and support of midwives." This place in childbirth that is incredibly spiritual was described as a sort of portal between worlds, or the "rainbow bridge," as it is often referred to in the natural birth community. The mama from Kona (Interview 47) also explained how spirituality and social connection in birth are part of getting to the core of self and how important the energy of her midwife was in this space:

> I think when you're present in that being, when you're so in your own center, you have the most clarity and connection to a source that's not only outside of you. It's that internal source of power. It's that external source of power and beyond. You really can channel that and feel comforted, wise. You can feel able to focus and make decisions and have the most calm... just like Zen... through anything. (Interview 47)

> Me: Yeah, so do you feel like through labor and birth, you were able to get to that center and feel that presence and that source within yourself?

Yes, and I also felt like I went through a door. I went through a very amazing space. My labor was about six and a half to seven hours only, and the first half of that, my practice of being present felt like the like warmest hug. I literally had no anxiety when my body would feel very close contractions. (I was) just breathing. I'd say it got me through it so amazingly. And then at one moment when it was getting a little harder and I was having very bad muscle spasms where the clary sage and the dim room… I was having huge, massive body spasms and locking… at that point, I had a girlfriend of mine… she was a teacher of mine for Hawaiian Studies… she became that presence of that sisterhood, and also with my midwife's energy, I felt like I was allowed to go through a threshold and leave that physical part of my pain behind.

And I felt like every part of me was in this area just outside of my head where all of my energy was there, and the rest of my body was allowed to be at ease, and it was almost as if I completely left that pain behind and felt like it was very mentally and spiritually grounded at that time. But those were the two parts of my being that I needed to focus with the most and the physical part is not where I needed to be focused. My body was doing it for me. My baby was doing her job. I had people of support around me, and I could just release that physical attachment and go through a beautiful spirit door, I call it. (Interview 47)

This mother also went on to talk about how that spiritual door is muddied during a hospital birth. She connected this to the concept of 'ike, a Hawaiian word for knowledge, and how our understanding of knowledge can allow for that which is beyond the physical realm:

I hear so many stories about moms with these hospital births where they're woozy and they're tired, and they don't remember anything about it, and their milk doesn't come in, and they didn't get to see their baby, and it was traumatizing. Things were shoved into them, and the list goes on and on and on… your body was born to feel these things, and when you go through experiences, and you didn't feel something, you don't get that 'ike, and you can get 'ike physically. There are three of it… epistemology of mind, body and spirit that I learned from Hilo. He's a director of Hawaiian studies on O'ahu. (He) was speaking about those forms and culturally what those terms are. So, we have 'ike of a knowing that is beyond us that we receive. We have an 'ike of things that we know from research and speaking to one another, and then we have a form of 'ike of our knowing of our beings experiencing something and gaining that knowledge.

If you're going through a birth experience, and you're not embodying in your mind, your body or your spirit soul that experience, then you're leaving out that knowledge of it, and, in a sense, you're almost blurring it, you're numbing it. It becomes a blurry experience. It becomes a numbed experience. It becomes a cut-off experience. Your spirit didn't get that connection because your mind and body were numbed and bound, and you weren't free and open to the literal vibrations and the energy that happens when you give birth… you did not internalize in your body. It basically went in, and it hit a door, and it caused you pain, and you numbed the pain, and then it was over, and then you woke up, and you're like, "What, I'm a mom now?"

I see the connections with the children being so
different. Mommies that I see that have had a connection with their birth, whether its hospital or not,
when I see mommies who go through hospital births
with midwives where they don't do Pitocin, and
they don't have those things. I super congratulate
those mothers, those midwives and those doulas, and
those hospitals for giving women the ability to have a
hospital birth that feels like a home birth or a birthing
center birth. (Interview 47)

This mum knows that pain is spiritual. The full experience of
childbirth not dulled by pain medication is one that requires the full
presence and the full embodiment of the experience to integrate the
spiritual aspect of birth. She explains the importance of midwives
and birth workers to the birth experience and how important it is to
the connection between mum and baby as well as to holding space
for such a spiritual experience.

Generally, the first connections we have in the world are with
our birth mothers, pending any emergency situations, and this, as
many mums explain, informs how we are in the world, how we
connect with one another, and how we are shaped as humans. When
we are embraced in loving support, our children can enter into the
world in a loving environment and a loving space that honors the
birth portal (the rainbow bridge).

Birthing in this way is the most natural and loving way, according
to these mamas. Yet, birthing at home requires a level of surrender
to pain and discomfort to reach this spiritual portal. I sometimes
imagine that birth is this huge trial, and we have to work through
the pain to open the spiritual portal to bring a soul through and into
human form. It feels like the same portal that souls exit and enter life.
The energy around a birthing mama must, therefore, be protected
and honored, for it is sacred. The O'ahu mama of four children, two
of whom were birthed at home (described in Interview 52) shared

the following about home birth, as she connected these themes of pain, ancestral support, and spirituality:

> It is a place of deep trust and knowingness. The way that I experience it is just this deep knowing, almost in a sense that no matter what happens in the birth, everything is going to unfold in the way that nature has intended it to, in a sense. Not in a disempowered way of, oh, just you know, whatever happens, happens, but a real settling into the surrender to the mystery, and the way that transferred over in my body… feeling the kind of energy that I sense would be how the ancestors helped to open the channel of me to be able to birth a human into creation. The way that I experience that in my body is just this very deep surrender of being able to relax and allow my body to truly be in the flow of creation.
>
> It's funny because I think that for some people, that looks a certain way. Even in the pain and discomfort of birth for me was, an actual knowingness, to go toward that, and to face all that as something that our ancestors have always done. And that's part of the process of self-initiation. You go through this initiatory process of going into that which I fear the most, which would be dying from childbirth. (Interview 52)

Going into those places of doubt, pain and discomfort was described as an initiatory process of self and becoming a mother. Many mothers explained that their midwives helped guide them through this process through their loving and knowledgeable support. Many mothers also explained that this process is nearly impossible with a medical doctor because of the socio-cultural ways in which clinical providers interact with patients. That is, there is little to no focus on relationship building, spirituality and emotions. On the other hand, midwives may offer that level of empowerment, community, love, trust, spirituality and knowledge that support home birth mothers. It is truly a sacred vocation.

Perhaps there is something in the midwifery model of care that offers an allowance of humanity and spirituality in the patient-provider interaction. It is perhaps less "professional" in the Western sense of the term, but it is more effective for these mothers and their desire to have a care provider that supports their choices and their spiritual journeys in birth. While not all midwives offer such care and spiritual support, many do.

Unfortunately, there have been attacks on the profession of midwifery for far too long. And often, the response to this is to create more programs, more training, more certification programs, more education, etc. I wonder, however, if all these measures to prove the "professionality" of midwifery end up being more harmful than good. That is, trying to establish a profession rather than focusing on the mothers and the spirituality of childbirth can dilute and change the way midwifery is practiced. This can also have the negative effect of limiting access to particular midwives who practice in more autonomous, spiritual and culturally relevant ways.

For instance, one Hawaiian mother from Maui was in tears when describing that there were no more traditional Hawaiian midwives. She explained that there was a traditional Hawaiian midwife in her husband's family and even had family birthing stones in Lahaina, but that it was difficult to find a Hawaiian practitioner of birth on Maui. She explained:

> There are no practicing Hawaiian midwives who continued that learning from their ancestors, and so that was... I mean, honestly, just saying it out loud still makes me emotional. To think of just such a beautiful tradition that really doesn't exist anymore (pauses to weep). But we did find a Hawaiian birth worker who was apprenticing under a white midwife here on Maui. And so, they really created a perfect

blend of modern Western midwifery with traditional
Hawaiian worldview and concept. And she's a mi—a
medicine and Hawaiian massage practitioner. She
really incorporated all of the medicines, and every
month at my prenatals, I would get an hour-long
lomi lomi massage, too. You couldn't even really
dream of a better prenatal team and situation.

We had a really, really low risk, low intervention…
actually all three of our births were really, really
smooth. My first actually came so fast that my midwife actually missed the birth, and my Hawaiian birth
attendant, who I hired, was the one who helped my
husband catch the baby. It was almost meant to be
because it really thrusted her into birth work (and)
has the confidence to take more primary roles. It
also really inspired me and my husband to continue
learning about Hawaiian practices and educating the
community about Hawaiian birth practices. (Interview 6)

The trauma of losing the Hawaiian birth traditions, practitioners
and practices affected this mama deeply. The lack of a Hawaiian midwife
or practitioner—and even the loss of birthing practices—affects the
birth journey, the spirituality and the ceremony of birth. This mama
was quite resourceful, and although she did not have a Hawaiian
midwife, her midwife—a white woman—practiced Hawaiian birth
practices and partnered with a Hawaiian birth practitioner as well.
In a sort of hybrid fashion, she was able to reclaim some of those
birthing practices, which she brought back to her own community
as well. Certainly, colonization even affects access to care providers
and birthing practices. Reviving these practices is one way of healing
colonial trauma and restoring culture, self-identity and community.

Midwives were often described as essential in the birthing
space, allowing mothers to feel safe and empowered and to trust in

birth. Sometimes, the midwife's role was more spiritual and harder to describe in scientific terms. That is, the presence of the midwife allowed the baby's soul to come through more peacefully. Not only was this important for the birth portal or rainbow bridge but also for the general support of the mother's spiritual, physical, and emotional health and wellness. The mama in Interview 54 described a spiritual birth experience and the presence of her midwife as follows:

> It was amazing because time stopped, and the color of the room was dusty pink with sparkles from the sunshine, and it was like this: you know they say the "rainbow bridge" …it really was. I'm really transformed, and it was this amazing moment in time where, when she came through, I understood the importance of a midwife instead of a doctor. They're guiding a spirit into a body, and if you don't understand that component, I don't know how you scientifically can (laughs)… how that can scientifically be proven except for stillbirths… healthy fetuses that all of a sudden are not alive at birth. I've asked Medra… that was one of my fears and anxieties during my pregnancy… the stillbirth of healthy fetuses and why they're not born alive, and she told me that sometimes she had to travel with a baby a spirit to the other side and retrieve them and coax them. (Interview 54)

The importance of midwifery in the spiritual side of birth remains somewhat of a mystery. Perhaps this is an area in which the medical gaze cannot penetrate. Certainly, the clinical gaze and the function of medicine are to continually uncover, discover, classify, pathologize, treat and diagnose. Freidson (1970) and Foucault (1973) describe this process of peeling back or uncovering the body, revealing the deepest parts of the body to study, pathologize and discover how our bodies function.

In its goal to discover more about the human body and how it functions or malfunctions, medicine must uncover what lies beneath the skin. In pregnancy and birth, we see this process manifest as routine blood tests, amniocentesis, ultrasounds, C-sections and electronic fetal monitoring. These are the processes by which doctors and medical professionals are able to look inside mothers' bodies, to discover what is going on with their babies, and to pathologize and diagnose when need be. Yet, this process cannot account for the various ways in which women experience birth, the spirituality of birth, the connections between mothers and midwives, and even the various impacts that colonization and patriarchy have on women's birthing spaces.

This scientific medical gaze upon the body cannot objectively discover and uncover all our experiences as humans, including our spiritual experiences. It cannot uncover the mysteries of birth and how/why many women have spiritual experiences during childbirth. It cannot explain fully why something so primal as home birth can also be so revolutionary in terms of spiritual, gendered, cultural, physical and personal growth.

Lee Maracle (1996:113) resists this scientific medical gaze upon our spirituality as humans. She writes, "To possess a spirit is to be alive. It does not mean that we strip spirit of its mystical cloak and look at it in the cold light of reality." And even if we were to somehow try to fully capture such experiences in a scientific or medical way, it would be nearly impossible to explain them in scientific terms. Science and medicine have limited methods and tools to measure such things. Science and medicine have also failed to monetize intuition and spiritual experiences; therefore, such things are unsurprisingly dismissed. "Science has not yet unraveled the mystery of the spirit; thus, no dollars are allocated to such research. This does not negate spirits' existence, it only shrouds it in mystery," as Maracle confirms (1996:113).

From the interviews, the personal experiences of many mothers, and the stories they shared with me, there is something in birth that lies beyond the physicality of birth, beyond scientific measurements, beyond our language and perhaps beyond our ability to articulate. There is ancestral strength, gut wisdom, love, connection, pain, pleasure, resilience, constraints, challenges and triumphs that bring babies into this world. All of these things bring us back to the womb.

Back to the Womb

We all come from the womb, and so much of this book has been about how to honor the womb. The uterus is sometimes equated with the womb, although reducing it to an organ when it is so much more than that almost seems comical. The uterus is, nevertheless, a fascinating organ. It stretches from the size of a lemon to a watermelon during pregnancy. And it nourishes and houses a whole new human being (sometimes more than one). So, when the womb is mentioned, I am certainly talking about the uterus. But the womb also evokes more than that. The womb can be a place of love, creation, ancestral connection, healing, respite and safety. The womb is our collective birthplace.

My midwife calls the place that women go to retrieve their babies the "rainbow bridge." It is the spiritual place where souls come in, and souls go out. It's the bridge between the living and the spirit realm, essentially. The womb makes this possible. The womb and its contractions can bring a woman to this bridge to get her baby. Of course, this is hard to scientifically measure, but many women have claimed to experience spiritual births. They claim to have almost psychedelic experiences, transformative experiences and spiritual experiences during birth in which they experience existence beyond their physical bodies. They go to a different place—the rainbow bridge. Home birth is important in this process as it has the potential to hold space for a woman to travel on this bridge in the most spiritually protected, women-centered way.

We don't really know exactly where we all come from, although many theories and books exist on this. We can only say for sure that all of us come from the womb. We can trace that womb back, in theory, to the original mother. Some people think that is Eve. Others think it's an African woman. Some think there was no original mother. Many of us believe God is our first womb; God is the birthplace of creation, and from there, we will live and once again return. Like a child running back to its mother for safety, we all must return to the womb eventually.

On a spiritual level, I think protecting birth is so important for this reason. We don't just want or need good physical outcomes. We also need good spiritual, mental and emotional outcomes. Protecting the mother, in this sense, is so important. To have a deeply spiritual experience be interrupted by unnecessary interventions, fluorescent lights, coercion, etc., is so unfortunate. Of course, not all hospital births are like this, but many are. And, of course, many home births have adverse outcomes.

So, I do not mean to sensationalize the spirituality of birth in every instance. Yet, I have never heard of a woman having the same deep, loving relationship with an OB as she has with her midwife. That loving relationship is vital to the spirituality of birth as well.

There are many things about the womb and birth that offer us pathways to healing as well as deep recognition of the ills of society. I'd like to address at least a couple of these, as I do believe birth is a metaphor for so many things in life. The way we treat birth and experience birth paves the way for our relations, our personalities, our gendered expectations, etc.

One issue I've been researching and thinking deeply about is the issue of disconnect. By disconnect, I mean a few different things: circumcision, immediate cord-cutting and taking baby away from mum. In the birth community, many people understand that our nervous systems are shaped by those first couple of moments and days we are alive. What do you think happens to our nervous systems when we are whisked away from our mothers, or when our umbilical cords are cut before our iron-rich blood and stem cells have a chance to be absorbed by our little bodies, or when we are stuck with a needle, or when (for the males) the foreskin is cut off? What message are we signaling to babies when this happens? These traumas shape babies' brains and nervous systems and can affect their personalities. Dysregulated nervous systems can breed disconnect, pain, dis-ease and harm.

Calm nervous systems breed peace. Peace on earth really does begin at birth, and it is our responsibility to protect babies and their nervous systems. In the hospital, this becomes a big task if your birth team doesn't support your plans. We know we have huge issues with stress, violence and trauma in our world today. I wonder if we treated birth differently and made it the most welcoming, loving and safest celebration a human being can go through in their first moments of life, our society might heal and become a more peaceful place.

Our bodies are truly all we have. We are born into a body with its complexities, hormones and life cycles. It is amazing! Life is amazing! Bodies are amazing! Birth is amazing! The essence of the home birth community I witnessed is a collective of people who truly honor birth, life and our bodies. Part of this essence of honoring birth also involves honoring our hormones in pregnancy, birth and beyond. I believe that's why so many women I interviewed were so committed to their healthy lifestyles, their health care with midwives, their spirituality and their bodies. They were aware of the importance of hormones, particularly during birth and breastfeeding. They were well aware of the need to honor our hormonal fluctuations during our menstrual cycles as well. Many women talked about how society doesn't honor our need for rest during menses and during the postpartum time. Mums also talked about how hospital settings disrupt the natural flow of oxytocin needed for the natural progression of labor, birth and even breastfeeding.

Honoring the essence of the womb, with the hormonal fluctuations that make menses, pregnancy, birth and breastfeeding possible, meant that the home birth mums chose to live a slower-paced life. The American lifestyle and hospital birth setting, for instance, were regarded as disruptive to this natural flow. Honoring birth means going slower and keeping in balance with our natural energy and hormonal flows. Many issues with health, stress, infertility and even burnout, were mentioned by several mums when they referred to how our society functions. That is, the pace of society is not at the pace in which we should live for the best health and most optimal hormonal balance.

This idea of slowing down a bit also transcended into the birth space and into the idea of honoring the womb. From references to how women used to rest during their blood (period) to not using hormonal birth control to how birth should not always be rushed (unless of an emergency), many mothers talked at length about really feeling the essence of birth and their bodies. This meant that they were prepared for longer labors. They did not wish to rush birth and labor or mute it with pain medications. They wanted to soak up and feel the entire experience. Home birth offers us a pathway, then, to really honor the womb in this way and also to honor this gift we call life by slowing down, entering into the fear and pain, transcending the pain and fear, and feeling our hormones and our birth contractions.

What if we could bring these lessons outside of the birth room? What if we could honor our natural fluctuations, pain and capacity? What if we enter every challenge with courage, breath and trust? Wouldn't that be the best way to honor life and to honor the womb? After all, we all return to the womb of creation. What better way to return with a lifetime of experience and to surrender unto life? Home birth is the single most significant experience I have found that teaches me to honor the womb and to honor life. I believe it was the same for the mamas I interviewed as well.

Chapter 7:
Conclusion

I wanted to uncover the miracle of home birth, understand who home-birth mothers are, and get to know why mums chose home birth in Hawai'i. I wanted to understand them (being one myself). I wanted to know why they make this unpopular choice and what that means for them. I wanted to understand why this decision held so much importance in their lives. I wanted to understand how home birth can shape an entire way of life. I wanted to know how this way of birthing can heal our souls. I wanted to understand how these mums live, what their values are, and what is important to them. I wanted to know how we view and treat birth informs society and social relations and how women understand medical freedom, autonomy, authority and informed choice.

In total, I talked with fifty-nine home-birth mamas. It became clear that they shared beliefs about the importance of birth, women-centered care, birth choices, midwifery, protecting the microbiome, using plant medicine, spending time connecting to family and 'āina, and living a healthy lifestyle. While racial and indigenous identities, class, marital status and education level provide nuance, it was clear that this group of mothers collectively value holistic health, empowerment, medical individualism/choice, plant medicine, spending time in nature and exercise. They also had various worldviews that often overlapped and complemented one another,

243

such as anti-colonialism, anti-patriarchy, family-centeredness and indigenous worldviews.

The mums chose not to fully interact with or be subject to the authority of the medical establishment for birth. Instead, home birth offered them an opportunity to be safe from the various harms they associated with the hospital setting. Birthing at home protected mothers from sexism, racism, continued colonial traumas, unnecessary medical interventions, violence and mistreatment. Birthing at home also allowed mothers to honor their cultures and histories, to feel loved, and to protect their bodies and babies from harm.

Many mothers expressed, for instance, that they did not want their babies to be vaccinated right away, poked, given medications, circumcised (for male babies) or even taken away from them right after birth. They did not want their babies bathed right away as the vernix (the protective layer of white substance on babys' skin) serves as a protective effect; mums wanted to determine when the cord was cut so babies received more stem cells and iron through the umbilical cord (protecting them against a myriad of diseases); and they wanted to pass their microbiome onto their babies without interruption.

The hospital setting disrupts much of this, and the mums explained that the midwifery model honors mothers' wishes as it is woman-centered care rather than doctor- or hospital-centered care. Birthing at home was about empowerment, certainly, but it was also about protection for these mothers and their babies.

Home birth was also described as a process of reclamation of one's power, sovereignty and culture through connecting to one's own strength as well as cultural birthing traditions. For instance, most of the mothers expressed some level of political action against the midwifery regulation bill. Many viewed birth as women-centered and family-centered, and many viewed birth as a natural process for which their bodies were designed. Additionally, they viewed birth as a spiritual experience but found that medical settings do not honor the spiritual, emotional, mental and physical aspects of birth. As a result, these mothers were inclined to seek out alternative care practitioners like midwives (or chose to birth unassisted) who view health as holistic and live a life that supports spiritual, family, and women-centered values.

Further, many mamas explained that birth was part of an empowering experience that allowed them to feel sovereign, particularly in the context of colonized Hawai'i. Part of this experience also included honoring their connection to place through spending time connecting with 'āina, growing herbs and food, and avoiding too much time in the city. Practicing spirituality through meditation, prayer, connecting with kūpuna, honoring ancestral strength, honoring the natural rhythms of life, and following intuition were also part of this experience. Healthy lifestyles were also valued, and this was represented through living a non-toxic lifestyle in terms of food, cleaning products, spending time in nature, exercising, purchasing local, organic foods, using plant medicines, and valuing informed choices, evidence-based practices and medical individualism.

They saw birth as a normal life process. They saw it as healthy and part of their lifestyle choices. They saw it as an opportunity to have empowered choices, to reaffirm concepts of holistic health, and to honor balance and spirituality. Not only did mothers trust in the natural process of birth, but their home births also provided an opportunity to trust in themselves and their midwives. Patient-provider interactions are generally described as hierarchical and clinical, with males more likely in positions of power as doctors. However, the midwifery model provided mothers a more equitable, closer, more trusting relationship with their care provider (i.e., midwife). This model of care humanizes us and is important, particularly for mums.

The mamas described birth as natural, and generally described the hospital setting as unnatural by using words such as "sterile, cold, clinical, loud." They also viewed the American lifestyle, diet and culture as unnatural in that it is filled with pavement, fast lifestyles, toxins, harm to health, and patriarchal values. On the other hand, things like attachment parenting, non-toxic lifestyles, organic foods and home birth were described as natural. The mums viewed health as holistic; that is, health is not just physical; it is mind, body, and spirit, and there is a need for balance, connection to 'āina, clean eating, exercise, outdoor time, spirituality, family and community connections, and avoidance of toxins to achieve holistic health.

These mamas formed a collectivity and shared similar worldviews as well. These shared values influenced their lifestyles, practices, consumption patterns and choices that shaped their lives and those of their families. Their lifestyle and birth choices were connected to deeper meanings such as cultural reclamation, sovereignty, natural living, self-sufficiency, and a rejection of mainstream consumer behaviors. In other words, the cultural and spiritual connection to land, particularly for Hawaiian mothers, informed their decision to birth at home as 'āina is intimately connected to cultural and medicinal practices—including birth. This is also spiritual in that 'āina provides a connection to kūpuna, community, mana, Akua (God), ancestral knowledge, plant medicine, clean food, cultural reclamation and sovereignty. Place, therefore, is such an important part of our lives.

Finally, the mums voiced the importance of spirituality, ancestral strength, pain, gut wisdom/intuition and the microbiome. The microbiome was described as passed from mother to baby. The microbiome has a protective effect on health and, at all costs, should be protected during birth. It carries wisdom, intuition and ancestral knowledge. I also addressed how women rely upon spirituality, ancestral strength, midwifery support and sisterhood to navigate the unknowns, the surrendering, the trust and the pain of childbirth.

The mums chose home birth for a variety of reasons. At times, they felt they were spiritually called to do so. But, more often, they chose home birth because they saw birth as a natural life process. They did not subscribe to the idea that birth is an emergency or is somehow something that needs to be pathologized. Many expressed that they chose a home birth for safety or to escape sexism, racism, and/or colonialism and because hospital births were more risky in terms of interventions and patriarchal, paternalistic experiences. Those who had previous hospital births also informed me that they chose a home birth because they felt like their choices were taken away from them in the hospital and that they lost authority over their own bodies. This stripped them of their power and their voice. They talked about things being done to their bodies without informed consent as well.

Mums conceptualized home birth as something that is deeply connected to who they are as people and as mothers. Their home birth choices were connected to their concepts of health. The holistic health concept that seeks balance in mind, body and spirit that supports informed consent and empowered choices and that honors natural healing all aligned with their choice to have a birth at home. They did not define health as something to be achieved through doctor's visits or a pill. Rather, health was defined as wellness, vitality, balance and awareness. When they went to care providers for health ailments or tune-ups, they generally visited complementary and alternative medicine practitioners. This aligned with the choice to hire a midwife and choose the midwifery model of care as it is based on a holistic health approach to the mother's health and to family health.

In contrast, while hospitals and doctors were described as necessary, and many mothers were grateful for their expertise and tools in emergency situations, they viewed biomedicine as overreaching in the birth space. They viewed hospital birth as an experience that is not as safe for those who want empowered choices and informed consent in their births. Sometimes, the hospital and its policies were viewed as dangerous for women and colonial in nature, especially for African Americans and Native Hawaiians.

For example, one of the Hawaiian mothers who had her first

child in the hospital said it was a terrifying experience and that she did not feel empowered or even like she was part of the process. That is, things were done to her, and she was not an active participant in the birth process because of the medications they gave her and the things they did to her without explaining or asking for consent. She contrasted this with her home birth, where she was able to feel supported, where Hawaiian ways of birthing were honored, and where she was able to connect to 'āina and make choices for herself.

Mothers certainly viewed home birth as aligned with their concept of health and as part of their lifestyles. They saw birth as "natural," that is, birth is viewed as something that women's bodies are naturally designed to do without intervention, just as they see their health practices as natural (that is, their practices are rooted in ways of living that are connected to nature, land, clean foods that come from the earth, and plant medicines that aren't synthetically altered). Anything that was toxic (i.e., fragrances, conventional soaps, GMO foods, too much screen time, not enough time in nature, etc.) was generally avoided to the extent possible. Likewise, eating clean, maintaining healthy stress levels, getting outside, utilizing CAM, exercising, and maintaining positive family relationships were all described as health practices that mums engaged in routinely.

Their natural/healthy consumption patterns reflected their reluctance to be dependent on the standard American lifestyle and everything it represents. By being "natural" and choosing birth at home and eating natural foods, they felt they could protect the natural environment, engage in traditional farming, reclaim cultural practices, practice aloha 'āina, and show their love for family by reproducing healthy children to enhance the future of humanity.

Additionally, home birth was viewed as part of reclaiming cultural practices for many mothers, particularly Black and indigenous women (but not limited to this group). Similarly, healthy lifestyles were often viewed as reclaiming cultural practices of growing one's own food, connecting to 'āina, living off the land, honoring ancestral ways of being and knowing, and connecting with family. The relevance of place, 'āina, and Hawai'i played a significant role in the choice of home birth and healthy lifestyles. 'Āina offered the opportunity for health, for Hawaiian culture to be practiced, for ancestral connection, for growing healthy food, and for balance.

The colonization of Hawai'i has certainly disrupted the connection to 'āina. However, the mums practiced ways to reconnect, such as birthing on their 'āina kūpuna (for some Hawaiian mothers), growing their own food, swimming and spending time in nature. Place is also important here as Hawai'i has various customs and cultural diversities that shape lifestyles. For many, place was significant in shaping practices and lifestyles aimed toward health.

Home birth is stigmatized, nuanced, rooted in various identities and experiences, and is a choice that has a relationship to nature, spirituality, health, colonization, 'āina, patriarchy and culture. Home birth can bring mums back to tradition and ceremony – to nature, to connectedness, to love, to relationship with self, other, spirit, etc. It resonates in our gut wisdom, engages ancestral strength and creates the deepest of human bonds. Home birth has the capacity to break open lies of the violence we've endured. It breaks open the medical gaze and embarrasses it with its embodied, female expansive power and has the capacity to return us constantly back to who we are—to the cervix, to the root, to the source of our lives, to the womb.

Accordingly, the stigmatization of home birth is certainly something that needs to be reevaluated in society and through legislation. In Hawai'i, legislators who seek to pass bills restricting lay and cultural midwives should be educated about home birth and why women make this choice before they are allowed to legislate on birth. They should also be educated about the importance of home birth choice as a cultural and spiritual experience as well, particularly in Hawai'i.

At the hospital level, it is clear that many women are making choices to distance themselves from Western medical care. Certainly, mistreatment during childbirth, the patriarchal atmosphere of medicine, the staggering statistics of infant and maternal mortality, particularly for BIPOC mothers, and the unnecessary interventions that occur to satisfy for-profit and efficiency policies (i.e., medically unnecessary C-sections) need to change to make birth more comfortable and safe for mums and babies in the hospital setting.

We could change policies that allow midwives to oversee hospital births. Currently, many hospitals allow nurse midwives to oversee birth. However, lay and cultural midwives do not have hospital privileges to oversee birth in the event a mum has to transfer to the hospital. The way that medicine is taught perhaps needs a paradigm shift. That is, rather than integrate doctors into a broken "health" care system (and perhaps subjecting such doctors to institutional and interpersonal stress), systemic changes need to happen. Changing the way medicine is taught, restructuring medical culture and work ethic (i.e., no more overworked doctors and nurses), reconsidering what healing means, changing the way we view birth, allowing for indigenous medicines and practices in hospital, and addressing how the medical model can improve/shift are all ways might help make hospitals more friendly for mums and babies.

Perhaps patient choice, whether someone wants a male or female doctor, a midwife, a person of their own cultural or racial background, etc., should be considered in policy-making. Doctors could also make care more collaborative and less top-down (I understand many doctors are shifting to collaborative care with their patients already). It would also be useful for hospitals and insurance companies to reevaluate policies dictating that various interventions must be used, especially when particular interventions may be unnecessary, harmful and not evidence-based. Perhaps insurance could start covering home births and care from cultural practitioners and healers of all kinds. Of course, this all must be evaluated on a legal level, as many policies are designed to avoid litigation.

While home birth generally has positive outcomes, especially for low-risk women, there is always the potential for hospital transfers. The testimony in response to "SB1033 SD2 HD2 Relating To The Licensure Of Midwives" revealed that women were often mistreated during hospital transfers, with nurses and doctors treating them poorly for attempting home births. Arguably, this erupts out of the stigmatization of home birth and the framing of home birth mums as risky, selfish, and perhaps anti-medicine.

Also, this transfer from home to hospital disrupts the continuum of care. Hospitals usually do not allow lay and cultural midwives to have hospital privileges and to oversee their clients/birthing mums' care. This, of course, adds stress on the mother during a crucial time. For Hawaiian mothers, this stress could be compounded if they experience the hospital as a colonial place as well.

On a broader level, teaching everyone about the history and spirituality of birth would certainly allow people to view home birth in a less stigmatized way and reduce the burden on crowded hospitals. Introducing young women to the midwifery model of care would also help to normalize birth, pregnancy, menstruation and even menopause. This could be done at the educational level.

For instance, I remember watching a birth on video during sex-ed in middle school. Back then, we had large televisions and VHS videos that rode on carts to each classroom. The video was grainy, and it appeared that the birthing mama was having the worst time of her life. This was the first birth I had seen. This was my first experience watching a baby come out of a vagina. This was to scare us into abstinence or avoiding pregnancy during the teenage years. And, yet, there was no talk of what pregnancy and childbirth were about on a physical, emotional, mental and spiritual level or what it means to be a parent. There was no talk about how contractions feel or what they do in the body. No visual showed that this mother was supported in mind, body and spirit. Further, there was absolutely no education about hormonal health.

Perhaps if I had seen a home-birth video with midwives and the mother's partner supporting her or even a hospital-birth video where the mother was given comfort measures and people weren't screaming at her to push, I would have had a different view of childbirth in my younger days. Perhaps I would have learned how to assert myself in medical contexts if I had seen a birth plan at a young age. Perhaps I would have even viewed mothers differently, and women differently if they didn't appear to be in crisis and in need of a male physician to control their bodies. Perhaps, if we allowed our young people to learn more about birth, there would not be so much fear about it; perhaps our youth and our society would honor mamas and babies during pregnancy, birth and postpartum.

Birth, which is undoubtedly the basis of our survival as a human race, should be given the most honor and reverence, in my opinion. It is not only the start of life; it is the birthplace of our entire existence. Honoring the womb means honoring all these things. We must respect and honor birth to even find peace in the world. That is, if we cannot honor the birth of a beautiful soul into this world, it is much easier to be violent and hate others. If we do not honor babies, how can we honor children? And if we don't honor children, how can we honor mothers? And the elderly? If we bring trauma to babies, we bring trauma to our world. If we do not honor the rainbow bridge and the pain it sometimes takes to get there, we cannot honor birth, life and death—our essential human experiences.

After both of my births, I was often reminded of these sentiments. Seeing a newborn baby, holding them, smelling them, and looking into their eyes makes you realize just how precious life really is. When we understand that, our healing begins. We break open in the best ways possible. I leave you with a short epiphany I had when reflecting on my home birth with my son Noah.

> Birth... it will shatter you into a billion pieces and
> pull you through all of time, all of space, of all life,
> and all of death until you arrive at the gates of souls,

where words don't exist anymore, where you and
your baby open the locks and come back to earth—
together, if you are lucky. And you both come back to
the womb. And you will never be the same.

References

American College of Obstetrics and Gynecologists. 2017. "Planned Home Birth." Committee Opinion. Number 697. https://bit.ly/3RgelYV

Attanasio, Laura B., and Rachel R. Hardeman. 2019. "Declined Care and Discrimination During the Childbirth Hospitalization." *Social Science & Medicine* 1982 (232):270–277.

Baker, Mary Tuti, 2021. "Gardens of Political Transformation: Indigenism, Anarchism and Feminism Embodied." *Anarchist Developments in Cultural Studies* 1:133–165. https://bit.ly/3v2ew2k

Bird, Chloe, Peter Conrad, and Allen M. Fremont, eds. 2010. *Handbook of Medical Sociology.* 5th Ed. New Jersey: Prentice Hall College.

Block, Jennifer.. *Pushed: The Painful Truth About Childbirth and Modern Maternity Care*. Cambridge, MA: De Capo Press.

Bobel, Chris. 2002. *Paradox of Natural Mothering*. Philadelphia, PA: Temple University Press.

Brown, Wendy. 2016. "Sacrificial Citizenship: Neoliberalism, Human Capital, and Austerity Politics: Neoliberalism, Human Capital, and Austerity Politics: Wendy

Clemente, Jose, Luke Ursell, Laura Wegener Parfrey, and Rob Knight. 2012. "The Impact of The Gut Microbiota on Human Health: An Integrative View." *Cell* 148(6):1258–1270. https://bit.ly/46PkG3a

Cockerham, William C., Thomas Abel, and Gunther Luschen.

1993. "Max Weber, Formal Rationality, and Health Lifestyles." *The Sociological Quarterly* 34(3):413:28.

Cockerham, William C. 2005. "Health Lifestyle Theory and the Convergence of Agency and Structure." *Journal of Health and Social Behavior* 46:51–67.

Cockerham, William C. 2011. "Health Sociology in a Globalizing World." *Política y Sociedad* 48(2):235-248. doi: 10.5209/rev_POSO.2011.v48.n2.1

Cockerham, William C. 2013. "Bourdieu and an Update of Health Lifestyle Theory." Pp. 127–154 in *Medical Sociology on the Move: New Directions in Theory.* William C. Cockerham, Ed. New York, NY: Springer.

Craven, Christa. 2007. "A "Consumer's Right" to Choose a Midwife: Shifting Meanings for Reproductive Rights Under Neoliberalism." *American Anthropologist* 109(4):701–712. https://bit.ly/3REgQWg

Craven, Christa. 2010. *Pushing for Midwives: Home birth Mothers and the Reproductive Rights Movement.* Philadelphia, PA: Temple University Press.

Davis, Dána-Ain, and Christa Craven. 2016. *Feminist Ethnography: Thinking Through Methodologies, Challenges, And Possibilities.* Lanham: Rowman & Littlefield. Print.

Davis-Floyd, Robbie. 1992. *Birth as an American Rite of Passage.* Berkeley, CA: University of California Press. Print.

Dill-McFarland, Kimberly, Zheng-Zheng Tang, Julia Kemis, Robert Kerby, Guanhua Chen, Alberto Palloni, Thomas Sorenson, Federico Rey, and Pamela Herd. 2019. "Close Social Relationships Correlate With Human Gut Microbiota Composition." *Scientific Reports* 9(703):1–10. https://bit.ly/3RlKcqT

Dye, Nancy Schrom. 1980, "History of Childbirth in America." *Signs* 6(1): 97–108. *JSTOR*, https://bit.ly/4ahEXkH. Accessed 17 May 2021.

Ehrenreich, Barbara and Deirdre English. 2010. *Witches, Midwives, and Nurses: A History of Women Healers.* New York, NY: The Feminist Press.

Freidson, Eliot. 1970. *The Profession of Medicine: A Study of the Sociology of Applied Knowledge.* New York, NY: Dodd, Mead, & Company.

Foucault, Michel. 1973. *The Birth of the Clinic.* New York, NY: Pantheon Books.

Foucault, Michel. 1978. *The History of Sexuality:* First American edition. New York, NY: Pantheon Books. Print.

Goodyear-Ka'ōpua, Noelani. 2017. "Reproducing the Ropes of Resistance: Hawaiian Studies Methodologies." In *Kanaka 'Ōiwi Methodologies.* Pp. 1–29. University of Hawai'i Press. https://bit.ly/3GB6PTz

Green, Laura C., and Martha W. Beckwith. 1924. "Hawaiian Customs and Beliefs Relating to Birth and Infancy." *American Anthropologist* 26(2): 230–246.

Hawai'i State Legislature. 2019. "SB1033 SD2 HD2 Relating To The Licensure Of Midwives." April 2019. https://bit.ly/3NnRnOo

Hawai'i State Legislature. 2019. Testimony in response to "SB1033 SD2 HD2 Relating To The Licensure Of Midwives." https://bit.ly/46XX-zmW

Heberle, Amy E., Elsia A. Obus, and Sarah A. O'Gray. 2020. "An Intersectional Perspective on the Intergenerational Transmission of Trauma and State-perpetrated Violence." *Journal of Social Issues* 76(4): 814–834.

History, Art, and Archives: The United States House of Representatives. Historical Highlights. The Sheppard–Towner Maternity and Infancy Act. November 23, 1921. https://bit.ly/47TZcU3

Hofmann, Mathias, Christopher Young, Tina M. Binz, Markus R. Baumgartner, and Nicole Bauer. 2018. "Contact to Nature Benefits Health: Mixed Effectiveness of Different Mechanisms." *International Journal of Environmental Research and Public Health* 15(1):31–.

Keli'iholokai, LeShay, Samantha Keaulana, Mapuana C. K Antonio, Ikaika Rogerson, Kirk Deitschman, Joseph Awa Kamai, Luana Albinio, et al. "Reclaiming 'Āina Health in Waimānalo." 2020. *International Journal of Environmental Research and Public Health* 17(14):1–14.

Kobayashi, Joy. 1980. "Early Hawaiian Uses of Medicinal Plants in Pregnancy and Childbirth." *Journal of Tropical Pediatrics*

22(6): 260–262. https://bit.ly/48x3j8L

Korp, Peter. 2008. "The Symbolic Power of 'Healthy Lifestyles.'" *Health Sociology Review* 17(1): 18–26. Web.

Lake, Ricky and Abby Epstein. 2008. *The Business of Being Born.* [DVD]. Burbank, CA: New Line Home Entertainment.

Mack, Ashley Noel. 2016. "The Self-Made Mom: Neoliberalism and Masochistic Motherhood in Home-Birth Videos on YouTube." *Women's Studies in Communication* 39(1):47–68.

Maina-Okori, Naomi Mumbi, Jada Renee Koushik, and Alexandria Wilson. 2018. "Reimagining Intersectionality in Environmental and Sustainability Education: A Critical Literature Review." *The Journal of environmental education* 49(4):286–296. Web.

Maracle, Lee. 1996. *I Am Woman: A Native Perspective on Sociology and Feminism.* British Columbia, Canada: Press Gang.

Mathur, Vani A, Theresa Morris, and Kelly McNamara. 2020. "Cultural Conceptions of Women's Labor Pain and Labor Pain Management: A Mixed-Method Analysis." *Social Science & Medicine 1982* (261):113240–113240.

McElfish, Pearl, Rachel Purvis, Monica Esquivel, Ka'imi Sinclair, Claire Townsend, Nicola Hawley, Lauren Haggard-Duff, and Joseph Keawe'aimoku Kaholokula. 2019. "Diabetes Disparities and Promising Interventions to Address Diabetes in Native Hawaiian and Pacific Islander Populations." *Current Diabetes Reports* 19(5): 1–9.

McMullin, Juliet. 2005. "The Call to Life: Revitalizing a Healthy Hawaiian Identity." *Social Science & Medicine* 61:809-820.

McMullin, Juliet. 2016. *The Healthy Ancestor: Embodied Inequality and the Revitalization of Native Hawaiian Health.* Walnut Creek, CA: Left Coast Press.

Morrison, Sheena M, and Elizabeth Fee. 2010. "Nothing to Work with but Cleanliness: The Training of African American Traditional Midwives in The South." *American Journal of Public Health* 100(2):238–9. doi:10.2105/AJPH.2009.182873

Oakley, Ann. 1986. *The Captured Womb: A History of the Medical Care of Pregnant Women.* Hoboken, NJ: Blackwell Publishing.

Oakley, Ann. 2016. "The Sociology of Childbirth: An Autobiographical Journey Through Four Decades of Research." *Sociology of Health and Illness* 38(5):689-705. doi: 10.1111/1467–9566.12400.

Okamura, Jonathan Y. 1980. "Aloha Kanaka Me Ke Aloha 'Aina: Local Culture and Society in Hawai'i." *Amerasia Journal* 7(2):119–137.

Oparah, Julia and Alicia Bonaparte, eds. 2016. *Birthing Justice: Black Women,* Pregnancy, and Childbirth. 1st Ed. New York, NY: Routledge.

Pacific Birth Collective. 2020. "Birth in Hawai'i. Accessed on November 3, 2021. https://pacificbirthcollective.org/page-18118

Pinto, Pua 'O Eleili Kelsi. 2019. "Pua Kanikawi Kanikawa: The Intimacy of Hawaiian Childbirth." ProQuest Dissertations Publishing. Print.

Roots Kalihi. 2021. "Ka Lahui O Ka Po: Birthing a Nation." Accessed on June 5, 2021. https://bit.ly/47RMUM8

Rothman, Barbara Katz. 2014. "Pregnancy, Birth, and Risk: An Introduction. *Health, Risk and Society* 16(1):1–6.

The Hawai'i Home Birth Task Force. 2019. "A Report to the Governor and the Legislature of the State of Hawai'i Per Act 32, Session Laws of Hawai'i, 2019 from the Hawai'i Home Birth Task Force. The Hawai'i State Commission. https://bit.ly/3RFR9V6

Torri, Costanza and Jennie M. Hornosty, eds. 2017. *Complementary, Alternative & Traditional Medicine: Prospects and Challenges for Women's Reproductive Health.* Vancouver, Canada: Women's Press.

Trask, Haunani-Kay. 1999. *From a Native Daughter: Colonialism and Sovereignty in* Hawai'i. Honolulu, HI: University of Hawai'i Press.

Tritten, Jan. 2014. "Home birth and the Microbiome." *Midwifery Today* 110:5–5. Print.

Vedam, Saraswathi, Kathrin Stoll, Tanya Khemet Taiwo, Nicholas Rubashkin, Melissa Cheyney, Nan Strauss, Monica McLemore, Micaela Cadena, Elizabeth Nethery, Eleanor Rushton, Laura Schummers, and Eugene Declercq. 2019. "The Giving Voice to Mothers Study: Inequity and Mistreatment During Pregnancy and Childbirth in the United States." *Reproductive Health* 16(77):1–18

Weiss, Gregory L. and Lynne E. Lonnquist. 2003. *The Sociology of Health, Healing, and Illness.* 4ᵗʰ Edition. Upper Saddle River, NJ: Prentice Hall.

Wellcome Trust Sanger Institute. 2019. "Babies' Gut Bacteria Affected by Delivery Method: Vaginal Delivery Promotes Mother's Gut Bacteria in Babies' Gut." *Science Daily*. Retrieved October 5, 2021, from https://bit.ly/47UHpMx

Wilson, Elizabeth A. 2015. *Gut Feminism*. Durham, NC: Duke University Press. Web.

Worman-Ross, Kathryn and Tamara L. Mix. 2013. "'I Wanted Empowerment, Healing, and Respect': Home birth as Challenge to Medical Hegemony." *Sociological Spectrum* 33:453–481.

Acknowledgments

In the profound journey of crafting *Back to the Womb*, I am filled with gratitude for the tapestry of support that has woven this work into existence. To the fifty-nine courageous home birth mamas in Hawai'i, your stories are the heartbeat of this book—thank you for entrusting me with your narratives. To the dedicated midwifery community in Hawai'i, your wisdom and commitment to nurturing life are invaluable. Gratitude extends to mothers worldwide for every birthing soul that shapes the human tapestry. A heartfelt acknowledgment to our ancestors, who birthed us into existence. The spirit of Hawai'i, with its boundless aloha, adds a unique richness to this work, for which I am filled with gratitude.

Special appreciation to my exceptional editorial team at Calumet Editions, especially Ian and Susan, who shaped and refined words with a mastery that exceeded my own. To my family, thank you for all your support these many years. I could have never done this without you. To Henry, your unwavering support is my anchor. Finally, to my cherished children, Bella and Noah, you are my world, and my love for you surpasses anything else. This journey is a collective endeavor, and each of you has left an indelible mark on its pages. I am truly grateful.

About the Author

Dr. Alexandra Kisitu is a devoted wife, mother and accomplished writer with a PhD from the University of Hawai'i. As a passionate advocate for home birth, she draws inspiration from her own experiences as a mother of two wonderful children. Driven by a desire to deepen human connections, her writing reflects a profound understanding of the human experience. In addition to her role as a writer, Alexandra is an intuitive, bringing a unique perspective to her work.

Beyond her literary pursuits, Dr. Kisitu is the founder of Infinite Expansions, a company dedicated to personal and collective growth. With a keen interest in fostering a sense of interconnectedness, her writing serves as a catalyst for bringing humanity closer to itself. Outside of her professional endeavors, Alexandra finds joy in sharing life's adventures with her husband, Henry. They bond over their love for movies, travel, hiking and cooking.

www.ingramcontent.com/pod-product-compliance
Lightning Source LLC
Chambersburg PA
CBHW031427270326
41930CB00007B/596